FORMS OF DISAPPOINTMENT

SUNY series in Latin American and Iberian Thought and Culture
———————
Jorge J. E. Gracia and Rosemary G. Feal, editors

FORMS OF DISAPPOINTMENT

CUBAN AND ANGOLAN NARRATIVE AFTER THE COLD WAR

LANIE MILLAR

Published by State University of New York Press, Albany

© 2019 State University of New York

All rights reserved

No part of this book may be used or reproduced in any manner whatsoever without written permission. No part of this book may be stored in a retrieval system or transmitted in any form or by any means including electronic, electrostatic, magnetic tape, mechanical, photocopying, recording, or otherwise without the prior permission in writing of the publisher.

For information, contact State University of New York Press, Albany, NY
www.sunypress.edu

Library of Congress Cataloging-in-Publication Data

Names: Millar, Lanie, 1979– author.
Title: Forms of disappointment : Cuban and Angolan narrative after the Cold War / Lanie Millar.
Other titles: Realigning revolution
Description: Albany : State University of New York Press, [2019] | Series: SUNY series in Latin American and Iberian thought and culture | Revision of author's thesis (doctoral)—University of Texas at Austin, 2011, titled Realigning revolution : the poetics of disappointment in Cuban and Angolan narrative. | Includes bibliographical references and index.
Identifiers: LCCN 2018045646 | ISBN 9781438475912 (hardcover) | ISBN 9781438475905 (pbk.) | ISBN 9781438475929 (ebook) Subjects: LCSH: Cuban literature—20th century—History and criticism. | Angolan literature (Portuguese)—20th century—History and criticism. | Angola—History—Civil War, 1975–2002—Participation, Cuban. | Angola—History—Civil War, 1975–2002—Literature and the war.
Classification: LCC PQ7378 .M466 2019 | DDC 860.9/7291—dc23
LC record available at https://lccn.loc.gov/2018045646

10 9 8 7 6 5 4 3 2 1

Contents

List of Illustrations   vii

Acknowledgments   ix

Introduction   xiii

Part I
Allegory and Aesthetics in the Post-Revolution

1. Silence and the People in Boaventura Cardoso's *Maio, Mês de Maria* and *Mãe, Materno Mar*   3

2. Postwar Cinematic Politics and the Structures of Disappointment   27

Part II
The Mobility of Form

3. The War Abroad and the War at Home: Eliseo Alberto's *Caracol Beach*   51

4. Revolution from the South in J. E. Agualusa's *O Ano em que Zumbi Tomou o Rio*   81

Part III
Genre, Style, and Empire

5. Deferred Time and Belated Histories in Leonardo Padura's *El hombre que amaba a los perros*   109

6   Post-Revolutionary Pastiche in Pepetela's Jaime Bunda Novels   139

Epilogue   169

Notes   179

Works Cited   193

Index   207

Illustrations

Figure 3.1   Public mural in Havana, Cuba. Photo by the author.   52

Figure 3.2   Unión de Jóvenes Comunistas de Cuba (the Young Communist League of Cuba) at the 1st of May parade in 2010. Photo by the author.   53

Acknowledgments

I owe the existence of this book to many communities of scholars, writers, artists, colleagues, and friends. My first thanks go to the authors, filmmakers, and critics whose work appears in the pages of this book. I am very grateful to my editor Rebecca Colesworthy for her support and guidance, to Michael Rinella for taking on this project, to Jorge Gracia and Rosemary Feal for including it in the Latin American and Iberian Thought and Culture series, to Eileen Nizer, Rafael Chaiken, and to the rest of the staff at SUNY Press. I owe enormous thanks to the anonymous reviewers for their generous, insightful, and constructive readings of the manuscript.

    I am extremely grateful for research support from the Kluge Center at the US Library of Congress, the Fundação Luso-Americana para o Desenvolvimento and the Arquivo Nacional Torre do Tombo in Lisbon, and the Oregon Humanities Center. Travis Hensley and Mary Lou Reker provided invaluable logistical support during my time at the Kluge Center, and together with the other fellows made each day there a joy. I owe many thanks to Mattye Laverne Page in the African and Middle East Reading Room at the Library of Congress for facilitating my access to archives on Angola. Thank you to Maria Remédios Amaral at the ANTT and Miguel Vaz at FLAD for making my research in Lisbon possible. Paul Peppis, Julia Heydon, Melissa Gustafson, and Peg Freas Gearhart are responsible for a wonderful and productive quarter writing at the OHC. My research has also benefitted enormously from conversations and events throughout the years organized by the wonderful staff at the Fundación Alejo Carpentier in Havana, especially the inimitable Luisa Campuzano. Thank you to Constance Arvis at the US Embassy in Angola for facilitating my research in Luanda, and to Eric Benjaminson for making the connection. I am also grateful to the Embassy staff and the administration, faculty, and students of the English Department at the Universidade Agostinho Neto for my reception there.

SOCE—Amanda Doxtater, Karen Emmerich, Leah Middlebrook, Fabienne Moore, and Casey Shoop—have been incisive and indefatigable readers and patient cheerleaders; the book has benefitted enormously from their brilliant eyes. Ex-Socista Marc Schachter, Nathalie Hester, Roy Chan, and Stephen Henighan all read portions of the manuscript, and I am grateful for their suggestions. Mayra Bottaro provided invaluable discussion, encouragement, and solidarity. Other colleagues have offered bibliography, provided feedback on works-in-progress, modeled outstanding scholarship, or offered encouragement as I wrote and revised the manuscript, including Annette Rubado-Mejia, Michael Gibbs Hill, Samira Mehta, Pedro García-Caro, Gina Hermann, Cecilia Enjuto Rangel, Sonja Boos, Cory Browning, Sergio Rigoletto, and Kirby Brown. A special thank you to Robert Long for helping make the research opportunities that supported this manuscript possible. The rest of the Romance Languages department and colleagues in Latin American and African Studies at the University of Oregon have been unfailingly supportive. Thank you.

This book got its start as a dissertation project in the Program in Comparative Literature at the University of Texas. I am grateful to my adviser Jossianna Arroyo-Martínez, who encouraged and shaped this study from its earliest inception, and has continued to support its development. Thank you to Hélène Tissières, my co-adviser, who provided invaluable guidance and perspective on African and postcolonial literatures. I owe a great deal to César Salgado, whose mentorship and scholarship through my graduate training and in the years since has greatly influenced my work. I benefitted from direction and conversations with Inocência Mata at the Universidade de Lisboa and from Sonia Roncador and Niyi Afolabi at the University of Texas, as well as Elizabeth Richmond-Garza, who always guided me in the right direction. My graduate student colleagues in Comparative Literature and Spanish and Portuguese were a source of vital support during my time at UT, especially Lorna Torrado, Naminata Diabate, and Nandini Dhar.

I am also indebted to discussions, collaborations, and conference invitations from Charlotte Rogers, Anne Garland Mahler, Jerry Carlson, Pilar Cabrera, José Antonio Michelena, Kerry Bystrom, and Magalí Armillas-Tiseyra. A special thanks to Emilio Óscar Alcalde for supplying me with a copy of his film *El encanto del regreso*. I appreciate weekly discussions over the past three years with Susan Stein-Roggenbuck and Tom Grano, who have kept me on track with research and writing. The students of my seminars "Runaways, Rebellions, and Revolutions in the Black Atlantic" and "The Cuban Revolution in Context" at the University of Oregon supplied enthusiastic and insightful discussions which benefitted early drafts of several chapters. Thank you to Elizabeth Peterson and the UO Library Services and CMET staff with their technological expertise, and to Alyson Millar-Blevins for proofreading work.

Acknowledgments

I appreciate Magalí Armillas-Tiseyra, Kerry Bystrom, and Joseph Slaughter for their editorial work on previous versions of chapters in this book. My thanks to the publishers for permission to reprint material that appeared as follows: an early version of chapter 2 was published as "Postwar Politics in *O herói* and *Kangamba*" in *The Global South Atlantic*, Ed. Kerry Bystrom and Joseph Slaughter, Fordham UP, 2018, pp. 207–24. A previous version of Chapter 3 appeared as "Circling the South Atlantic: Revolution in J. E. Agualusa's *The Year That Zumbi Took Rio*" in *The Global South*, vol. 7, no. 2, 2014, pp. 87–109. Subvention support from the Oregon Humanities Center and the University of Oregon College of Arts and Sciences helped make publication of this book possible.

Finally, thank you to my family, especially my parents and sisters for your unfailing encouragement, and most especially to Felipe.

Introduction

Forms of Disappointment traces significant connections between Cuban and Angolan post-Cold War narrative and film, particularly their reconsiderations of past revolutionary forms, texts, and cultural politics. In this book, I argue for the relevance of disappointment as a concept that describes both the negative feelings associated with the collapse of confidence in the promise of ongoing revolutionary transformations after 1989, and the continued longing for the inheritances of revolutionary transformation and interlinked anti-imperial solidarity among artists and writers from Cuba and Angola. Both Cuba's collaboration with Angola's leftist MPLA party during Angola's civil war and broader discourses and portrayals of racial, political, and cultural solidarities across the Global South significantly impacted Cuban and Angolan culture, leaving traces even after the period of close internationalist collaboration came to a close.[1] In thinking through these historical contexts, this study places Cuban and Angolan novels and films into conversation via a set of textual practices that I call techniques of disappointment, means by which disappointment shapes the form of cultural texts in the post-Cold War era. For Cuban and Angolan narratives, this disappointment is rooted not solely in the collapse of the global socialist dream after 1989, but in the specific legacies of battles fought in the name of third-world solidarity. By demonstrating that these Cuban and Angolan narratives share techniques even after the era of close trans-national collaboration has come to a close, I show the ongoing impact of Global South networks that remain invisible when we only consider these cultural histories through the binary global politics of the Cold War or the vertical axis between metropole and colony. These texts are, I show, conditioned by Cuba and Angola's history of internationalist collaboration and allegiance across the Global South.

I would like to begin by reading a scene from Angolan director Maria João Ganga's film *Na Cidade Vazia* (*Hollow City*) that encodes disappointment in the affective and formal registers that constitute the grounds for my analysis. Released in 2004, two years after the end of Angola's brutal civil war, *Na Cidade Vazia* portrays the young war orphan N'dala's difficult initiation into the often-hostile urban environment of the capital city of Luanda. Toward the end of the film, Zé, an older boy who has befriended N'dala, performs the title role as another war orphan in *As Aventuras de Ngunga* (*The Adventures of Ngunga*), a school play based on renowned Angolan novelist Pepetela's didactic children's story written on the battlefield as the author fought against the Portuguese in 1972. The sequence cuts back and forth between Zé's performance and N'dala's participation in a home robbery orchestrated by Joka, Zé's cousin. This parallel structure presents N'dala and Ngunga as undergoing analogous processes of initiation; the play's protagonist learns revolutionary sacrifice for the common good, while N'dala, coerced into shooting the homeowner, is initiated into a post-revolutionary scheme of violence and cynical opportunism that ultimately ends in his own death. My interest in this sequence lies in how the multilayered refraction of the allusions to the dual processes of initiation transforms the meaning of both scenes and forms of representation. The film abruptly shifts between the play and the robbery, a text associated with the past and a performance in the present. The director thus focuses our attention on the film's ironic repetition of prior historical moments and associated narrative forms. This repetition highlights the disjunction between Pepetela's objective to form Socialist New Men who would construct the revolution to come and the film's portrayal of N'dala's foreclosed future. It also signals a gap between the seeming coherence of Pepetela's didactic text with the social objectives it sought to inculcate in its actors and audience, and the multiple valences and plastic possibilities of cinema in the post-war moment.[2]

N'dala's death at the end the film provoked both controversy and disappointment in the viewing public, which the director acknowledges in a 2016 interview:

> o público angolano, até porque já estávamos a entrar numa fase de esperança, de ver o nosso país a renascer, as pessoas, de certa forma, aqui, prefeririam que tivesse dado um fim mais agradável. Mais soft. Aquela criança sofreu e as pessoas sofreram com ela. Recebi algumas críticas e encontrei mesmo pessoas que me diziam: "deste-nos tanta poesia, tanta beleza e depois matas aquela criança". . . . Se o fiz foi porque, na altura, se todos estávamos com muita esperança no futuro, eu tinha a certeza que essas crianças não tinham futuro. (M. Gomes)

(The Angolan public, especially because we were just entering a hopeful phase, seeing our country being reborn, the people, in a way, here, wanted me to give it a happier ending. Softer. That child suffered and people suffered with him. I was criticized and some people even told me "you gave us so much poetry, so much beauty and then you kill that child" . . . If I did it was because, at that time, even though all of us had so much hope for the future, I was certain that those children had no future.)

The sense of disappointment that Ganga discusses in this interview stems from the repetition of the young initiate's death seen through two different modes of representation (play and film), responding to two different historical moments (the 1970s and the 2000s), whose irreconcilable asynchronicity results in what Ackbar Abbas calls a "miss[ed] . . . appointment with meaning" ("Erotics" 219). The final scenes of *Na Cidade Vazia* manifest what Abbas goes on to describe as the effect of layered historical references and aesthetic forms whose juxtapositions call our attention to historical discontinuities that are in plain view but tended to remain unacknowledged (219).

I have chosen to read the final sequence of *Na Cidade Vazia* because it exemplifies some of the ways that feelings of disappointment about the present take the form of textual revisiting of the revolutionary past. *Forms of Disappointment* makes use of both the grandiose implications of "disappointment" as an expression of disillusionment or disenchantment, as well as its more mundane implications of the everyday gap between expectations and lived reality, in order to capture the complex range of political stances and aesthetic practices that the Cuban and Angolan texts analyzed here encode. Laura Quinney, in her examination of a poetics of disappointment in nineteenth- and twentieth-century poetry, notes how the etymology of "disappointment" reveals the specific vector of an individual's engagement with the public sphere:

In its first use, disappointment meant "to undo the appointment of; to deprive of an appointment, office, or possession" (*O.E.D.*, 1483). Disappointment in this sense entailed losing one's hold on public identity and public space, losing a goal for one's energies and an occupation for one's time. Most primitively, disappointment meant ceasing to be "*à point*," in the right place at the right moment, and thus implied a break-down in one's relation to time, a falling out and away from a recognizable order. In the seventeenth and eighteenth centuries, disappointment came to have its more familiar meaning, "the frustration or nonfulfillment of expectation, intention or desire." (1)

For Quinney, disappointment wrests subjects from both their *place* in the world, as well as from their *time*: "To cease to believe in the destiny of the self empties time of its teleological promise . . . the disappointed subject thrust into a temporal void feels himself to be surrounded by nothing but time, in effect, to be drowning in time" (8). Quinney's discussion illuminates several features of disappointment that are central to my study: the first concerns the relationship among communities in the social sphere, and speaks to how after the collapse of global socialism, upon withdrawing from Angola, Cuba is "dis-appointed" from its leadership role in the Global South, while Angola is "dis-appointed" as a center of global revolutionary solidarity. Quinney thus also signals how the sense of historical displacement and the lack of fulfillment of expectations effect a subjective experience of the world. These features are encoded in how Cuban and Angolan narrative texts published during and after the post-Cold War transition systematically revisit the cultural history of the revolutionary past.

While Quinney is concerned with individual subjecthood, the disappointment presented in works by contemporary Cuban and Angolan novelists and filmmakers is a fundamentally collective feeling; it is perhaps no surprise, then, that this expression of disappointment is well-developed in the polyphonic genre of the novel and in the collectively produced visual and narrative medium of film. In the following chapters, I analyze novels by Cubans Eliseo Alberto and Leonardo Padura and by Angolans Boaventura Cardoso, José Eduardo Agualusa, and Pepetela, as well as films by Cuban Rogelio París and by Angolan Zézé Gamboa. These literary and visual works engage two primary historical narratives that link representations of the Cuban and Angolan revolutions: they represent revolution as a form of anticolonial and anti-imperial resistance, and they establish connections between the Caribbean and Africa on the grounds of racial solidarity and histories of economic underdevelopment. Produced following the post-Cold War transition and focused on a process of historical reckoning, these narratives of disappointment revisit the question of the radical future possibilities of revolution through techniques of citation and imitation such as allegory, satire, pastiche, and historical re-writings. These works' disappointment emerges, in part, from a realization that the revolutions, the events that were supposed to enact an indefinitely ongoing transformation of the totality of social life, do, in fact, become history. By citing and imitating this history, they interrogate how the meanings and cultural value of signs, forms, or events associated with past revolutions have changed in the post-1989 world. In other words, they examine the process through which the revolutions are made historical, and, in so doing, uphold literary and cinematic works of art as privileged sites for dealing with the feelings of disappointment.

The Contexts of Disappointment

Cuba and Angola share a long history of Iberian colonization dating from the fifteenth century, as two poles of the trans-Atlantic slave trade, and, more recently, a history of twentieth-century leftist revolutions—Cuba's, of course, triumphed in 1959, while Angola's anticolonial revolution won independence from Portugal in 1975. The mass forced displacement of enslaved Africans to the Americas fundamentally determined the course of both nations' postcolonial histories, and despite differences in Cuba and Angola's individual colonial processes, this shared history occupied a central role in the public rhetoric that justified Cuba's support for Lusophone African independence. In both places, the link between the colonial past and the threat of a neocolonial present provided an ongoing rhetorical basis for seeing Cuba and Angola as involved in similar ideological and literal battles for sovereignty, racial equality, and anti-imperial resistance as a corrective to the colonial past: symbolically, Cuba's early Angolan mission was named "Operación Carlota" (Operation Carlota) for the leader of a nineteenth-century slave rebellion in Cuba. A 1976 speech by Fidel Castro commemorates the anniversaries of the Cuban victory over US invaders in 1961 at Playa Girón (the Bay of Pigs) and Angola's independence from Portugal in 1975, laying out the rhetorical underpinnings of the long-entangled geopolitics linking the two nations:

> En Girón se derramó sangre africana, la de los abnegados descendientes de un pueblo que fue esclavo antes de ser obrero, y fue obrero explotado antes de ser dueño de su patria. Y en África, junto a la de los heroicos combatientes de Angola, se derramó también sangre cubana, la de los hijos de Martí, Maceo y Agramonte, la de los que heredaron la sangre internacionalista de Gómez y el Che Guevara. Los que un día esclavizaron al hombre y lo enviaron a América, tal vez no imaginaron jamás que uno de esos pueblos que recibió a los esclavos, enviaría a sus combatientes a luchar por la libertad en África. La victoria de Angola fue hermana gemela de la victoria de Girón. (Castro "Discurso . . . 1976" n/p)

> (In Girón, African blood was spilled, that of the selfless descendants of an enslaved people who were slaves before becoming workers,

and exploited workers before becoming owners of their country. And in Africa, together with the heroic combatants of Angola, Cuban blood was also spilled, that of the sons of Martí, Maceo, and Agramonte, of those who inherited the internationalist blood of Gómez and Che Guevara. Those who one day enslaved men and sent them to America, perhaps never imagined that one of those nations that received slaves would send its combatants to fight for liberty in Africa. The victory of Angola was the twin sister of the victory at Girón.)

This discursive strategy of equivalence has continued to have purchase long after the era of military collaboration came to an end. In 2007, during a state visit to Havana, then-Angolan president Eduardo dos Santos invoked similar rhetoric that collapses the "shared inheritances" of colonialism's violent displacement of African bodies to the New World and the Cuban sacrifices on the contemporary battlefields of Angola when he remarked: "la amistad [entre Cuba y Angola] ha sido forjada con sangre" ("Presidente de Angola" n/p) (the friendship [between Cuba and Angola] has been forged with blood).

Other Lusophone African intellectuals share Castro's and dos Santos's rhetoric of placing together two moments of national revolution against colonial and neocolonial forces as parallel events in a worldwide fight against colonialism and imperialism. Nine years before Cuba's official entrance into the Angolan conflict, at the First Tricontinental Congress in Havana in 1966, Bissau-Guinean revolutionary Amílcar Cabral had used almost the same language as Castro of retracing the routes of the slave trade in the shared interest of decolonization.[3] After lauding the accomplishments of the "Cuban miracle" of the early revolutionary years, Cabral declares:

> estamos prontos para mandar para Cuba tantos homens e mulheres quantos sejam necessários para compensar a saída daqueles que, por razões de classe ou inadaptação, têm interesses e atitudes incompatíveis com os interesses do povo cubano. Repetindo o caminho outrora doloroso e trágico dos nossos antepassados (nomeadamente de Guiné e Angola) que foram transplantados para Cuba como escravos, viremos hoje como homens livres, como trabalhadores conscientes e como patriotas cubanos, para exercer uma atividade produtiva nesta sociedade nova, justa e multirracial; para ajudar a defender com o nosso sangue as conquistas do povo de Cuba. Mas viremos também para reforçar tanto os laços históricos, de sangue e de cultura que unem os nossos povos ao povo cubano, como essa desconcentração mágica, essa alegria visceral e esse

ritmo contagioso que fazem da construção do socialismo em Cuba um fenômeno novo à face do mundo, um acontecimento único e, para muitos, insólito. (*Documentário* 172)

(we, the peoples of the countries of Africa, still completely dominated by Portuguese colonialism, are prepared to send to Cuba as many men and women as may be needed to compensate for the departure of those who for reasons of class or of inability to adapt have interests or attitudes which are incompatible with the interests of the Cuban people. Taking once again the formerly hard and tragic path of our ancestors (mainly from Guinea and Angola) who were taken to Cuba as slaves, we would come now as free men, as willing workers and Cuban patriots, to fulfill a productive function in this new, just and multi-racial society, and to help and defend with our own lives the victories of the Cuban people. Thus we would strengthen both all the bonds of history, blood and culture which unite our peoples with the Cuban people, and the spontaneous giving of oneself, the deep joy and infectious rhythm which make the construction of socialism in Cuba a new phenomenon for the world, a unique and, for many, unaccustomed event). ("The Weapon of Theory" n/p)

Anne Garland Mahler has specifically traced the origins of theories of the Global South to the ideologies of the Tricontinental Congress, and to its origins in Cuba's symbolic and material leadership in third-world notions of liberation and decolonization in the second half of the twentieth century (*From the Tricontinental*). Angola was the site of Cuba's largest internationalist military and humanitarian mission, and Stephen Henighan has shown that contact and collaboration between Cuba and Angolan revolutionaries dates to the early 1960s ("Cuban fulcrum" 236). Over the course of their military collaboration from 1975–1991, tens of thousands of Cuban soldiers served in Angola as allies to the leftist MPLA. Cuba's initiatives included education for African students on the island in a range of specialties; teachers, engineers, and medical personnel numbered among the Cuban volunteers sent to Angola. Cuba's leadership affirmed the two nations' solidarity, and Angola's politicians and intellectuals expressed their gratitude publicly. The two writers' unions, the Unión de Escritores y Artistas Cubanos (UNEAC; The National Union of Cuban Writers and Artists) and the União dos Escritores Angolanos (UAE; Angolan Writers' Union) signed an agreement of mutual publication in 1978.[4]

The public rhetoric in national and international publishing venues around the South Atlantic emphasized a process of mutual self-recognition, articulated through notions of Africa-diaspora siblinghood as well as through anti-imperialist leftist solidarity. This feeling of solidarity is perhaps no more clearly demonstrated than in Nelson Mandela's famous 1991 visit to Cuba the year after he was released from prison. In his speech accepting the José Martí Medal, Mandela declared, "The Cuban people hold a special place in the hearts of the people of Africa. The Cuban internationalists have made a contribution to African independence, freedom, and justice, unparalleled for its principled and selfless character" (17–18). The political discourse, films, and literature written about the revolutions are emblematic for their expressions of enthusiasm, seen as a contagious feeling of affinity that spreads among revolutionaries and spectators alike.[5]

The argument that post-Cold War literature by Cuban and Angolan writers is linked to feelings of "desencanto" (disenchantment), "desilusión/desilusão" (disillusionment), "desengaño"/"desengano" (disillusionment or disappointment) or "decepción"/"decepção" (disappointment) is well established in the critical canon, as I discuss below, though with Casamayor-Cisneros, I believe that "desencanto" is not the only mode of post-Cold War literature (35–36).[6] My use of the term "disappointment," to which each of the Spanish and Portuguese terms listed above could be translated, is not solely predicated on capturing a feeling associated with the political crises after 1989, but is also linked specifically to third-world solidarity and to moments in the 1970s when enthusiasm for internationalist allegiance in effecting revolutionary transformation around the decolonizing world overlapped with ideological purging and the escalating civil war in Angola, and censorship and bureaucratization of the aesthetic spheres in Cuba. Therefore, in *Forms of Disappointment* the term signifies a feeling associated with, on one hand, a historical crisis that begins in the 1970s and culminates in the early 1990s, and the subsequent search for narrative forms to help bring that history into view. On the other hand, "disappointment" refers to the everyday negotiations of the new worlds that these crises have engendered, especially as registered in affective relationships both with other subjects and with the past. Because it is characteristic of the decades of post-Cold War transition, disappointment can be read as a "para-critical mode" of feeling as well as one associated with emergent "cultural hypotheses" (Abbas "Dialectic of Deception"; Williams). I identify disappointment as a "feeling" deliberately. First, I use it to invoke Raymond Williams's concept of structures of feeling, which can be seen as the set of "cultural hypotheses" that are both felt and thought, produced in response to conditions and experiences that continue to be lived. In *Marxism and Literature*, Williams explains that a structure of feeling "cannot without loss be reduced to belief-systems, institutions, or explicit general relationships, though it may include all these as lived and experienced" (133). As Sean Matthews argues, in Williams's work, structures of feeling emerge at moments of social change, where the ways of articulating the new realities may still be coming into being, while Johnathan Flatley notes that Williams's concept is "useful not only because it enables us to talk about the sociality of affect, but because it enables us to describe those structures that mediate between the social and the personal that are more ephemeral and transitory than set ideologies or institutions" (Matthews 186; Flatley 25). The "ephemeral" or "emergent" nature of structures of feeling are precisely why I find the concept useful for understanding disappointment. I see disappointment as a feeling produced in the struggle to make sense of an international solidarity located in the past, and therefore as a feeling that might produce a range of political and affective responses, from disenchantment to melancholy, to the revitalization of revolutionary enthusiasm at another time or in another place.

More recently, theorists of feeling, following Fredric Jameson's configuration of affect as free-floating "intensities" that characterize the postmodern age (10–16), have debated a distinction between emotion—produced by a subject—and affect—a generalized, disembodied, or subjectless feeling.[7] In *Ugly Feelings*, Sianne Ngai argues that certain negative feelings that "[draw] our attention to the politically charged predicament of suspended agency" can thus exist as both emotion and affect (12). That is, she accounts for feelings which are both felt by a subject—a character in a literary work, for example, as is the case of Iván in Leonardo Padura's *El hombre que amaba a los perros*, or by the swindled churchgoers in Boaventura Cardoso's *Mãe, Materno Mar*—and those which, desubjectified, might exist as an "unfelt but perceived feeling," which results from interaction with the work of art, and whose primary repository is its form (28). Drawing on Adorno's account of aesthetic autonomy as self-reflexive guilt, Ngai sees the negative feelings that she examines as "allegories for an autonomous or bourgeois art's increasingly resigned and pessimistic understanding of its *own* relationship to political action" (3). Of course, art in revolutionary Cuba and Angola was conceived and theorized as politically engaged, part of the project of social transformation; here, Ngai's reading is referring to the capitalist context of bourgeois artistic autonomy. Nonetheless, Ngai's analysis of "ugly feelings" as allegories for this uneasy relationship between art and politics can help illuminate disappointment, and I draw from her methodology of uncovering "ugly feelings" in formal elements of literature. The disappointment traced in the Cuban and Angolan works in this book are conditioned by a changing relationship between art and the public sphere: that is, with the dis-integration of public institutions and artists, and the sometimes troubled relationship between works of art and the polis in the post-1989 period. Esther Whitfield has compared the accompanying cultural boom as Cuban literature entered the global marketplace in the 1990s to a new postcolonial paradigm, in which Cuba remained on the margins of globalized markets (17–18). A similar anxiety about Angola's place as a belated consumer of globalized mass-market culture and the corrupting effects of its post-Cold War petrocracy are central to both J. E. Agualusa's *O Ano em que Zumbi Tomou o Rio* and Pepetela's Jaime Bunda novels. Disappointment is a central expression of this sense of displacement.[8]

Both internal and external fascination with the struggle to understand the aesthetics and cultural histories of the Cuban and Angolan revolutions generate anxieties that are evident in works of disappointment. Ackbar Abbas proposes a similar dialectical relationship between two modes, fascination and deception—we recall that "decepción" and "decepção" are two common translations of "disappointment" in Spanish and Portuguese—to examine the entry of cultural products from formerly colonized spaces into global circulation. For Abbas, fascination is a "para-critical" mode of apprehending an event or situation, in that it occurs when something captures our attention but eludes our understanding (348). The promise of understanding may, in fact, be a deception, but it is that promise that also holds our fascination:

> Deception in the sense I am giving it signifies not a love of trickery or obscurantism; it indicates that cultural phenomena always appear to us, to begin with, without the stamp of approval, with no clear value, unrecognised or misrecognized . . . The para-critical function of fascination is that it prompts us through the enigma to attend to what our culture or even we ourselves do not want to recognise. (356)

Abbas argues that attention to fascination is particularly relevant for "emergent" sites of cultural production; attending to site-specific "secret" histories of a space like Hong Kong reveals the "problematic nature of a colonial space making the transition from imperialism to multinational capitalism, a space where all the rules have quietly and deceptively changed" (363). Abbas is primarily concerned with a critical reception that attends to the specific histories that may not be evident to an uninformed global audience consuming cultural products from places like Hong Kong. In his discussion of fascination and deception, Abbas is capturing a similar sense of contingency that Williams's concept of structures of feeling describes. We can observe the same kind of fascinated struggle for understanding thematized within works of disappointment, a struggle that also underlies the critical responses of an international readership. Each of the authors examined in this book has achieved market success following the post-Cold War contraction of state-sponsored publishing in their respective places of origin by contracting with international publishing houses, often in Spain and Portugal, and thus write under the pressures of the rubrics of "representativeness" and "subalternity" that Abbas rightly notes predominate discussions of cultural products from emergent sites of production.[9]

This sense of "subalternity" is a central theme in the postcolonial Angolan works analyzed here, which examine the ways in which the post-independence era cites the colonial past. Similarly, Cuba's image of itself as an ally to the Third World and its solidarity with Angola and other decolonizing nations in the mid-to-late twentieth century was predicated on its own history as a former colony and its projection of itself as the ongoing object of imperialist desire. This ideological link between the two sites is central to understanding the literary techniques that characterize narratives of disappointment originating in these spaces. While textual features such as ironic citation, the blending of genres, pastiche, and parody are central to a broad range of postmodern texts, theorists have distinguished postcolonial African and Latin American literatures from postmodern works on the basis of their long tradition of rewriting colonial histories and their politics, which focus on contestation and revision. For example, Cuban critic Margarita Mateo Palmer argues that the postmodernist "discovery" of Latin American literature operated as a kind of new critical imperialism, ignoring the historical roots of Caribbean and Latin American literature as speaking back against the colonial record from the time of the Spanish chroniclers through the twentieth century.[10] Similarly, Antonio Benítez Rojo notes that Caribbean textual features analyzed in the late twentieth century through the tools of poststructuralism have a long continuity through the centuries of Caribbean colonial history (39). Therefore, while postmodernist critical frameworks help elucidate some of these texts—such as Alberto's *Caracol Beach* or Pepetela's Jaime Bunda novels—I distinguish works of disappointment precisely because of their historical consciousness. This historicity and what Kwame Anthony Appiah calls a political "space clearing" marks a difference between narratives of disappointment and the sort of Jamesonian postmodernism experienced as an undifferentiated and apolitical present. While the textual strategies analyzed in the following chapters share aspects with techniques identified with postmodernism, I argue that for texts conditioned by south-south allegiances and the concomitant engagement with postcolonial politics, postmodernism is not the critical framework that can best illuminate the full range of texts in which we see these practices. Rather, these works maintain a dual awareness of how revolutionary aesthetic projects have occupied a place at the vanguard of an alternative narrative of the twentieth century centered on third-world allegiance. They also record a sense of precariousness in relation to their cultural and political sovereignty that is specifically related to their former colonial histories.

From Enthusiasm to Disappointment

As I have signaled, disappointment is closely related to the structures of revolutionary enthusiasm. A brief examination of the intellectual and political histories of Cuba's and Angola's early years of enthusiasm for revolutionary change will thus help to delineate how and when this feeling of possibility gives way to disappointment. In his article "Anatomía del entusiasmo" (Anatomy of Enthusiasm), Cuban historian Rafael Rojas examines an intellectual history of the Cuban Revolution through the moment in the late 1960s and early 1970s in which two important ideological turns took place: first, the turn of the Euro-American Left away from its support of the revolution, catalyzed by the series of high-profile censorship cases beginning in the late 1960s and Cuba's subsequent rapprochement with the Soviet Union. Second, he identifies the Cuban turn toward support and identification with other revolutionary movements in Latin America and Africa, in what Rojas calls an ideology of "Third-Worldism" most clearly theorized in Roberto Fernández Retamar's seminal essay *Calibán* (1971). For Rojas, the early revolution represented a "spectacle of ideas," in which the Euro-American and Latin American Left could observe and participate in the debates about the implementation of revolutionary ideals. To describe the newness of the feeling associated with this spectacle of ideas, Rojas draws on Jean-François Lyotard's 1986 essay *Enthusiasm: A Kantian Critique of History*.

For Lyotard, as for Kant, the French Revolution of 1789 serves as a philosophical touchstone in an Enlightenment history of democratic progress. In *Enthusiasm*, Lyotard analyzes Kant's discussion of enthusiasm as the political analogue to the aesthetic feeling of the sublime invoked by an idea such as "the maxim of patriotic virtue, or of friendship, or of religion" (Kant 57) that can come about due to unprecedented political events like revolution. While for Kant the French Revolution serves as the foundational event that inspires this feeling, in Lyotard's reading, the relevance of Kantian enthusiasm in the twentieth century is the possibility of heterogeneous unanticipated events that would provoke new feelings similar to enthusiasm, which, in turn, would lead toward yet-unnamed ends. In Lyotard's postmodern world, those ends cannot be the singular idea of human progress conceived by Kant, but rather are multiple: human rights, the rights of peoples, the dictatorship of the proletariat, etc. (63–67).[11]

In "Anatomía del entusiasmo," Rojas examines the intellectual history that leads to an interpretation of the Cuban Revolution as an event that inspires enthusiasm for, among others, the idea of decolonization, ironically developed in (often mistaken, in his view) observations about Cuban history by thinkers from the Euro-American Left. Rojas focuses on two of the ideas that took hold among Cuban intellectuals through their contacts with international theorists: first, the narrative of the Cuban Revolution as a decolonizing event, and second, the thesis of Cuba as an underdeveloped nation. He particularly finds in Ernesto "Che" Guevara's landmark 1965 essay theorizing the revolution "El socialismo y el hombre en Cuba" (1965) (Socialism and Man in Cuba) a strong influence from Jean-Paul Sartre's essays on the revolution published in *France-Soir* and collected in Spanish as *El huracán sobre el azúcar* (*Hurricane over Sugar*) (1960), as well as Frantz Fanon's *Les Damnés de la Terre* (*The Wretched of the Earth*) (1961).[12] For Rojas, the result of the theses regarding decolonization and underdevelopment among Cuba intellectuals, however, was an increasing distance between the Cuban architects of the revolution and their Euro-American spectators: these observers did not identify with Cuban social conditions. This distance became for many a definitive split after the state denounced poet Heberto Padilla's and playwright Antón Arrufat's prizewinning works in 1968; Padilla was forced to publicly confess to crimes against the revolution (the infamous "Caso Padilla") in 1971. These events were accompanied by Cuba's rapprochement with the Soviet Union after Castro refused to condemn the Soviet massacre of protesters in Prague in July of 1968, marking Cuba's definitive turn toward the Soviet bloc. The island's subsequent geopolitical position allowed Cuba to see itself as no longer "behind" the then-called "First World," and to serve instead as a symbolic leader to the "Third World":

> Desarrollarse y descolonizarse implicará, entonces, romper con el humanismo occidental y con la izquierda democrática del primer mundo. En 1971—año del encarcelamiento de Heberto Padilla y del Primer Congreso Nacional de Educación y Cultura, en el que los líderes de la Revolución rompieron públicamente con aquella izquierda occidental—cuando Roberto Fernández Retamar escribe *Calibán*, ya aquella relocalización geopolítica de la Isla ha sido consumada. El bárbaro que hablará entonces podrá mirar su entorno antillano y latinoamericano sin sentirse amenazado por una identidad subdesarrollada que cree haber dejado atrás. Representar a Calibán, hablar en su nombre, vindicar la lengua del colonizador será, a partir de ahí, intervenir en la constitución de otro lugar, no exactamente caribeño ni tercermundista: el Segundo Mundo socialista, la alternativa global al mercado y la democracia, desde el cual se divisa y evalúa la marcha de la humanidad. (Rojas "Anatomía" 13)

(Development and decolonization would imply, from then on, a break with Western humanism and with the democratic Left of the First World. In 1971—the year of Heberto Padilla's imprisonment and of the First National Conference on Education and Culture, in which the leaders of the Revolution publicly broke with the Western Left—when Roberto Fernández Retamar writes *Calibán*, that geopolitical relocation of the Island had already been achieved. The barbarian who would speak from then on could look at his Antillean and Latin American surroundings without feeling threatened by an underdeveloped identity that he believes he has left behind. To represent Caliban, to speak in his name, to vindicate the language of the colonizer would mean, from then on, intervening in the constitution of another place, not exactly a Caribbean or third-world one: the socialist Second World, the global alternative to the market and to democracy, from which one could discern and evaluate the march of humanity.)

In Rojas's analysis, the consolidation of the Cuban Revolution as a decolonizing event and its turn to the Global South is paired with subsequent expressions of "desencanto" in the turn toward censorship and bureaucratic control of the intellectual sphere. For Jorge Fornet, "disenchantment" was largely located in the gap between the revolution's utopian dream and the concrete failures of the bureaucratic state to realize that dream, rather than in the loss of the dream itself. That loss, he argues, came "late" to Cuba—late relative to much of the rest of the world—after the crises of 1989. Following Rojas and Fornet, I therefore locate the roots of post-1989 disappointment in a series of events of the late 1960s and 1970s, though it does not fully manifest until the post-Cold War period.

What remains outside of Rojas's analysis is the enthusiasm that the Cuban Revolution generated for intellectuals from across Africa and Latin America. Therefore, I am arguing for a more nuanced relationship between enthusiasm and disappointment than a strictly chronological one—that enthusiasm precedes disappointment. I am also signaling something more specific than a widely generalizable structural argument that revolutions inevitably fail to fulfill some part of their promise—for what revolution across the globe and throughout time has lived up to its utopian imaginary? Rojas points to an ideological barrier between the Euro-American observers of the revolution and their Cuban counterparts, a barrier that fed the thesis regarding decolonization: the fact that international Western intellectuals had no intention of reproducing Cuba's revolutionary action back at home. However, this is the opposite of the case for many observers from across the Global South, who explicitly looked to the Cuban model as their own decolonizing movements accelerated in the 1960s and 1970s.

When Castro and Cabral cite Cuba and Angola's "shared blood" and the "routes of slavery," they are pointing to the ways that Cuban and Angolan society have both been profoundly shaped by the enslavement of African and African-descended people and the forced migration of enslaved people from the continent to the American colonies. Yet their differing colonial processes point to how by the 1970s, Cuba occupied a geopolitical position relative to the Lusophone African colonies imagined both horizontally as third-world solidarity and as social, political, and cultural vanguard. Both nations underwent processes of belated independence in relation to their surroundings, though eighty years apart; Spain and Portugal were loath to lose the wealth from extraction and agricultural export economies supported largely by slave and coerced labor.[13] In Angola, late colonial policies of strict social apartheid limited education and social mobility to an extremely small elite. A valuable extraction economy based on petroleum, diamonds, and cash crops with cruel forced labor conditions accelerated under Portugal's Estado Novo dictatorship (1933–1974), deepening and exacerbating the divisions among factions that battled the colonial regime until 1975.[14] Cuba's comparatively well-developed criollo land-owning class and urban bourgeoisie at the time of independence and during the republic (1902–1961) as well as its early twentieth-century national ideology of *mestizaje* (racial mixing), distinguished Cuban prerevolutionary conditions from Angola's both economically and socially. However, during the 1960s, Cuba's revolutionary leadership sustained the theses of decolonization and underdevelopment by pointing to the dominance of US economic interests on the island and US political intervention during the republic, increasingly recognizing the racism and social inequalities inherited from slavery and the colonial system. Cuba could thus simultaneously project images of subalternity and of third-world leadership—images the United States, Portugal, and other colonial powers saw as threatening—though they were enthusiastically acknowledged by communities around the Global South.[15]

The origins of disappointment in the late 1960s and 1970s temporally overlaps with an ongoing appreciation for Cuba's leadership across the Global South. Alfredo Margarido notes that the Chinese and Cuban Revolutions served as ideological models in the Portuguese colonies in the 1960s as anticolonial ideas turned to direct action (14), a position that Henighan affirms, noting that eventual MPLA administrators had sought contact with Fidel Castro in the late 1950s ("Cuban fulcrum" 236). Mário Pinto de Andrade cites the Cuban Revolution as a model for cultural liberation in his reflections on the 1968 Congreso Cultural de La Habana (Cultural Congress of Havana) ("Reflexions").[16] The rhetoric of the iterability of revolutionary liberation is evidenced in many key documents from the early years of revolutionary third-world solidarity: from Che Guevara's "Message to the Tricontinental," in which he argues for the tricontinental ideology of multi-continental allegiance in the fight against imperialism, and calls for the creation of "two, three, many Vietnams"; to Andrade's characterization of the Cuban Revolution as a model of the "poetic act" of cultural liberation for the tricontinental ("Culture" 4); to Nelson Mandela's gratitude to Cuba for its contribution to the fight against apartheid. Cuba's turn away from the Global North to embrace African and Latin American liberation movements in the 1960s precipitates among some of its theorists a new genealogy of revolution, one founded in a radically anticolonial interpretation of the enslaved and the oppressed taking charge of their historical future.[17] In many ways, post-1989 disappointment encodes a longing for the traces of that enthusiasm: the reinvigoration of the revolutionary hero in Agualusa's *O Ano em que Zumbi Tomou o Rio*, addressed in chapter 4, is an example of this longing, while the protagonists of Eliseo Alberto's *Caracol Beach* (chapter 3) and Leonardo Padura's *El hombre que amaba a los perros* (chapter 5) lament cultural worlds lost after 1989. Rather than simply following enthusiasm, disappointment is entangled with it.

As its prefix indicates, disappointment is ineluctably contingent; it follows or works in tandem with another possibility, an "enchantment," or "illusion"; a hope for a future that comes to an end, or that never comes to pass in the first place. In this sense, disappointment exists in a dialectical relationship with enthusiasm: if the feeling of revolutionary possibility before its effects are cognized and judged is one of enthusiasm, disappointment is necessarily reflective, removed in time, and sometimes in space, from the events and situations that spur it. It is relational, and therefore formally linked to one of its dominant modes of irony, which depends on shifting meaning comprised in both utterance and context. The specific literary techniques I analyze in this book as the sites of disappointment, such as allegory and pastiche, are figures of multiplicity: they depend on other uses and meanings that they reconfigure. Practices of disappointment are where revolutionary allegiances live on, though in altered forms.

In Cuba and Angola, though political transitions do not follow the same phases of colonial occupation followed by globalized capitalist present that Abbas describes, the question of the "rules that change" in the post-1989 transitions is fundamental to disappointment. The constant revisiting of times and texts from prior eras makes that transition one of the primary features that links these works together. Enzo Traverso argues that this revisiting is a global symptom of a twenty-first century which began with no new utopias on the horizon to replace those that dissipated in the final decade of the twentieth, precipitating inevitable reconsiderations of both "closed" histories and living memory, as two converging temporalities (9–10). The temporalities that converge in works of disappointment, however, are not just those of history and memory. These works also engage an acute awareness of the relationships, sometimes overlapping, and other times divergent, among revolutionary movements and histories of resistance and rebellion that mark the Cuban and Angolan experiences. Works of disappointment are often characterized by anxieties about the asynchronicity between the postcolonial world and former colonial and neocolonial powers, in the case of Angola, or between the then-called Second World, where I place Cuba as a representative space of the socialist alternative for formerly colonized places, and its relationships to both the First and the Third Worlds.

Susan Buck-Morss refers to the mechanism of that dialectical relationship between enthusiasm and what I am calling disappointment as a "colonization" of time. Using the example of the Soviet Union, she argues that the process of implementing enthusiastic dreams of a possible future carries real risk, including violence:

> Utopian visions, 'castles in the air,' are scientific, Lenin wrote, when they motivate a 'new people' to realize a revolutionary plan. Historical actualization thereby becomes the criterion for the acceptability of socialist dreaming. It seems to give proof that the dream was no mere fantasy. But in the process, history itself becomes a dreamworld. The voluntarism of the vanguard party, including the arbitrariness of its revolutionary violence, is rationalized as history striding forward. Using the masses as an instrument for realizing the dreamworld of history, the armed vanguard 'submits' to a conception of time that, so long as it remains victorious, legitimates its own rule . . . But when their logic, in compensating for the disappointments of today, becomes a 'plan' that locks in future meaning, time's indeterminacy and openness is colonized, and the utopian dream becomes a reality of oppression. (*Dreamworld* 67)

Iván de la Nuez, in his discussion of "postcommunism" in Cuba from 1999, identifies a similar process of "colonization of the future" by an overwhelming nostalgia for the pre-revolutionary past. For de la Nuez, this idealization risks reactivating the authoritarian and imperialist regimes prior to 1959 in the contemporary moment of Cuba's conversion into a "theme park" of ideological consumption (169). De la Nuez's discussion reveals how the metaphor of "colonized time," the fixing of the historical future, thus has a different valence for communities that see their political and cultural revolutions as decolonizing efforts. The significance of the sector of the Cuban Revolution's theorists who reinforced a narrative of intellectual inheritance in the decolonizing movements of the twentieth century over a genealogy that links it to the bourgeois revolutions of the eighteenth through nineteenth centuries is fundamental to understanding Cuba's investment in Angola and Latin America and Africa more broadly. In the Angolan case, this link is even more explicit: in a place of colonial violence time is already colonized; the future of the colonial subject is already foreclosed. In agreement with many of the first-generation African leaders who embraced socialism as an alternative to forms of governance predicated on their colonizers' traditions, Aimé Césaire famously argued in 1949 that "capitalist society, at its present stage, is incapable of establishing a concept of the rights of all men, just as it has proved incapable of establishing a system of individual ethics" (37). Disappointment is, therefore, not solely a term that reduces leftist revolutionary utopianism to its most repressive actions, or sees its failures at the close of the twentieth century as inevitable. Disappointment is repetitive: it is the condition that both brings about revolutions ("the disappointments of today") and the one which might follow in their wake. It is linked, discursively, to expressions of enthusiasm as the evidence of better possible futures, and sometimes mourns the dissipation of that enthusiasm. In its literary incarnations, this repetitive nature takes the central form of citational practices focused on history, literature, and other cultural media. Acts of citation—in parody, satire, and pastiche, but also in historical novels and remappings of history—become the central modes in which disappointment is written.

Entangled Political Histories

A trans-national poetics of disappointment is uncoincidentally rooted in the periods of internationalism—Cuba's deepest engagement with third-world politics of revolution and internationalist missions, and Angola's presence on the world stage of Cold War politics in the Global South—and yet deployed at a time when world events provoke a profound reconsideration of the sociocultural place of Cuban and Angolan literature in the world. The 1960s and 1970s in Angola, also a tumultuous period of profound political and social changes, paralleled phenomena in Cuba in a number of significant ways. Angola's anticolonial war, which began with a series of violent attacks in the north of Angola in 1961, spread throughout the colony through the 1960s, before independence was negotiated in 1974 following Portugal's Carnation Revolution. In the 1960s and 1970s differences over the ideological model that national liberation would follow and eventually among the leadership of the MPLA resulted in the alienation and exile of some of the most important anticolonial intellectuals, including intellectual historian Mário Pinto de Andrade, poet and cultural critic Mário António Fernandes, and *negritude* poet Viriato da Cruz. Angola's civil conflict between 1975 and 1976, following the turnover of sovereignty to the Angolan people, resulted in a single-party government under the MPLA, which was disputed among the other parties, notably Holden Roberto's FNLA and Jonas Savimbi's UNITA.[18] The subsequent South African invasion of Angola's borders, seen as the apartheid government's attempt to stop the spread of communism in Africa, also had the effect of helping to escalate the civil conflict, as each of the major parties depended on international support: the MPLA from Cuba and the Soviet Union, and the FNLA and UNITA from the United States and South Africa.

Just as the early years of Cuba's post-1959 changes brought intense scrutiny from international observers and catalyzed both support and condemnation, the South African invasion of Angola attracted international attention as well, albeit on a smaller scale. As David Birmingham notes, the conflict was cast internationally in terms of two of the most important political debates of the moment: the Cold War and South African apartheid; "profound horror" with South Africa's apartheid regime resulted in increased Western support for Angola's MPLA government (*A Short History* 84). However, as in the case of Cuba, the institutionalization of communist ideals of the revolution in Angola brought a rapid end to the short-lived enthusiasm surrounding independence, as Fernando Arenas notes: "It can be argued that the beginning of the end of these utopias occurred immediately after the institutionalization of the political regimes that set in after independence. In the case of Angola such a utopia was stillborn in 1975 given the deep fractures within and between the anticolonial movements" (xxx). In 1977, the young radical Nito Alves attempted a coup with support from the Soviet Union and the popular classes against MPLA leader and Angolan president Agostinho Neto, backed by Cuba and seen as a representative of the urban *mestiço* (mixed-race) class and the intellectual and political elite.[19] The failed coup led to a crackdown and period of violent purges of perceived enemies of the party, a subject addressed Boaventura Cardoso's *Maio, Mês de Maria* in chapter 1, and in José Eduardo Agualusa's *O Ano em que Zumbi Tomou o Rio* in chapter 4.[20]

If the disappointment that *Forms of Disappointment* traces is rooted in the cultural politics of the 1970s, the events of 1989–1991 precipitate the widespread reconsideration of the changing meaning of the cultural and political history of prior decades. According to the New York Accords signed in 1988 and the Bicesse Accords signed in 1991, troops were to demobilize, foreign powers including Cuba were to withdraw from Angola, and multiparty elections were scheduled; nevertheless, they failed to secure peace. UNITA leader

Jonas Savimbi's refusal to accept the MPLA's dominance in the 1992 elections triggered a second phase of devastating and violent civil war centered in the nation's cities, rather than the rural hinterland where battles had taken place in prior years. In 1989, Cuban general Arnaldo Ochoa pleaded guilty to money laundering, corruption, diamond smuggling in Angola, and drug trafficking in Cuba; he and three other military officials were executed. Piero Gleijeses argues that Ochoa's gains were limited and his corruption anomalous (494–95), though critics both on and off the island have accused the Cuban leadership of widespread involvement in these crimes.[21] In a series of interviews with writers including Cuban authors Karla Suárez and Yoss (José Miguel Sánchez Gómez), Raquel Ribeiro points to how the Ochoa trial marked a public crisis of legitimacy that has had lasting effects on how the war was memorialized:

> 'Uma guerra não acaba com os acordos de paz,' escreve Suárez. Porque não se pode falar de Angola sem falar do Verão de 89. Yoss também disse: 'Entre Cuba e Angola, há um antes e um depois de Ochoa.' Antes, exibiam-se as medalhas com orgulho. Depois, esconderam-nas. A sociedade cubana estava paralisada, dividida com o julgamento, a acusação . . . conta Karla: '. . . E quando acabou foi um silêncio total. Foi o ponto final da guerra. Custou muito: crescer com o discurso dos heróis e depois descobrir que os heróis também se fuzilam.' (Ribeiro n/p)

> ('A war does not end with peace accords,' writes Suárez. Because you cannot speak about Angola without speaking about the Summer of '89. Yoss also says: 'Between Cuba and Angola, there was a before and an after Ochoa.' Before, medals were displayed with pride. After, they were hidden. Cuban society was paralyzed, divided by judgement, accusations . . . Karla recounts: '. . . And when it ended there was total silence. That was the end point of the war. It really cost us: to grow up with the discourse of heroes and then discover that heroes are also executed.')[22]

The silence surrounding the war extends back across the Atlantic as well: Eliseo Alberto has written caustically about the absence of Cuban officials and representatives at the signing of the Bicesse Accords, the tripartite peace agreement among the Angolan parties and South Africa in Lisbon (*Informe* 170–71). Angolan writers Ondjaki and Ana Paula Tavares, both of whom are among the subjects Ribeiro interviews, note how in Angola the generalized silence about the MPLA's purges and the broader violence of the war has extended to a widespread suppression of discussion about Cuba's role

(Ribeiro). Ochoa's execution and the ethical crisis that accompanied the end of the war exemplifies the deep implication of internationalist allegiances in the broader post-Cold War crises in both Cuba and Angola. As the collapse of the communist bloc brought an end to the socialist experiment in Angola and ushered in Cuba's economic crisis known as the Special Period in Times of Peace, the transition initiated what Iván de la Nuez calls "la cancelación del futuro casi tocado y el nuevo porvenir, desconocido, que ahora se imponía pensar" (165) (the cancelation of the almost-touched future and the new unknown future that now had to be considered).

Literature of Disappointment

Both Cuban and Angolan critics have seen disenchantment as a post-Cold War cultural paradigm. Jorge Fornet's paradigmatic discussion of disenchantment in the literature of the 1990s in his article "La narrativa cubana entre la utopía y el desencanto" (Cuban Narrative Between Utopia and Disenchantment) defines disenchantment as a specifically historical process, rather than an affective one (11); in Ambrosio Fornet's response to his son's analysis, the older Fornet analyzes how "desencantamiento" (the process of becoming disenchanted) is both historical and ideological, capable of projecting new kinds of utopian thinking, and precipitating a new consideration of the post-1989 canon of Cuban literature both on and off the island ("La crítica" 20). Both Inocência Mata's discussion of Angolan poetry of the 1990s and Fernando Arenas's analysis of Angolan narrative of the same era discussed below capture the broad ideological and historical contours of this theorization of "desencanto." However, in her detailed analysis of the revolutionary New Man, Marta Hernández Salván draws particular attention to how both Ambrosio and Jorge Fornets's analyses elide the affective component of disenchantment, arguing that melancholy—the displacement of a feeling of loss—is the most important element of disenchantment. Hernández Salván shows that this melancholy is from the beginning a constitutive aspect of the revolutionary project itself, since the longing for utopia was always centered on an impossible object of desire—utopia's "no place"—and thus the melancholia of the post-Soviet era, in which the Cuban subject cannot mourn a lost object that never existed, takes the form of the loss of the self (77–81).

My intent here is not to contest these conceptualizations; in fact, they enrich my discussions of particular aspects of some of the narratives analyzed in this book. Rather, the aim of my analysis is different: my discussion of "disappointment" moves in a different direction than the project that the primary theorizations of "disenchantment" have engaged—that is, in the comprehensive characterization of a generation of writers who come of age in the late 1980s and early 1990s within national boundaries.[23] In my discussion, I take advantage of the mobility of the feeling of disappointment shared among trans-national communities, as well as the range of connotations of disappointment from its global implications to the local and personal. I see these as apt figures for how the texts I analyze engage not solely with the constitution of a national canon or a national hero, but with the broader trans-regional reach of the internationalist projects of the 1970s, and the more localized affective ties of communities and relationships forged through these allegiances. This mobility of feeling produces texts and textual features that address silences about the Angolan war and associated coordinated projects of internationalism. Their techniques of multiplicity demonstrate the difficulties of making these projects historically and artistically legible. In their techniques of citation and doubling, these works bridge past and present, origin and exile, literature and archive.

In Jacqueline Loss's examination of the enduring mark that Soviet cultures and Soviet imaginaries left on Cuba, she finds complex signifiers of racial difference, empire, and solidarity. Similarly, Christabelle Peters argues that the "Angolan experience" had an even more transformative effect on Cuban culture, consolidating, on the one hand, a neutralization of the most radical strains of black liberation; on the other, she contends that it produced sublimated outlets of radical racial thought in key cultural essays and texts. On a wider scale, it is also no accident, for example, that the Haitian Revolution and its leadership appear in literary and historical works as an alternate sign of the Age of Revolutions in novels and works of history; works discussing slavery focus on acts of rebellion and resistance, rather than romantic depictions of suffering. Toussaint L'Ouverture, along with other black revolutionary historical figures such as the Brazilian Zumbi dos Palmares, and the Angolan Queen Nzinga appear in Angolan literature as historical predecessors and founders of traditions of resistance. I draw from both of these characterizations my claim for a more nuanced relationship between the entangled origins of enthusiasm and disappointment in the internationalist projects of the early revolutionary years.

The period of 1971–1976, labeled the "quinquenio gris" (the gray five years) by Ambrosio Fornet, is remembered as the sharpest period of censorship and bureaucratic management of the artistic and intellectual spheres in Cuba. As Desiderio Navarro explains, this period marked a deep division between the intellectual class (though not all intellectuals) and the political leadership that had profound effects on the aesthetic realm, producing a "particular Soviet version of Socialist Realism that was . . . hostile to social critique" (191). Navarro argues that the relative loosening of administrative control over cultural production during the 1980s cultivated a generation of artists' reengagement with the public sphere, albeit frequently in extra-institutional spaces; this trend intensified during the economic crisis of the 1990s when writers were permitted to sign contracts with foreign presses. Along with Navarro's observations that the 1980s marked a de-institutionalization of especially visual arts in Cuba, Hernández Salván, focusing on poetry, argues that the post-1985 state policy of "rectificación de errores y tendencias negativas" (rectification of errors and negative tendencies) introduced a new kind of conservatism to revolutionary ideology that had the effect, for many writers, of a similar kind of withdrawal from the public sphere. She argues that the period of the "postrevolution" thus begins in the late 1980s: "Postrevolutionary poetic works focus on the limits of language's representation, which is a notion that actually challenges the idea of public sphere itself" (5). As Esther Whitfield has shown, nostalgia, disaffection, and *desencanto* became the "Cuban currency" in the international sphere during the post-Soviet era. The use of the metaphor of currency thus suggests an intersubjective valence to the structures of feeling, signaling how disappointment operates in a public space or commonplace.

In Angola, the 1980s also saw works that began to employ the techniques that define the poetics of disappointment. Manuel Rui's now-classic *Quem Me Dera Ser Onda* (1982) (*I Wish I Were a Wave*) satirizes the reduction of political engagement to a proliferation of revolutionary slogans and rules, though its affectionate tone sympathizes with the child protagonists trying to navigate the new post-independence world. By the early 1990s, however, the dreams of the 1970s are portrayed as definitively lost or indefinitely deferred. Inocência Mata, focusing on the poetry of the 1980s and 1990s, notes a movement away from the strategies for constructing a "political nation" toward constructing a civic one. Speaking of the poets José Luís Mendonça and Botelho de Vasconcelhos, she observes strategies of silence and images of black metal to argue that Angolan poetry at the turn of the twenty-first century has a decidedly dystopian tone:

> [T]here is already a note of nostalgia for a future that has been announced but not yet fulfilled: silence and the black metal reveal evident melancholy and regressive, dystopian nostalgia. The semantic-pragmatic form favoured by the two poets is the elegiac mode so as to better express their perplexities about the world, the country and themselves. (56)

Pepetela's novel *A Geração da Utopia* (1992) (The Generation of Utopia) laments the crisis of the independence generation as they see their utopian dreams fade; Fernando Arenas sees *A Geração da Utopia* and Boaventura

Cardoso's *Maio, Mês de Maria* (1997) (*May, the Month of Mary*) as the central texts of this utopian loss:

> [They] have become paradigmatic novels of profound disenchantment with the ideological, political, and socioeconomic trajectory of the postcolonial Angolan nation. These novels share a degree of skepticism on a worldwide scale with regard to some of the metanarratives that prevailed throughout the twentieth century (and still today), such as state-sponsored Marxism, neoliberal capitalism, and religious faith of various stripes. (170)

Works of disappointment encompass both the desire for historical recuperation and reckoning and the tone of disenchantment that characterizes their engagement with these pasts.

Cuban and Angolan works of disappointment often locate new sites of meaning-making in alternative communities distant from the grand narratives of nation or internationalist solidarity that guided the teleologies of the latter half of the twentieth century. In the context of Angolan literature, Fernando Arenas notes that characters who display small acts of generosity and social responsibility in the midst of violence and corruption serve as "critical microutopian horizons of hope" (200). Similarly, in her analysis of post-Soviet Cuban fiction, Guillermina de Ferrari argues that the values of fraternal sociability often metonymically replace the integration of public and private selves in the work of post-1991 intellectuals (18–19). Odette Casamayor-Cisneros's study *Utopía, distopía e ingravidez* (*Utopia, Dystopia and Weightlessness*) explores the continuities among post-Soviet Cuban works that she associates with the three titular concepts of utopia, dystopia and weightlessness as different manifestations of an ethical concern for community and humanity across a wide range of Cuban authors, both before and after 1989. My book builds on Hernández Salván's, de Ferrari's, Casamayor-Cisneros's, Mata's and Arenas's works tracing the melancholic and disenchanted postures of post-1989 texts, but reorients the direction of these feelings in the works I analyze away from solely a national sphere to track them trans-nationally, and link them specifically to the internationalism and transnational solidarities of the 1960s–1980s. In this sense, the formal figures of doubling and multiplicity in works of disappointment signal the movement and repetition of these figures across the South Atlantic, but also comprise the vestiges of feelings of trans-national solidarity. My analysis also builds beyond these characterizations to show that these works systematically acknowledge historical loss while refusing to see literature and culture as meaningless or illegible. The intersubjective ties that constitute the grounds for feelings of disappointment result in systematic propositions for textual strategies on which community-building can take place: uncovering silenced histories, revisiting the colonial archives, reviving the revolutionary hero, or reencountering the exiled other.

Each of the six chapters that follow—grouped into three parts—focuses on specific strategies that exemplify the deformation, disintegration or recasting of forms and texts associated with revolutionary enthusiasm. The chapters in part I, "Allegory and Aesthetics in the Post-Revolution," examine how novels and films explicitly cite common artistic techniques and styles associated with the early years of revolution, showing how the relationship between context and text give these techniques new meaning in the post-Cold War world. In chapter 1, "Silence and the People in Boaventura Cardoso's *Maio, Mês de Maria* and *Mãe, Materno Mar*," I discuss Cardoso's portrayal of the Angolan community's political transformations in the post-independence years through religious allegory. I analyze *Maio, Mês de Maria* (*May, Month of Mary*), a novel which narrates the anguished disappearance of a whole Luandan neighborhood's youths in the 1977 purges, and *Mãe, Materno Mar* (*Mother, Maternal Sea*), which narrates how the passengers aboard a 15-year-train journey to Luanda are defrauded by evangelical Christian "prophets," as two halves of a sustained historical critique. I show how Cardoso's techniques of historical ellipses, unmarked shifts in narrative perspective, competing voices, and narrative diversions reveal a search for an ordering process in Angola's postcolonial history. By focusing on how political discourses of progress alienate the everyday existence of common people, I analyze the ways in which Cardoso denounces inheritors of neocolonial forms of social control, both the repression following 1977's attempted coup, and in the proliferation of prophetic churches, to argue for the power of the "people" to frame both Angola's present and its past.

Chapter 2, "Postwar Cinematic Politics and the Structures of Disappointment" explores how two early twenty-first century films, *O Herói* (*The Hero*, Angola, 2004) and *Kangamba* (Cuba, 2008) cite documentary cinematic styles and the rhetoric of revolutionary collaboration and friendship from the 1960s and 70s but give them new meaning in the post–Cold War period. *Kangamba*'s war epic focused on humanitarian collaboration between Cubans and Angolans and Cuban heroism in a decisive 1983 battle presents a post–Cold War restorative impulse that remembers the early years of Cuban revolutionary orthodoxy as stable and purposeful. A more critical take on the legacy of the war, *O Herói* tells the story of an Angolan ex-soldier struggling to reintegrate into civilian society and the relationships he builds with a former prostitute and a presumed orphan. Considering the two films together exposes how both films assert the importance of understanding the relationship between past politics of south-south solidarity and postwar paradigms of neoliberal development, in which notions of ideological solidarity are blunted, made less visible, or disappear altogether. Taken together, the two films show how disappointment can manifest in the disjointed deployment of revolutionary style and form in a post-revolutionary context: what in the past had been a revolutionary style, both innovative and linked to leftist politics, has in the present become convention, vacated of its transformative potential.

Part II, "The Mobility of Form," addresses novels in which the interpenetration of film, music, and other literary genres, authors, and artists allows the novels to project new historical paths that break revolutionary teleology. In both chapters 3 and 4, these techniques constitute a politics of reconciliation, imagined both geographically between the Cuban island and exile communities, and ideologically, where the failed Angolan revolution can be re-staged in Brazil. Chapter 3, "The War Abroad and the War at Home: Eliseo Alberto's *Caracol Beach*" addresses the contradiction between Cuba's visual and mass media portrayals of the idealized revolutionary and racial and ideological solidarity between Africa and Latin America, and the lived experience of social divides in the Angolan war and at home. Alberto's work narrates the night a veteran of the Angolan war exiled in Florida kidnaps a group of teenagers to commit suicide by police. The novel portrays exile as both a bodily and an aesthetic experience that interrupts limits imposed by geographical boundaries, proximity, and political allegiance. Far from Ernesto "Che" Guevara's Socialist New Men, the novel's characters are haunted by how inherited social divisions including racial prejudice, hypermasculinity, homophobia, and tribalism manifest in the "hyper-reality" of the revolution as seen on large and small screens. My analysis examines how the novel constantly resorts to styles and references drawn from cinematic and other media, deforming the novel genre. I propose that in the novel, wartime violence, whether experienced firsthand or vicariously through media consumption, is presented as a kind of contagion counteracted in the novel through the trans-national ritual practice of Santería. Santería's focus on bodily manifestations of spirits' and deities' will in the material world bridges the novel's affective, political, and genre divisions, not by positing ritual as a counterpoint to visual media, but by emphasizing how Santería's transformative capacities can operate *through* media. This technique serves as a formal manifestation of the novel's call for counteracting the violence of divided communities on and off the island.

In chapter 4, "Revolution from the South in J.E. Agualusa's *O Ano em que Zumbi Tomou o Rio*," the revolutionary hero is resuscitated as a diachronic historical figure of resistance. José Eduardo Agualusa's novel *O Ano em que Zumbi Tomou o Rio* (*The Year that Zumbi Took Rio*) stages an imagined violent revolution in the marginalized, racialized communities of twenty-first-century

Rio de Janeiro through the collaboration of Angolan and Brazilian subjects displaced by war, racism and other forms of social violence. The novel retells the story of the messianic figure of Zumbi dos Palmares, the seventeenth-century king of the Brazilian maroon city of Palmares, who lead the city's final failed uprising against Portuguese and Dutch colonialists. In the Zumbi mythology, the Afro-Brazilian figure's eventual return will initiate a new revolutionary cycle, vindicating and reversing the community's fall. The chapter calls upon Boaventura de Sousa Santos's notion of "epistemologies of the South," which argues for a process of intercultural translation or knowledge exchange. This exchange operates through the cracks in hierarchical boundaries that restrict the circulation of knowledge reinforced through organizing concepts such as nationalism, colonialism, and racism. I show how the novel's complex system of citation of myriad historical, poetic, narrative, and cinematic sources enacts a cynical critique of the failures of the Angolan post-revolutionary regime to deliver on its pledges of peace and prosperity. The novel locates hope in the promise of a trans-Atlantic community of actors by reimagining the Angolan and Brazilian presents through collective resistance in a colonial past that had previously linked Angola to the Americas.

Part III, "Genre, Style, and Empire," analyzes works which interrogate the larger colonial and imperial histories against which south-south allegiances sought to resist in the mid-twentieth century, suggesting the Soviet Union as a neo-imperial power in Cuba and the new Angolan bureaucratic state as a contemporary model of coloniality in Angola. In this way, the novels of the final two chapters signal that the conditions that drove Cuba and Angola's horizontal solidarities in the mid-twentieth century remain relevant in the contemporary globalized world. Chapter 5, "Deferred Time and Belated Histories in Leonardo Padura's *El hombre que amaba a los perros*," places Padura's controversial novel *El hombre que amaba a los perros* (*The Man Who Loved Dogs*) in the context of Cuba's cultural politics of the 1970s–1990s, casting the consequences of Cuba's sovietization as a kind of ideological coloniality. I argue that *El hombre que amaba a los perros* revisits the inheritances of this relationship on the first Cuban generations who grew up with the Revolution. The novel follows the overlapping stories of Leon Trotsky from the time of his exile to his death, Trotsky's assassin Ramón Mercader, and the fictional Cuban writer Iván, focusing on the touchstones of the 1970s cultural crackdown in Cuba and the post-1990s transition. Padura's work stages the reconsideration of Cuba's relationship with other revolutionary movements and powers from the literal and ideological margins. For Padura, the suppression of histories such as Mercader's and Trotsky's is directly linked to the suppression of aesthetic experimentation in favor of a single model of socialist realism, both of which he blames on Soviet influence. I show that Padura's interlinked portrayals of exile and "insile" in the novel reveal the text's debate over whether a positive model of future reconstruction can arise via a belated knowledge of the past, even as it argues for the importance of a disperse mode of community formation predicated on the informal, surreptitious circulation of knowledge.

The final chapter, chapter 6, "Postrevolutionary Pastiche in Pepetela's Jaime Bunda Novels," analyzes the two Jaime Bunda detective novels by renowned Angolan author Pepetela (Artur Carlos Maurício Pestana dos Santos). Pepetela's sharp social criticism takes a satirical form in these two novels of the early twenty-first century, one which narrates the inept detective Jaime's failed investigation of the murder of young girl, and the other of an American engineer. This chapter shows how the Jaime Bunda novels, as literary pastiches of crime genres, critique the parallel importation of global capitalist ideology and English-language cultural products to Angola after 1989. I argue that an important unacknowledged referent of the novels is the nineteenth-century Portuguese writers Eça de Queirós and Ramalho Ortigão's literary parody *Mistério da Estrada de Sintra* (*The Mystery of the Sintra Road*) (1870), the first detective story to appear in the Portuguese language. The phantasms of the Portuguese colonial regime, symbolized by the unacknowledged Portuguese literary source, permeate the social world of the Jaime Bunda novels, even as that world is saturated with the influx of American products and influence. The Jaime Bunda novels portray American crime fiction conventions as inadequate to solve the crimes the titular character investigates, and thus to narrate the realities of the neo-colonial Angola he inhabits. The keys to Jaime Bunda's social world remain in plain sight, however, as literary excess that fails to fit the mold of the crime fiction the titular character consumes. Finally, in the Epilogue, I address several recent works that contain both disappointment and other affective responses to Cuba and Angola's histories of internationalist solidarity across the Global South.

The notion of horizontal, trans-geographical solidarities and resistance is built into cultural texts whose development under the twin rubrics of the postcolonial and globalization undergird many of the studies of Angolan literature in the final decades of the twentieth century and the first decades of the twenty-first. Similarly, critical readings of post-Soviet literature in Cuba require systematic analysis of Cuba's mediation between former third-world leadership, second-world solidarity and its location as a new site of tourist consumption in the post-transition global marketplace. Each of the narratives considered in the following chapters traces the geographies of the Global South—the former colony in Southern Africa, those peripheral areas of the former Soviet bloc, the peripheral spaces of the Southern United States, and Southern Europe. Taking them together emphasizes the necessity of examining the legacies of prior eras' linked political and cultural projects. The textual and cinematic strategies of disappointment analyzed in this book thus clarify the legacies of the entangled trans-national histories that characterized Cuba's and Angola's revolutionary and post-revolutionary eras, and show that studies of their post-Cold War literature and film require a deeper engagement with the horizontal solidarities and alternative visions of Cold War centered on the Global South.

Part I

Allegory and Aesthetics in the Post-Revolution

1

Silence and the People in Boaventura Cardoso's *Maio, Mês de Maria* and *Mãe, Materno Mar*

Boaventura Silva Cardoso (b. 1944) is the author of two novels fundamental to tracing a post-Cold War feeling of disappointment in Angola: *Maio, Mês de Maria* (1997) (*May, Month of Mary*) and *Mãe, Materno Mar* (2001) (*Mother, Maternal Sea*), which won Angola's National Prize for Culture and Art in 2001. These two novels address the twin crises of the MPLA's crackdown on suspected followers of Nito Alves after the coup attempt in 1977 and the opportunism and corruption that accompanied the transition to capitalism in the 1990s; both novels end with scenes of collectively experienced and communally expressed disappointment. The particular novelistic devices that encode this disappointment in Cardoso's two works—allegory, nonlinear temporality, collective narration, and a range of linguistic registers and codes—expose two fundamental features that I have traced in the introduction: how the feelings of enthusiasm and disappointment mutually implicate each other, and how the concept of disappointment links historical disenchantment with the affective register of large and small failures in the fulfillment of expectations. These techniques emphasize the collective and widespread impacts of the violent reaction to the coup, the devastation of the war, and the subsequent extensive internal displacement of people, as critics have noted.[1] I maintain, however, that the literary devices that mark these novels also become the repository of a new political potential still struggling to find a form among the rapid changes in the decades after revolution. In this sense, the inherent multiplicity of the figures and techniques that shape Cardoso's two novels is a formal analogue to the social structures of feeling emerging in the violence that accompanies the transitions from colony to independent nation, and single-party socialist rule to ruthless capitalism.

Though his first publications were poems and short stories published during the 1960s and 1970s, Cardoso is best known as a novelist who draws from his formal training in social sciences and his research into contemporary popular religious phenomena in Angola (Chaves, et al. 26). A lifelong public servant, Cardoso was a founding member of the Angolan Writers' Union and has served in a variety of public posts, including as director of the Instituto Nacional do Livro e o Disco (INALD; National Book and Disc Institute), Angola's ambassador to France and Italy, Minister of Culture from 2002–2010, and president of the Angolan Academy of Letters, founded in 2016. His early narratives focus primarily on the injustices of the colonial system, while the novel *Noites de Vigília* (2012) (*Sleepless Nights*) traces the rise of an unlikely revolutionary hero in the war for independence. *Maio, Mês de Maria* and *Mãe, Materno Mar* are two works that consider the post-independence era in depth.

Maio, Mês de Maria centers on the protagonist João Segunda's desperate search for his son Hermínio after the youths of his Luanda neighborhood disappear en masse, presumably due to their clandestine political activities under the leadership of a young radical in the early years of independence. João Segunda, a wealthy *assimilado* who moves from his rural home to Luanda, finds himself caught between the old colonial world in which his clear path to social advancement—cultural assimilation among the white Portuguese—vanishes at independence, the point at which João Segunda no longer understands his social role.[2] As Inocência Mata points out, João Segunda is "dolorosamente iniciado no novo regime político" ("MMM: as águas em movimento" 155) (painfully initiated into the new political regime), "painfully" because he had always thought of himself as Portuguese, and is unable to grasp the new manners, values, and customs that take hold during the post-revolutionary transition. The novel traces his ultimately futile attempt to find his son, and presents the community's desperation and agony over their disappeared children as sublimated in the ecstatic and syncretistic celebrations around the cult of Our Lady of Fátima, the patron saint of Portugal.

Maio, Mês de Maria has a circular movement in both time and geography: the first and last chapters narrate differing interpretations of the same scene of João Segunda's death. By contrast, *Mãe, Materno Mar*'s movement is primarily linear. The latter novel is an allegorical portrayal of the scramble to reorganize displaced communities in the chaos created by Angola's post-independence war. The novel captures this history through the interactions of the passengers aboard a train that takes fifteen years to travel from the interior city of Malanje to the capital of Luanda, symbolically originating in the same province where the Baixa de Cassanje revolt initiated the anticolonial war against the Portuguese in 1961. Cardoso notes in a 2005 interview that the train journey that dominates *Mãe, Materno Mar* allegorizes a post-independence national development that is frequently derailed, delayed, and re-routed through explosions of wartime violence, political confrontation, and internal displacement ("Entrevista"). The formal technique of a collective and plurivocal narrator in the novel parallels the rise of a diverse array of prophetic Christian and syncretic sects, whose leaders compete for bodily and monetary capital, amassing followers and accruing profits from donations and their multiple business ventures. The confusion and constant detentions of the train due to mechanical failures and infrastructural problems with the railroad, the looming war, and the resultant social upheaval and disorganization among the passengers is the locus of Cardoso's critique of the ruling class's large-scale abandonment of disadvantaged communities as the war escalated during the 1980s and the nation transitioned from single-party to multi-party rule in the 1990s. The novel builds to a final crescendo in which the train arrives in Luanda, where the Prophet Simon, leader of the most successful church, defrauds thousands of passengers and waiting faithful. The text also juxtaposes and intermixes religious and political ritual: party ideology is frequently cast as a competitor to other circulating discourses of the religious leaders. *Mãe, Materno Mar*'s portrayal of a market of ideas/ideologies thematizes the community's oft-frustrated attempt at making meaning from the plurivocal social milieu, rather than making a definitive proposal for Angola's post-transition future. The term "prophet" is thus significant, as the Prophet Simon does indeed preview Angola's wholesale conversion to an exploitive market economy in the post-Cold War era.

Both novels systematically deploy techniques that deposit linguistic and history-making authority with the people, an authority that is evident in the texts' shifting narrative perspectives, collective interjections, and use of orally-inflected popular language. Jorge Macedo argues that the strategy of privileging the experiences and perspectives of the marginalized constitute the author's political engagement: "Ao escritor, preocupa a emanação de uma literatura de permanente intervenção social (literatura engajada), envolvendo sobretudo os extractos sociais mais desfavorecidos e que constituem o subúrbio humano" (48) (The author is concerned with creating a literature of permanent social intervention [engaged literature], involving above all the least favored social constituents and those that constitute the margins of humanity). I thus read the two novels as dual parts of a structural social criticism of Angola: *Maio, Mês de Maria* takes place just before and just after the moment of transition from colonial rule to independence in Angola, while *Mãe, Materno Mar* narrates the decades after independence; *Maio, Mês de Maria* is primarily set in Luanda while almost all of *Mãe, Materno Mar* takes place in the small cities and countryside east of the capital; *Maio, Mês de Maria* addresses the Angolan syncretistic interpretation of the Catholic cult of Our Lady of Fátima while *Mãe, Materno Mar* critiques charismatic Christian churches as they are reinterpreted and adapted to Angolan society.³ The parallel alliteration of the two titles serves as an additional link between the two novels, proposing narrative and structural continuity. In Cardoso's two novels, collective religious belief and religious ceremony function as repositories of communal feeling and popular authority that evidence the residue of collective enthusiasm for the revolution's promised transformations. As both Carmen Lucia Tindó Secco and Rafael Cesar have noted, the religious practices around which both novels center also provide a mode of re-privileging traditional African cosmologies (Secco "Entre mar e terra"; Cesar). Popular religious ceremony thus becomes a strategy to deal with the widespread yet silenced trauma of the disappearance of thousands of suspected participants in 1977's failed coup and the mass displacement of rural populations to the urban centers due to the war. Cardoso's novelistic project suggests an analogic political power that rests with the people, where their simultaneous political, social, and economic marginalization nonetheless establishes an overwhelming creative potential to remake their social world.

Political Subjects After the Revolution

Cardoso's strategies that vest the populace with the power of "social intervention," to use Macedo's phrase, suggest a configuration of the collective that resists the colonial vision of the undifferentiated colonized masses as non-subjects of history, and also moves beyond the "povo" (people) of party politics as conceived during the era of single-party rule. Jacques Rancière's concept of the "people" helps to elucidate how Cardoso's treatment of the collective in the two novels can be linked to the potential for radical transformation of their reality, which takes the form of the reconstitution of a fractured community. For Rancière, the people are "a collective body in movement, an ideal body incarnated in sovereignty" which "dispute the forms of visibility of the common and the identities, forms of belonging, partitions, etc., defined by these forms" (*Dissensus* 93). The people as an "ideal body" is an empty concept only ever visible in its specific instantiation; that is, defined in opposition to the parties and identities available in a given order, which by definition limit and exclude.⁴ Rancière elsewhere argues that this process of political subjectification takes place via language: it is in enunciation of their presence and/or their demands that a "people" stages its terms for equality within an order, and thus opens the grounds for transformation of that order (*Disagreement* 22–26).⁵

The 1977 coup demonstrates how the performative power of enunciation can operate to consolidate and to contest power. Nito Alves, a seasoned guerilla fighter from the anticolonial war and member of the MPLA Central Committee, was concerned about what he saw as the abandonment of Angola's most disadvantaged groups by a socially elite mixed-race and highly educated party leadership. He organized and led study groups in Luanda's poor neighborhoods for debate on "the ideal of independence, the belief in equality, and the strategy for finding employment" after independence, and was eventually expelled from the party (Birmingham *A Short History* 88). On May 27, 1977, loyalists to Alves broke into prisons to free Alves allies and killed six MPLA leaders, while the Cubans defended Agostinho Neto's MPLA leadership (George 129). The transfer and subsequent reconsolidation of power was staged over the radio airways: supporters of the coup took over the radio station and declared Alves the new president of Angola; within hours, Cuban general Rafael Moracén Limonta interrupted the broadcast of a biography of Alves, forcing the presenter to proclaim support for Agostinho Neto on air. Moracén Limonta then announced that the coup had failed, and that the MPLA remained under Neto's control (George 129–30). The challenge to the MPLA staged by the dissidents was subsequently silenced: not only were those suspected of allegiance to the factionists repressed, but a generalized reticence around the episode has pervaded the Angolan public sphere. This is one of the primary foci of J. E. Agualusa's criticism of Angola's process of historical reckoning in the novel *Teoria Geral do Esquecimento* (2012) (*General Theory of Forgetting*), which also captures the contested memory and silence specifically around discussing the Cubans' role in the events of 1977.⁶ However, the larger context cannot be reduced simply to a popular revolt suppressed by a political oligarchy: the Soviet Union backed the Alves coup attempt and it was the Cuban allies who helped to restore Agostinho Neto to power, leading Henighan to argue that the success of the coup would have represented a new phase of European imperialism via the USSR in Angola ("Cuban Fulcrum" 238).

Cardoso's novels address this silencing and the performative power of enunciation by instilling linguistic authority among the people through collective narration and the deployment of an orally-inflected, Angolanized Portuguese, connecting his texts to earlier examples of foundational anticolonial writing. Born in Luanda, Cardoso spent fourteen years of his childhood in the interior city of Malanje; as such, he has noted the influence on his literature of Kimbundu and varieties of spoken language drawn from both the rural areas of Angola and the neighborhoods of migrants and transplants in the capital city. Cardoso observes:

Desde muito cedo nutria uma grande simpatia, uma grande paixão pelos falares angolanos da língua portuguesa. Debrucei-me de debruço-me principalmente sobre os falares das populações de língua bantu—Kimbundu de Malange e de Luanda. São esses falares que constituem a base da minha língua literária assumida e o meu "prazer de escrita," parafraseando Barthes. . . . De notar que o português norma e o angolanizado fazem parte do meu discurso estilístico. (Cristóvão and Cori 61–62)

(From a young age I cultivated a great sympathy, a great passion, for Angolan variants of the Portuguese language. I concentrated, and continue to concentrate, principally on the dialects of the Bantu language-speaking populations—the Kimbundu from Malange and Luanda. It is these variants that form the basis of the literary language I engage and my "pleasure of writing," to paraphrase Barthes. Note that both standard and Angolanized Portuguese form part of my stylistic discourse.)[7]

The opening sentences of *Maio, Mês de Maria* provide an example of these linguistic tendencies: "Igrejas tinham novamente mundo de gente, sobretudo de mulheres que, joelhando, fatimavam ardentemente Nossa Senhora de Fátima. Os cânticos ecoavam então unissonamente e se fiapavam por entre portas e janelas das igrejas. . . . As águas revindas constantes. Vinham vindo de todos os cantos sem chamamento" (11). (Churches once again had worlds of people, especially women who, kneeling, fervently fatimaed Our Lady of Fátima. The canticles then echoed in unison and threaded their way out among the doors and windows of the churches . . . Constant waters coming again. They came coming from every chant without being called). This passage demonstrates a number of linguistic features that appear systematically throughout Cardoso's two novels: rhythmic repetition ("todos os cantos sem chamamento"), orally-inflected syntax, including the typical Angolan repetition of the verb "vir" ("vinham vindo"), and morphological innovation ("fatimavam"). These features establish among the novel's concerns the poetics of the shared language and experience which assert as primary the novel's collective and multiple narrative voices. It is significant, however, that this creative enunciation is being staged in the church, one of the institutional weapons of colonial control. The novel, by performing the linguistic creativity of the people in the church, prefigures the people's linguistic conversion of their social spaces to search for a transformative political power at the end of the novel.

This use of Kimbundu- and orally-inflected Portuguese in rhythm, syntax, and lexicon connects Cardoso to earlier Angolan writers, particularly those associated with anticolonial literature such as Luandino Vieira and Uanhenga Xitu, as Franciso Soares notes (139). Luandino Vieira's groundbreaking story collection *Luuanda* (1963) showcases the writer's characteristic realist aesthetic and language grounded in the spoken mix of Portuguese and Kimbundu of the *musseques*, or shantytowns, where Vieira grew up; the work was censored until 1974 on political grounds. Vieira himself composed a "Nota de Censura Póstuma" (Posthumous Censorship Note) that appears before the main text of *Maio, Mês de Maria*, in which he emphasizes the "furação" (hurricane) of the revolution that unhinges João Segunda's identity from his social world— a central metaphor for revolution that appears in Agualusa's and Padura's novels as well—and the silence surrounding the 1977 purges in the "brutal repressão, surda-cega-e-muda, que acelerava a desagregação individual, social e nacional" (9) (brutal repression, deaf-blind-and-dumb, that accelerated individual, social, and national dissolution). Vieira identifies in Cardoso's literature similar linguistic features to his own: Vieira's work shares with Cardoso's the popular sources on which the authors draw for their literary language and thus establish Angolan Portuguese as its own protagonist in the history of the nation (10). Russell Hamilton observes of Vieira's prose from the 1960s:

> O leitor mais atento, mesmo não percebendo o kimbundu, fica ciente de que o narrador e as personagens se exprimem num português poeticamente transformado por um substrato linguístico africano, e que há, deste modo, um texto atrás do texto, ou um metatexto . . . Aqueles moradores de musseque que se encontravam em condições de ler as estórias, e que se davam ao trabalho de lê-las, sabiam que na altura, ou no futuro, poderiam sentir que o seu modo de ser—ou, pelo menos, a essência dele—era expresso numa forma estética válida. (132)

> (The attentive reader, even without understanding Kimbundu, is cognizant of the fact that the narrator and characters express themselves in a Portuguese that has been poetically transformed by an African linguistic subtext, and there is, therefore, a text behind the text, or a metatext. . . . Those *musseque*-dwellers who found themselves in sufficient conditions to read the stories, and who took it upon themselves to read them, knew that at the time, or in the future, they could feel that their way of being—or at least, the essence of it—was expressed in a valid aesthetic form.)

Vieira's use of a language influenced by the oral speech of the Luanda shantytowns he knew serves to humanize a population profoundly marked by scarcity and lack during the years of colonial dictatorship (Salgado 170). However, in *Maio, Mês de Maria* and *Mãe, Materno Mar*, political authority and transformative power is not solely vested in the "people" as speakers *when they speak*, the focus of Rancière's analysis, but also in their silence. Strategic silences or textual reticence in both novels not only mark the disappointment and devastation that accompanies the violence after the coup and the escalating civil war; these textual silences also signal a way out of disappointment. Phyllis Peres reads the strategy of what Doris Sommer calls "textual intransigence"—unrevealed secrets or guarded information—as a central element in the politics of Luandino Vieira's literary use of the Kimbundu *estória* form, or orally transmitted story, as a measure of taking linguistic power away from the colonizer to guard it among the informed, multilingual inhabitants of the *musseque* environments where he sets his literature and imagines his readers (28).[8] In both of Cardoso's novels, silence and ellipses play an equally important role to speech as a measure of staging contestation and thus taking political power, but thus signal the ambiguous nature of this political potential, which the people may or may not enact.

Maio, Mês de Maria

The initial protagonists of both *Maio, Mês de Maria* and *Mãe, Materno Mar* occupy privileged subject positions that are marginal to the larger communities around them: João Segunda by virtue of his status as *assimilado* and Manecas by virtue of his revolutionary high school education. The political and social transformation that Angolan communities undergo in the two novels take the shape of the re-education that each of the two protagonists experiences as they are thrown into contact with unfamiliar social milieus; in both novels, their individual narrative perspectives are eventually subsumed among the multiplicity of the people. In *Maio, Mês de Maria*, João Segunda takes pride in moving easily among the social strata enforced by the colonial system, but finds that his colonial worldview is maladapted to the kinds of new political knowledge in circulation after independence without the approving reinforcement of the white colonial class. Language is a primary site where Cardoso stages this tension:

> Apesar de não ter estudado mais do que a 4ª classe, João Segunda nas letras não tinha desconhecimento. Que ele escrevia bem bem, na escrituração comercial quem que lhe podia aldrabar?, e nas cartas de condolências, cartas de pedido de namoro e noivado, de casamento até, tinha tudo lembrado sabido de tanto ler um manual instrutor na escrita para todas ocasiões. Na faladura falada,

Segunda que também tinha habilidade dele. Quando estava na prosa com gente de sanzala se comunicava bem em kimbundo e umbundo, com provérbios e anedotas chalaçantes, ou então linguajava em pretoguês, que se fazia entender. No meio dos brancos João Segunda que afinava os putu dele, fia da mãe! donos da língua se conseguiam de lhe imitar? Sabia falar como os brancos de primeira e de segunda, bordava requebros nas falas do Minho, da Beira Alta, do Baixo Alentejo, do Algarve, ele que só conhecia a Metrópole no mapa. Então os brancos que lhe falavam assim você é só preto na pele, no coração você é branco como nós, e então ele se ria ridente vaidoso. (43)

(Despite not having studied beyond 4th grade, João Segunda was not unfamiliar with the language arts. He wrote so well, so well, in commercial recordkeeping who could touch him? and condolence letters, letters to ask someone for permission to court or for someone's hand, even for weddings, he remembered everything learned from having so carefully studied an instruction manual on writing for all occasions. In spoken speech, Segunda also had a certain ability. With people from the villages he conversed well in Kimbundu and Umbundu, using proverbs and witty anecdotes, or he'd chat in black-uguese, which he could get by in. With white people, João Segunda refined his Portuguese, good god! could masters of the language even come close? He knew how to talk like first- and second-class Portuguese, he could flirt extravagantly in the dialects of Minho, Beira Alta, Baixo Alentejo and the Algarve, he who only knew the metropole on a map. And the white people would tell him you're only black on your skin, in your heart you're white like us, and then he would laughingly laugh with puffed-up pride.)

This passage offers a prototypical example of how a collective narrative voice confirms João Segunda's authority through interjections ("fia da mãe! donos da língua se conseguiam lhe imitar?") and rhetorical questions ("quem que lhe podria aldrabar?"). However, it also subtly ironizes the insufficiency of his worldviews to accommodate his new lived realities, since his very authority is vested not solely in his ability to speak with the Portuguese, but with a diverse range of social groups. The narrator represents this fluency by privileging popular language constructions (the augmentative repetition of "bem, bem" or the redundant "faladura falada" and "ria ridente") over a formal peninsular Portuguese, thus presenting a tension between this narrative register and João

Segunda's vanity in being seen as "branco no coração" (white in his heart). Under the colonial system, João Segunda's mastery of languages, dialects, and registers permits him an easy mobility among different social circles, while his racial identification gives him access to those same social circles—insofar as he complies with the colonial value system as well. João Segunda's social capital comes from being *assimilado*—that is, through imitation of the colonizer and internalization of colonial values, while maintaining an irresolvable difference, racially coded in his non-white skin.

João Segunda's race operates as a signal of the limits of his assimilation in the colonial world, and his past assimilation marks the limits of his adaptation to the postcolonial one.[9] He carries over the fully internalized colonial affinity for the markers of social hierarchy into the post-independence system, collecting titles as president of the neighborhood association and the local soccer club, despite his disdain for the poorly-mannered inhabitants of his building and his total lack of knowledge of soccer.[10] He consents to his daughter's marriage to an uneducated Commander in the military, adapting to the new regime's clientelism by taking advantage of his new son-in-law's illicit business connections. He dreams that one day his children will receive a university degree in Portugal, though "não lhe importava nada os cursos que eles pudessem tirar, que queria só é que eles voltassem senhores doutores" (85) (it didn't matter to him what they studied, he just wanted them to come back with the title of graduate). For João Segunda, education is a signifier of social capital empty of content: the values it inscribes—for good or bad—are largely invisible to him. This is yet another representation of the tension between colonial education as inculcation in colonial values and revolutionary education as liberation. By contrast, João Segunda's son Hermínio, whom his teachers admire, takes seriously the educational work for citizens of the new system: "Crescido, com mais novos conhecimentos, leituras dele se orientaram para coisas mais sérias, romances volumosos, alguns clássicos do marxismo-leninismo cujas páginas sublinhava a lápis" (85) (All grown up, with the latest knowledge, his reading turned to more serious things, thick novels, some of the classics of Marxism-Leninism whose pages he underlined in pencil). Though this context is never made explicit in the novel, it is precisely the radical ideological debates and organization among the underprivileged neighborhoods in Luanda that drove the coup. The novel presents a sympathetic attitude to João Segunda not because of his colonialist values, but because of the pathos introduced by his internalization of them at the expense of his intellectual liberation. Similarly, it creates sympathy with Segunda's son Hermínio not necessarily because of his political views—which are never made explicit—but because, despite the seriousness with which he approaches the weight of the educational task after 1975, he disappears with the other young men and women of the neighborhood.

In eliding the historical contextual details, the focus of Cardoso's lament remains on the community's deep social fractures and their subsequent collective anguish, on the feelings of desperation and the process of disenchantment, rather than on explaining the events from the perspectives of the political leadership. In his reading of *Maio, Mês de Maria*, Pires Laranjeira criticizes Cardoso's symptomatic reticence as an extension of the widespread taboo on discussing openly the events of 1977 ("A Intentona" 171). This feature contrasts with the linguistic exuberance of the narrative voice; therefore, rather than a replication of public censorship, I see both textual strategies—strategic silence and narrative abundance—as contributing to the denial of a singular interpretive authority outside of the collective. Indeed, in *Maio, Mês de Maria* especially, the novel repeatedly signals secrets and unknowns without revealing their contents: João Segunda's clairvoyant pet goat as well as the spirit of his dead wife with whom he converses are the sources of secrets that the novel refers to but never reveals. The neighborhood's unconfirmed hypotheses about the disappearance of the youths due to packs of terrifying dogs establish the ambiance of fear and anguish that overwhelms João Segunda and the other families of the disappeared. However, the novel only references the human perpetrators obliquely in the final chapter when "cães começaram estavam se transformar em homens, bons cristãos" (228) (dogs began turning into men, good Christians). Throughout *Maio, Mês de Maria*, the chapters appear out of chronological order; the reader must make sense of them by tracking the presence or absence of the disappeared, especially Hermínio. A central demonstration of this technique takes place in the ecstatic scene of devotion to Mary during which the youths reappear in two overlapping parts as the first and last chapters of the novel. First, the novel presents the celebration with an outsider's view as believers mistake the priest's voice for the voices of their disappeared. The final chapter, however, revisits the same scene from the perspective of the believing populace as they first hear and then see their loved ones return. Narrating the celebration of Our Lady of Fátima over the first and last chapters thus enacts a historical and epistemological fracturing that pervades the rest of the novel.

In her reading of *Maio, Mês de Maria*, Inocência Mata sees in the repeated images of uncontrolled waters in the novel, including rains, oceans, and rivers, symbols of what she calls a process of "dechronicalization" of history. This dechronicalization at once halts the redemptive time of revolution and prophetically projects into the future the feeling of loss that took hold at the time of the coup and became widespread disillusionment by the end of the twentieth century ("*Maio, Mês de Maria*: as águas em movimento" 157). João Segunda's travels in search of his son effect this dechronicalization spatially as well: he retraces the route from Luanda to his home in Dala Kaxibo, and goes as far as Angola's remote border with Zambia, where he infiltrates a brutal work camp, returning home both times with no additional information. The silence around the circumstances of the youths' disappearance operates as a diegetic parallel to the narrator's historical reticence, exemplifying the climate of censorship and fear. After João Segunda's neighborhood is accused of fomenting ideas of independence, the inhabitants "continham penosamente a tradicional incontinência verbosa, não sei de nada, não vi nem ouvi nada, quem que imaginava nos tempos agora nossos a gente tinha de retrazer memoria esquecida do tempo do tuga, vigiar a palavra. . . . Na cabeça das gentes tinha sequer espaço para ver esse impossível?" (84) (painfully repressed their traditional verbal incontinence, I don't know anything, I didn't see or hear anything, who could have imagined in this day and age people would have to retrace forgotten memories of the time of the Portuguese, watch their words. . . . Was there even space in people's heads to imagine this impossibility?).[11] The people's repressed speech functions here as another effect of the process of "dechronicalization" of history: while they perform ignorance, they are simultaneously "retracing the forgotten memories" of the colonial period, where the overlapping experiences of before and after independence acquire a troubling and troubled similitude.

The final passages of *Maio, Mês de Maria* represent the ecstatic culmination of the people gathered in search of miraculous relief from their anguish, where Cardoso pairs the ambiguous power of the church to convene thousands of believers looking for relief with the apotheosis of plurivocal narrative voices which take over the novel. The people-as-narrators thus leave the imprint of a teeming power, though one that is ambiguous because this power might materially transform the community, enacting the return of the youths, or it might dissipate in mass hysteria and thus collective disappointment. *Maio, Mês de Maria* registers this imprint via the shift in perspective between the first and last chapters of the novel, each of which narrates the celebrations of Our Lady of Fátima on May 13th. The first chapter, which ends with João Segunda's death, recounts how the people begin to witness the miraculous appearance of their missing children's voices in the church; João Segunda eventually returns to his long-abandoned faith in the hopes of hearing Hermínio's voice. The perspective of the priest offers an explicit corrective to the syncretic beliefs of the congregation. For example, the image of Mary has been draped with cloths and offerings have been placed at her feet, "oferendas boamente trazidas, sincretices religiosas, que sô Padre cada vez vinha cada vez mandava deitar tudo fora, bruxarias, o povo cada vez que voltava mais fervoroso, sô Padre lhe falaram então estava profanar santidades populares" (12) (offerings brought in good faith, religious syncretisms, Father would always come and send everything to be thrown away, witchcraft, the people would return more and more zealous, Father, they told him, was profaning the sanctity of their popular beliefs). The priest, as someone who does not share a belief in the people's syncretic practices, offers an outsider's view on the miraculous reappearance of the voices of the disappeared during the church service:

> Palavra do orador, fulgurante, arrebatava sentimentos e, os crentes, no quase todo mulheres, copiosamente lagrimavam chorosos. Sentida, mensagem ecoava no fundo dos corações e atiçava a dor. Certo dia, no decurso de uma das pregações do jovem padre, que uma senhora irrompe no meio da multidão gritando: Meu filho! Meu filho! É ele o meu filho! É a voz do meu Quinzé! *No pensamento dela voz do padre era voz do filho que ela procurava fazia meses.* Essa ocorrência se generalizou depois. Cada vez mais senhoras caíam no desmaio *quando a voz do padre lhes trazia a recordação de vozes dos entes que elas buscavam.* (13; my emphasis)

> (The word of the preacher, flashing, raptured them and the believers, almost all women, tearfully cried copious tears. Mournful, the message echoed deep in their hearts and stirred up their pain. One day, during one of the young priest's sermons, a woman rushed forward in the middle of the multitude shouting: My son! My son! It's him, my son! It's the voice of my son Quinzé! *In her thinking the priest's voice was the voice of the son she had been trying to find for months.* The incident spread. More and more women fainted to the ground *when the priest's voice brought back memories of the voices of those they were searching for.*)

Here, the narrator offers an explanation for the phenomenon: the women *thought* they heard the voices of their loved ones; the priest *reminded* them of their memories of the disappeareds' voices. However, this interpretive framing from the perspective of the priest disappears in the last chapter, as the text turns over narrative authority to the collective of believers.

The final chapter symbolizes the shift to the narrative perspective of the believers who experience the miracles in a variety of ways. The setting is outdoors where the neighborhood processes the Virgin through the city as part of a demonstration, ending in a central plaza, rather than inside the controlled institutional space of the church. The people, initially frightened away by the pursing dogs, return to the plaza to celebrate the Virgin in ever-expanding numbers, and the priest's voice, which had provided an interpretive framing in the first chapter, is lost among the crowd. The effect of the people's takeover of the narrative is a shift in the material manifestation of their belief. Rather than hearing voices posited as a rationalized effect of memory, the people witness how the disappeared miraculously show up among the crowd:

> E mais outro desfalecido agora acompanhado de um grito, é ele! é o meu filho! Que a agitação começou estava tomar vários pontos do Largo e gritos a ecoarem nítidos, é o Juca!, está aqui o meu Nelito! é o Titico!, olha o Tó e a Bé! meu noivo!, oh, Santo Deus!, será possível, tu aqui?!, *sô Padre, todo cenhoso, sempre no centro do Largo, não estava perceber razão daquela toda desordem, estava fazer gestos para as pessoas se calarem, mas quem que lhe podia ouvir no meio daquela tanta numerosa multidão?* Depois vieram lhe falar qualquer coisa no ouvido, e não precisou de mais nenhuma explicação porque então as muitas todas vozes se levantaram uníssonas e se ouviu na toda largueza do Largo, milagre!, milagre!, milagre!, Nossa Senhora de Fátima ouviu as nossas preces!, os jovens do Bairro reapareceram!, os nossos filhos estão aqui! obrigado, Virgem Maria! *Jovens do Bairro do Balão tinham efectivamente misteriosamente reaparecido naquela manifestação, se misturando na multidão.* (229; my emphasis)

> (And another person fainted now with a shout, it's him! it's my son! Agitation began to set in in different places around the square and cries echoed sharply, it's Juca! my Nelito is here! it's Titico! look, Tó and Bé! my boyfriend! oh, Lord God! is it possible you're here? *Father, all scowls, stayed in the center of the Square, he couldn't see the reason for all that disorder, he was making gestures for people to calm down, but who could hear him in the middle of that numerous multitude?* Then they came to tell him something in his ear, and he needed no more explanation because all the many voices lifted up in unison and all along the length of the square could be heard, miracle! miracle! miracle! Our Lady of Fátima heard our prayers! our neighborhood kids have come back! our children are here! thank you, Virgin Mary! *The youths of the Balão Neighborhood had, in fact, mysteriously reappeared at the demonstration, mixing among the multitude.*)

In this passage, the individual voices of the families of the reappeared youths collectively overwhelm the priest, while the ideological effect of this technique establishes their perspective as primary. Central to this effect is their specifically syncretistic belief in the powers of the Virgin to intervene in their world, combining African belief with the infrastructure of the Catholic Church. Spatially, the return of the youths is an effect of shifting the collective experience from the circumscribed space of the church to the public square, where the priest's authority is ceded to the people; nonetheless, Hermínio arrives too late to reach his father before João Segunda's death.

Taken together, the first and last chapters present an ambiguous vision of the power of the believers. The return of the disappeared youths can simultaneously be read as the manifestation of ecstatic and mysterious belief in the hands of the people, as well as the desperate collective hallucination of a politically disempowered people suffering under a regime of fear and repression.[12] It is because of this ambiguity that I read the people's political power here as a possibility that is not fully activated or fulfilled. In this sense, the people's ability to bring back the disappeared connects to other moments in history when the collective has stood poised to take common action, especially as portrayed in pre-independence works of social protest. However, in the context of *Maio, Mês de Maria*, the immanent moment of transformation in anticolonial works like Vieira's—the inevitable independence from the colonizer—is sublimated in the *symbolic* act of social transformation in religious ritual. The people's collective narration and collective belief may or may not have the performative power to contest their reality. The novel's ambiguous presentation of these two equally-possible imaginative possibilities becomes another register of "textual reticence" in the novel.

Mãe, Materno Mar

In *Mãe, Materno Mar*, Cardoso's latter novel, the linguistic multiplicity that marks *Maio, Mês de Maria* remains an important feature, but the novel also makes use of the figure of allegory as another register of the ambiguity of Angola's political transformations in the post-independence era. In Walter Benjamin's analysis, allegory is an aesthetic figure that refers to history, rather than mythology, and thus that comes about in response to moments of historical crisis (*Origin* 166). The fifteen-year train journey around which the narrative revolves reveals the importance of allegory as central to the disappointment that the novel encodes. The novel is divided into three parts titled for the elements earth, fire, and water; as Secco notes, air, the fourth element central to many African cosmologies, is distributed throughout ("Entre mar e terra" 17–18). Air acquires an ambiguous charge: while it is associated with poetic imagination and divine authority, images of airs and winds in the novel also signal "a pesada e putrefacta atmosfera . . . que envolve a acidentada viagem do comboio, uma alegoria da história do pais" (18–19) (the oppressive and rotting atmosphere . . . that surrounds the bumpy train voyage, an allegory of the history of the country). In *Mãe, Materno Mar*, the young Manecas's initiation into the post-independence reality is different from João Segunda's tension between the colonial regime and the post-independence one. Rather, over the course of the allegorical train journey, Manecas's idealized expectations that stem from his post-revolutionary schooling come into conflict with the popular beliefs and practices incorporated into the religious leaders' theologies. These syncretistic belief systems both emphasize a popular and African-centered ontology and enable the pastors' chicanery. The way that the pastors manipulate these practices also offers a critical reading of the values of competition and profit-making that spread among the populace after the multi-party transition of the 1990s.

Early in the novel, these tensions take a biopolitical form, as the pastors vie for authority to perform the funerary rites for four passengers killed in a generalized brawl. In Hernández Salván's analysis of post-Cold War Cuba, biopolitics replaces ideology as the reason of state after the collapse of the socialist dreamworld; we can read a similar effacement of ideology in Manecas's initiation into the world of popular belief beyond his revolutionary education:

> Que uns, os da Igreja do Bom Pastor, defendiam que os mortos tinham de ser naturalmente enterrados na Terra, no cemitério, como era da boa santa tradição cristã; . . . a Igreja de Jesus Cristo Negro falava que não, que os corpos dos mortos tinham é de ser incinerados e as cinzas deitadas ao rio ao som de grandes batucadas, muita canjica e muita bebida, a rija festança; não, não, não, ripostou a Igreja de Jesus Cristo Salvador de Angola, a queima dos corpos significaria a queima das respectivas almas, que isso é uma prática que não se ajusta às nossas sagradas tradições . . . Manecas . . . não estava perceber porquê se estava perder tanto tempo com um assunto que lhe parecia tão simples de se resolver, que ele nunca tinha entendido nem se preocupado com as populares tradições. (51–52)

> (Some people, those from the Church of the Good Pastor, defended the position that the deceased had to be buried naturally in the earth, in the cemetery, in the good, sacred Christian tradition . . . the Church of the Black Jesus Christ said no, that the bodies of the dead definitely had to be cremated and the ashes spread on the river to the sound of batucada, with lots of canjica and lots of drinks, a giant celebration; no, no, no shot back the Church of Jesus Christ Savior of Angola, burning the bodies would

mean burning their respective souls, and that's something that doesn't conform to our sacred traditions . . . Manecas . . . couldn't understand why they were wasting so much time on an issue that seemed so simple to resolve, since he had never understood nor thought much about popular traditions.)[13]

In this passage, Cardoso is parodying the proliferation of charismatic and prophetic movements that begins to accelerate during the 1980s, each distinguished by its own rituals, often incorporating local traditions (Secco "Entre Mar e Terra" 12–13). By pairing the phenomena of social disruption and reorganization with that of the dead bodies as socioreligious capital, Cardoso also makes a clearly critical reference to the ideological stakes of the decades of war from 1975 until 2002. Manecas, like João Segunda, is caught in a position of uncomfortable unfamiliarity with what he witnesses, though, unlike João Segunda, Manecas is ignorant of rural and traditional culture: "Lá em Malange ele ouvia falar de certos rituais fúnebres que aconteciam nas sanzalas distantes da cidade, mas nunca manifestara interesse em conhecê-los. Não era ele um menino do liceu, educado nas boas educadas maneiras, que freqüentava os bons e os civilizados ambientes?" (56) (In Malange he had heard of certain funerary rituals that took place in the villages far from the city, but he had never shown interest in learning about them. Hadn't he attended high school, and been educated in good manners, spending his time in good and civilized places?). The religious practices are foreign to Manecas because he is urbanized, "civilized" and "educated"; his rhetoric reflects the MPLA's official policy of anti-tribalism and establishment of a national revolutionary culture that through the period of its single-party rule sought to deemphasize regional and cultural differences. They saw these differences as challenging to the development of a common national self-image, particularly as deployed as markers of political belonging.[14] However, the novel at times presents the Party as but another voice among the pastors: one of the narrative voices, in fact, accuses the Party member who vies for the rights to bury the dead in a properly revolutionary funeral as promoting another "pretensa religião surgida depois da Independência" (53) (supposed religion that came about after Independence). As the funeral rituals get underway, "No ar se ouviam já cânticos religiosos à mistura com cantos revolucionários, o que era previsível já que no Partido tinha muitos crentes, e, nas igrejas, militantes disfarçados em crentes" (56–57) (In the air could be heard religious canticles mixed with revolutionary chants, it was probable that in the Party there were many believers, and, in the churches, militants disguised as believers). The bodies of the train riders—the Angolan people—become the prizes of a tug-and-pull among the various political and religious figures, and lay bare the human impact of their corrupt dealings. By including the Party among the churches, the passage effects a sharply satirical literalization of the body-as-capital model of the state at war.

The effect of dechronicalizing history and elision of historical detail that Cardoso creates in *Maio, Mês de Maria* also occurs in *Mãe, Materno Mar*. The novel's central allegory of the train journey exposes the limitations of a historical imaginary that conceives a single path forward: the train at times becomes a prison as its passengers are trapped between origin and destination in what Ana Lúcia Sá calls a "não-lugar," a no-place (473). The utopian strain of teleological revolutionary views of history are encoded here: a utopia is, of course, Thomas More's idealized "nowhere," transformed in *Mãe, Materno Mar* into sites of suspension of action and of history, "espaços de transitoriedade nos quais essa vivência seria inormalizável, sensação adensada pela impossibilidade de contactos com o exterior e pelos riscos de guerra e das suas actuações terroristas de sabotagens e de minagem de terrenos, que impedem o abandono do comboio" (Sá 473) (spaces of transitoriness in which this existence would be un-normalizable, a feeling heightened by the impossibility of contact with the outside and by the dangers of war and acts of sabotage and mining of lands, which prevent [the passengers] from leaving the train). However, the train's immobility is not the only way that the novel disrupts the advance of linear time. The multiple messianic origin stories of the church leaders function as another ironizing mechanism of the singular direction of historical progress. A critical through-thread in the novel places political discourse in competition with the religious prophetic discourse. The foundational visions and visitations of the pastors thus operate as an act of displacement or divergence of a singular historical course for the people, a technique which connects the two novels both formally and thematically.

Maio, Mês de Maria's nonlinear narrative technique reappears in *Mãe, Materno Mar*. The latter novel accomplishes its effect of dechronicalization through a proliferation of possible foundational narratives that overlap or figuratively "speak over" the account of the train journey that originates in Malanje and travels to triumph in Luanda; Manecas represents one incarnation of this narrative. Another is the novel's griot figure, a blind old man named Ti Lucas, a former worker in the colonial railroad administration, and imprisoned in 1961, the date of the uprising that sparked the anticolonial war (134). The pastors each offer an additional foundational narrative, accompanied by the lofty promises and assurances of divine authority and authenticity that the ironic tone of the novel undermines throughout. The leader of the Igreja de Jesus Cristo Salvador de Angola derives his authority through his claims to have traveled abroad to Brazil and the United States, where he visited Harlem and Martin Luther King, Junior's Ebenezer Baptist Church in Atlanta,

Georgia. His rendition of the gospel anthem "Oh, Happy Day!" is interpreted and taught to his illiterate followers in "kinguelês," a phonetic mixture of Kimbundu, English, and Portuguese such that "Hué! Hué! Hué! Reconhecível era só mesmo a música. O resto quem que podia de entender?" (94) (Hué! Hué! Hué! Only the music was recognizable. Who could understand the rest?). Another of the leaders, the Prophet Simon Ntangu António, depends on his staff for his divine authority, "pois o bastão lhe tinha sido posto nas mãos no momento em que a Senhora das Boas-Águas lhe aparecera para lhe revelar a sua profética missão. Sem o bastão o Profeta era e não era, um simples Lukau Ntangu António, não mais Simon, o não-ser, os vagos ares" (152) (the staff had been placed in his hands at the moment in which the Lady of Good Waters had appeared to him to reveal his prophetic mission. Without the staff the Prophet was and was not, the simple Lukau Ntangu António, Simon no more, the not-being, the vacant air). The Pastor of the Igreja do Bomfim, the Profeta Simão Mukongo, in spite of being "uma figura humilde na aparência e nos modos" (172) (a humble figure in his appearance and his manner) begins to swell his numbers through his miraculous cures. The prophets' various foundational narratives invoke central practices that link historical prophetic movements in the Congo-Angola region, including visions and a divine call to witness and repositioning the center of religious authority in Africa and African bodies and voices. These types of churches thus often functioned as centers of anticolonial resistance.

The novel's rapid pace of the shifting points of view—the narrator is in one moment a member of the believing audience, and in another, the skeptical voice that reveals some point of trickery that the prophets employ in order to maintain their hold over their believers—captures both the rapid movement of the populace from one church and set of beliefs to another, as well as the accelerated pace at which new religious movements crop up and quickly find a core of practitioners. The fact that the pastors share a number of characteristics with historical church leaders as well as with the generalized expansion of charismatic movements during the 1980s and 1990s in Angola signals the double irony of their historical roots in the context of Cardoso's portrayal of their economic opportunism. Secco has analyzed characteristics that the prophets share with historical churches such as those founded by Simão Kimbangu in 1921 and Simão Gonçalves Tôco in 1949. As the Portuguese PIDE (Polícia Internacional e da Defesa do Estado; International Police for the Defense of the State), archives indicate, these churches were constantly under surveillance and accused of fostering anti-Portuguese sentiment and encouraging nationalism and independence among the populaces with whom they had contact.[15] Historically, movements such as the Tokoist and Kambinguist churches served as centers of the development of Pan-Africanist thought, anticolonial resistance and a theological alternative to colonial notions of Western modernity (Blanes and Sarró; Covington-Ward; Kandjimbo 165). And yet, their expanding presence and the proliferation of similar movements in the final decades of the twentieth century point to their similarly uneasy position vis-à-vis the postcolonial state (Blanes and Sarró).[16] The challenge that the churches pose to the social realms that the state is unable to fully occupy thus serves as a criticism of the post-independence political regime. However, the novel also condemns the abuses—both material and spiritual—that religious leaders are able to impose as a result of a lack of check on their power among communities in upheaval. In this sense, the people's disappointment bridges the competing systems of social organization.

As the Prophet Simão Ntangu António's perspective takes over the final chapters of *Mãe, Materno Mar*, the novel implicates the rise of his influence in his new purchasing power and accompanying financial opportunism that clearly references Angola's post-1991 transition to capitalism. The church opens supermarkets, department stores, bakeries, restaurants, butcher shops, and market stalls, all for the benefit of the believers. The narrator, in describing the litany of money-making enterprises that the Prophet operates in Luanda describes his "generous" and "magnanimous" works that parody the Prophet's profiting from the church in order to build his luxurious mansion, ostensibly for his "profundo e prolongado retiro spiritual" (253) (profound and prolonged spiritual rest). The people's confusion over his status—true Prophet or charlatan—continues through to his final arrival in Luanda after fifteen years proselytizing aboard the train. After the Prophet loses the staff that confers his powers and fails to appear before the crowds awaiting him in the capital, competing rumors of his divine healing powers and his trickery converge in the crowd's vacillating cheering and calls for his death. The people's voices thus replace the prophet's authority at the end of the novel.

The people's heterogeneous voices irrupt in the last pages of *Mãe, Materno Mar*, accompanied by their slow realization that the Prophet has betrayed his followers; this pairing links the novel thoroughly with the mode of disappointment in the last decade of the twentieth century. The return of the disappeared in *Maio, Mês de Maria* depicts the anguish of the repression of suspected factionists in the 1970s as tempered with a possible hope for a yet-undetermined future. At the end of *Mãe, Materno Mar*, that indeterminacy has morphed into a crowd of competing interests that effect the fracturing of the historical telos of the independence moment and explicitly implicates the pastors in the contagion of corruption at the expense of the people. And yet, it is again in the people's mosaic of voices and actions that Cardoso locates their potential—though not certain—redemption. The crowds, growing at every station as Prophet Simão Ntangu António's miraculous powers become known, explode as the train approaches Luanda. As in the final chapter of *Maio, Mês de Maria*, the people's voices occupy the material space of the novel and their competing interests accumulate among their pages, inscribing the ironic tone that pervades the text's treatment of the churches.

As the Prophet and the train arrive in Luanda, the people accumulate competing positions: they take over both the urban space of Luanda and the text of the narrative. In a five-page passage that lists petitions to the Prophet, businessmen ask for new opportunities, political opportunists request a Parliament seat, people beg for help with housing, educational scholarships, and jobs, a young beauty queen contestant seeks a crown, orphaned children search for their parents, the parents of disappeared youth request information about their loved ones, displaced peoples seek reparations for land and property lost, and even the family of a recently dead relative hope the Prophet will bring him back to life (278–82). The populace's requests capture both Angola's real social failures in the turmoil of the civil war and parody the prophet's own gains via his rise to power:

> Um camionista andava à procura de dinheiro para reparar os seus seis caminhões avariados todos na mesma semana. Aquilo só podia ser resultado de um mau olhado do vizinho! . . . Milhares de crianças de rua vinham organizados em bloco pedir ao Papá Simon lhes dissesse por onde andavam os seus papás e mamães. Os kimbandas e curandeiros, tendo em conta a grande procura dos seus serviços, vieram para pedir ao Profeta fizesse algo para que fossem oficialmente reconhecidos, com direito a casa e carro, parabólica, telefone celular e um vermelhinho passaporte. Xé! Alfinal, muitos dos que estavam lá em cima não lhes deviam o favor da sua pronta e eficaz intervenção? Haka! Que ingratidão! (281–82)

> (A truck driver was looking for money to repair his six trucks which had all broken down the same week. It could only be the result of his neighbor's evil eye! . . . Thousands of street kids came organized in a group to ask Father Simon to tell them where their fathers and mothers were. Diviners and witch-doctors, keeping in mind the great demand for their services, came to ask the Prophet to do something so they would be officially recognized, with rights to a house and a car, satellite TV, a cell phone, and a little red passport. Xé! In the end, weren't many of those present owed the favor of a swift and effective intervention? Haka! What ingratitude!)

The people's requests to the Prophet range from the mundane to the desperate to the opportunistic; the final request comes in the form of a mysterious stranger who presents himself at the airport and asks for help procuring, among other Angolan specialties, "uma brilhantes pedrinhas" (292) (some brilliant little stones). However, the Prophet—like the other church leaders—has absconded with the money gathered from his followers, leaving behind a generalized sense of disappointment: "assim aquele todo povo voltou nas suas casas no arrastar de pés e no declive dos ânimos" (293) (and thus all the people returned home dragging their feet with fallen spirits). The people's power of enunciation is left unanswered, and their unfilled petitions thus ironically reveal the fully internalized values of corrupt patronage and clientelism that operate in both formal and informal circles of power. The parallel between the recent political and economic history in Angola could hardly be clearer—the novel's accusations of opacity, corruption, forced national underdevelopment for the benefit of foreign investors, police abuse, and political indifference that *Mãe, Materno Mar* levies against the pastors have plagued the Angolan postcolonial political and social systems on a larger scale, but are often only obliquely acknowledged. The Prophet has been able to temporarily corral the various voices of the national and international community in a fleeting moment of unity as the people await the train's arrival, and yet just as quickly this unity dissipates, ending the novel with the crowd's exploding anger and disappointment.

Textual Reticence and Elliptic Futures

The believers at the end of *Mãe, Materno Mar* have been initiated in a difficult process of a second phase of enthusiasm and disappointment that ends with a revelation—just not the one that the people had hoped for. However, the novel suggests the potential for a more informed discernment among those defrauded by the Prophet as a necessary though painful lesson. In the final paragraph of the novel, Manecas, his small family, and Ti Lucas dip their feet in the sea: "E assim Manecas retornou às maternais águas" (293) (And thus Manecas returned to maternal waters). This final gesture of yet another undetermined foundation or beginning is an important indicator as to how we can read the final disappointment of the people in the context of both the historical elision that characterizes both novels and their fracturing of foundational narratives. Waters are an unstable signifier across the two novels: as I have argued elsewhere, unlike the "uncontrolled" waters of *Maio, Mês de Maria*, in *Mãe, Materno Mar* the "maternal waters" of the sea are long prefigured in Manecas's childhood obsession with waters, boats, and sea-dwelling beings. In this sense, his arrival to the edge of the sea is a sort of baptismal new beginning and the completion of a promise that has been foreshadowed throughout the novel (Millar "Águas inquietas" 21). However, as Rafael Cesar observes, the sea waters are not a neutral signifier: they are the means of arrival and conquest of the Portuguese and the routes of slavery and forced labor, but waters—especially river waters—are also the home of the traditional Angolan divinity Kianda. Citing Secco's observations that the sea both reinvigorates African values and carries African subjects to death, Cesar sees the sea as an ambiguous space where ancestral memories, the colonial occupation, and the recent wartime past converge (105–06). *Maio, Mês de Maria* ends in the public square with the people's voices raised in unison; in *Mãe Materno Mar* Manecas and Ti Lucas leave the masses behind to rest in the liminal space of the seashore. The novel's sudden end thus signals another locus of the secrets that the novel signals and yet does not reveal: the future. Ti Lucas, who accompanies Manecas to the sea, has powers of clairvoyance, though he refuses to speak of them since "a galinha só põe ovos quando ninguém olha para ela" (134) (the hen only lays eggs when no one is looking); Ti Lucas is also the one character who sees the true nature of the prophets and moves easily among the various classes and social strata of the train passengers. The pairing of the young man and the elder here points to a yet-undetermined future, as well as a potential process of revision of the foundations of the past. Ti Lucas's reticence to reveal what he may see of the present or the future thus relates to novel's sudden close on the liminal edge of the Angolan land, to the undisclosed secrets in *Maio, Mês de Maria* as well as to the historical silences in both novels.

    Doris Sommer characterizes literary techniques such as strategic silences and historical and narrative ellipses as textual "intransigence" and "reluctance." For Sommer, literary texts that announce silences or secrets whose contents are then denied to the reader enact a process of taking power: these strategies create a desire for information that is held permanently out of reach (415). As I have mentioned above, this is a strategy that is central to texts by anticolonial writers like Luandino Vieira, whose language use and literary style leave important marks on Cardoso's writing. However, Sommer also notes that such a strategy also has the capacity to posit "a politics of coalition among differently constituted positionalities, rather than the identity of interchangability of subjects as the basis for equality" (421). That is, Sommer sees in "textual intransigence" a distribution of power that is not predicated on a universally shared access to narrative, historical, or religious knowledge; textual silence thus operates not solely as a representation of repression, but also as one of carefully managing access to different kinds of knowledge. The people in Cardoso's novels are constituted in the collective narrators and the indirect discourse that represent the perspectives of multiple named and unnamed characters as well as numerous interlaced narrative threads, but they are also indicated as a series of absences: those who know the secrets, and those can read the silences. The tension between these two strategies opens up new ethical responses to disappointment in the novel vis-à-vis their reading of Angola in the post-independence era. As we have seen, Cardoso builds explicit criticism into the novels of both postcolonial forms of violence, as well as the corruption and clientelism that characterize the postcolonial state among other forms of social organization. In this sense, his works are very much in line with a wide range of writers from across the Global South who interrogate inherited forms of coloniality that they see as deeply embedded in local and national social, cultural, and political practices.

However, attention to the ellipses and contested voices in Cardoso's works also signals a way out of what Biodun Jeyifo calls the widespread perception of an "epistemic impasse" of "arrested decolonization" of contemporary spaces of former colonization that leads to a postcolonial disillusionment and subsequent historical melancholia of the present (125–27).[17] It would be reductive, I believe, to see *Mãe, Materno Mar* and *Maio, Mês de Maria* solely as documenting a particular Angolan iteration of a generalized postcolonial historical telos that ends in historical disaster. Rather, attention to the textual ellipses, to the creative power of Angola's linguistic imagination, to the novels' collective protagonism, and to the metaphoric valence of water, signal an implicit question: what other pasts, presents, and futures could be narratively constructed from these experiences? The disappointment registered in Cardoso's novels opens the possibility of a profoundly diverse series of narrative answers to this implicit question, in which the people can give form to its political power.

2

Postwar Cinematic Politics and the Structures of Disappointment

The first decade of the twenty-first century marked important turning points in Cuban and Angolan film production and the specific relationship to the legacies of the internationalist missions and the Angolan civil war. After state support for filmmaking evaporated in the years after independence, Angolan cinema reemerged on the international scene with the three fictional films released in 2004, including *O Herói* (*The Hero*) (Ferreira 222–223; Gamboa "Como Angola Está"; Moorman 112). Cuba's long public reticence to discuss Angola after the final withdrawal of troops in the early 1990s was broken in 2008 with the release of *Kangamba*. Both of these films thematize the Angolan conflict, but also make systematic references to the broader importance of filmmaking and the rhetoric of solidarity and heroic sacrifice that underpinned the revolutionary ideology linking the two communities, though in different ways. In both Cuba and Angola, literary and cinematic production were conceived in the early years as a fundamental realm of revolutionary action and internationalist collaboration; documentaries, fiction films, poetry, and narrative celebrating the war effort marked the early years of the military collaboration between Cuba and the MPLA. These texts were understood as examples of a larger project of international cooperation and examples of transatlantic solidarity that opposed colonial and imperialist incursions into the Global South. In this chapter, I explore how *O Herói* and *Kangamba* cite cinematic styles and the rhetoric of revolutionary collaboration and friendship from the 1960s and 1970s but give them new meaning in the post–Cold War period. In this sense, both contemporary films resonate with Walter Benjamin's discussion of a central feature of allegory as making explicit the process of textual "craftmanship" and re-signification as responsive to moments of historical crisis (*Origins* 179; 184).

Each of the two films refers to the revolutionary impulse of the early war years in the context of the post–Cold War confrontation with the global circulation of cultural and economic capital. *Kangamba* serves as an example of a film that portrays what Rafael Rojas identifies as a post–Cold War restorative impulse that casts the early years of Cuban revolutionary orthodoxy as stable and purposeful (*El estante* 55; 120–21). In *Kangamba*, this teleological purpose extends to international collaboration between Cuban and Angolan military and humanitarian military personnel during the 1983 battle in Cangamba, Angola, against an allied UNITA and South African coalition. A more critical take on the legacy of the war, *O Herói* tells the story of an Angolan ex-soldier struggling to reintegrate into civilian society. The film focuses on the relationships he builds with a former prostitute, a presumed orphan, and a young idealistic teacher. Considering the two films together exposes how both assert the importance of understanding the relationship between past politics of south-south solidarity and postwar paradigms of neoliberal development, in which notions of ideological solidarity are blunted, made less visible, or disappear altogether. *Kangamba* implies a continuity between the 1960s and 1980s internationalist projects and Cuba's updated international collaboration in "human" capital rather than material investment (Huish and Blue 8). However, an examination of *Kangamba*'s poetics reveals the fundamental impossibility of constructing a continuity of signification between early revolutionary and post–Cold War contexts, where the revolutionary styles have become cinematic convention. In its opposition to exploitive neocolonial relations between North and South, *O Herói*'s ironic allusions to past politics of solidarity point to the failures of these politics to realize the changes their architects imagined. Thus *O Herói* complicates the notion that histories of south-south relations are, in and of themselves, a sufficient basis for an ongoing politics and poetics of liberation. This chapter reads disappointment in *O Herói* as an affect and a citational technique internal to the film and closely linked to Angola's incomplete social transformation in the postwar years. Its conventional form—distinct from the revolutionary cinematic styles used in Cuban cinema of the 1960s and 1970s and cited in *Kangamba*—points to how the frustrated revolutionary process in Angola no longer takes as a point of reference the construction of a revolutionary future. Conversely, in *Kangamba*, disappointment is registered in the incongruity of the film's reactivation of now-familiar style and tropes of early revolutionary fiction and documentary film and its twenty-first-century social context. The two films thus suggest different readings of how to understand histories of internationalist, anticolonial, and anti-imperial collaboration in the contemporary moment.

Kangamba and Cuban Revolutionary Cinema

Kangamba portrays a seven-day battle that took place in the village of Cangamba, Angola, in 1983, eight years after official Angolan independence was achieved in 1975. The year 1975 also saw Cuban military troops' arrival in Angola and the transition from colonial war to civil war between the major battling political factions within the country. In the battle depicted in *Kangamba*, an outmanned, allied contingency of Cuban and FAPLA forces (Forças Armadas Para a Libertação de Angola/Armed Forces for the Liberation of Angola; the armed division of the MPLA) successfully holds off a much stronger and better-equipped UNITA and South African coalition. The film's director, Rogelio París, has noted in an interview that he intends to present not a testimonial view but rather a creative one, a fact he deliberately highlights in the spelling change from Cangamba the town to the film's title of *Kangamba* ("Rogelio, Aprendiz" n/p). The film inserts itself into the decades-long official Cuban rhetoric of African siblinghood and third-world solidarity through which the island nation's internationalist missions are narrated. París's resulting film, which references both Cuba's revolutionary cinematic innovation and its documentary tradition, draws its viewers into a melodramatic narrative, where the members of UNITA are cast as the puppets of a manipulative, racist, and greedy South African leadership and the Cuban soldiers as friends and defenders of Angolan freedom and national integrity. The film establishes notions of self-recognition and siblinghood among the Cuban and Angolan soldiers through the personal relationships, through interlingual practices mixing Spanish and Portuguese in conversation, and through a common concern for protecting the civilian communities from wartime suffering.

Both technically and thematically, *Kangamba* alludes to a narrative and an aesthetic in line with a revolutionary style developed through the 1960s and 1970s; it also follows a number of fiction and documentary films specifically about the Angolan experience produced between the 1970s and the 1990s. It is París's second film about the war, following 1990's *Caravana* (Caravan), and is the first in a trilogy of reconsiderations of the war named for three decisive battles, including *Sumbe* (2011) and a third film, expected to be titled *Cuito Cuanavale* (Izquierdo n/p).[1] *Kangamba* offers a nostalgic portrayal of the battle at Cangamba as the height of internationalist collaboration, and thus reasserts the place for utopian Cuban internationalism in the post–Cold War dissolution of binary global alliances. The film's political importance, therefore, also lies in its response to the silence around the Angolan mission following the ethical stain imposed by the Ochoa affair after 1989, as well as its release two years after Cuba had undergone its first major post-revolutionary transition, when Raúl Castro replaced Fidel as president. Consistent with a 1960s-'70s revolutionary narrative of trans-third-world solidarity, *Kangamba* insists on a narrative of continuity: an ongoing characterization Cuban and Angolan alliances as anticolonial, antiracist brotherhoods. The twenty-first-century context in which these revolutionary discourses are resurrected, however, points to a new neoliberal enemy—symbolized in the South African invading forces in Cangamba—who stands in for the imperialist capitalist world alliance. As Huish and Blue suggest, Cuba's ongoing internationalist projects can be "understood as a rejection of the sort of foreign relations that entail hegemonic processes of dependency and neo-colonialism" (8). Thus, *Kangamba* draws upon Cuba's unique history of internationalist collaboration to argue for an enduring difference in the post–Cold War era between the Global North's shift to neoliberal market-based assistance to the Global South and Cuba's collaborative approach to international solidarity and development.

Cuban film after the establishment of the ICAIC (Instituto Cubano de Artes e Industrias Cinematográficas/Cuban Institute of Cinematic Arts and Industries), the first cultural institution founded after the revolution, took revolutionary action as a primary subject of both documentary and fiction films.[2] This interest extended beyond Cuba to elsewhere in the world. The subject matter of these films is intimately related to the broader prerogative articulated by Cuban filmmaker Juan García Espinosa in his seminal essay "Por un cine imperfecto" (1967) ("For an Imperfect Cinema"). Imperfect cinema would erase the division between artist and viewer, making the production and reception of the artistic product part of the same revolutionary action; the function of the filmmaker or individual protagonist is suppressed in favor of a collective, allegorical protagonism. According to Michael Chanan, imperfect cinema fits into broader movements for "cultural decolonization" called for across the Global South, by articulating a new cinematic poetics driven by the new revolutionary context (*Cuban Cinema* 306). This poetics would be characterized by a film's explicit attempt to demystify the filmmaking process by making its collaborative nature visible, rather than relying on the myth of the single *auteur* filmmaker. It would thus reflect the values held by the broader social collective, rather than the vision of a director or producers alone and would conceptualize film as provoking a response from its audience, including them in its "action" (Burton 128–29; Chanan "The Changing Geography" 377). Imperfect cinema has much in common, therefore, with other contemporaneous theorizations of Latin American cinema, such as Fernando Solanas and Octavio Getino's "Hacia un tercer cine" (1969) (Toward a Third Cinema) which recasts the vocabulary of the "three worlds" in circulation during the mid- to late-twentieth century. Third Cinema, as a project of cultural decolonization, also calls for a similar participatory aesthetic that mobilizes and politicizes its viewers (Solanas and Getino 44). The ideas of these new conceptualizations of revolutionary cinema were put into practice in Cuba via collective showings of films accompanied by analysis and discussion (*cine-debate*) and mobile public showings, including film projections in rural areas without theater installations (*cine-móvil*). Techniques such as text questions posed to the viewers and incorporated into the film, didactic voiceovers and portrayals of roundtables, public meetings, and debates within the films themselves served as examples of how the viewing public could participate in the "imperfect" film.

Narratively and cinematically, *Kangamba* reflects the participatory artistic practice theorized in Espinosa's and in Solanas and Getino's essays. The film draws on a number of techniques to portray the Cuban Revolution's refrain of resistance to imperial powers and solidarity with African-descended peoples through a rhetoric of anti-imperial resistance, friendship across the Third World, and racial solidarity among colonized and formerly colonized areas of the globe.[3] Technically, the film reflects this discourse in a lack of differentiation between FAPLA and Cuban operatives: the Cuban and FAPLA soldiers speak to each other in a fluid mix of mutually comprehensible Spanish and Portuguese and wear similar fatigues. These details deemphasize differences among them and allow the Cuban viewers to see themselves as protagonists in world decolonization projects. One of the film's ironies, however, is that the Portuguese is subtitled for Spanish-speaking viewers: the "mutual comprehensibility" between Cuban and Angolan subjects does not smoothly translate to the extra-diegetic world. One of the film's primary characters, the Cuban Captain Mayito, develops a friendship with the Angolan medic João, as well as a romantic relationship with João's schoolteacher sister, Maria. Mayito and João's conversations, during which each character speaks his native language without confusion, contrast with the scenes in which the black UNITA commanders communicate with their white South African benefactors, who use Afrikaans for conversations to which the Angolans do not have access, and who demand English as a mutual language of domination.

In revolutionary films, especially documentary, individuals' testimonies about a given social or political situation are meant to serve as allegorical representations of the experiences of the broader public, and thus appear with minimal or no biographical information. The names of the two Angolan characters in *Kangamba*, João and Maria, are common to the point of generic, and therefore stand in for the larger Angolan community in the style of the anonymous testimonials common in Cuban documentaries of the 1960s–1970s. As protagonists, Mayito, João, and Maria represent three of the areas of development that have been the focus of Cuba's internationalist missions through the latter half of the twentieth century, including its aid to Angola: military assistance, education, and medicine. The three characters' intersecting collaboration in these areas reinforces the allegorical nature of their functions in the film.

The strategies of mutual identification and allegorical representation of the conflict as part of a global fight against colonialism and oppression appear in very similar form in Cuba's previous films about the Angolan war. By 1976, the first two documentaries about the Angolan intervention had appeared: *Angola, victoria de la esperanza* (1976) (*Angola, Victory of Hope*) directed by José Massip, which narrates the history of Portuguese colonialism that led to the war for independence, and *La guerra en Angola* (1976) (*The War in Angola*) directed by Miguel Fleitas. The two films were produced during a period of a flowering of documentary activity focused on internationalist solidarity around the world, and employed techniques that had come to mark Cuban cinema during the 1960s and 1970s. For example, in *La guerra en Angola*, Fleitas employs anonymous interview subjects accompanied by explanatory voiceover to establish a similarly allegorical function for the interviewees' testimonies. In one case, a young man identified as a FAPLA sergeant and former prisoner of UNITA testifies to having witnessed a number of Americans collaborating with UNITA, implicating the opposition parties in a larger project of global imperialism. He bolsters his observation by calling upon the townspeople to corroborate his identification of the foreigners. In a later scene, a woman testifies to witnessing UNITA's slaughter of a number of villagers, including the interviewee's father, for suspected collaboration with the MPLA.[4] In each of these cases, interpellation is key to the visual rhetorics of imperfect cinema. The scenes begin with close-ups of the interviewees' faces as they begin to speak, and as their testimony continues, the camera slowly pans out to include the interviewer and the filmmaking apparatus such as microphones, cameras, and camera operators. The documentary stages not only the testimony of the witnesses speaking as representatives of larger populations, but also the act of capturing the interview on film itself. In making the process of filming visible within the documentary, the focus remains on the collaborative process rather than the finished product. The expansion of the diegetic field thus suggests the viewers as additional participants in the process of documenting worldwide decolonization.

Fleitas's documentary also employs strategies that place the Cuban collaborators as part of a larger international collective that includes the Angolan people. Alongside Angolan witnesses, the filmmaker includes interviews with Cuban soldiers and doctors about their missions in Angola, as well as newsreels, montages of headlines, and speeches from both Fidel Castro and Angolan president Agostinho Neto. While the majority of the Portuguese in the film is translated into Spanish in subtitles, several scenes are left in Portuguese, including an Angolan news segment reporting on the MPLA's capture of South African prisoners as proof of South Africa's meddling in internal Angolan affairs, reported to a cadre of international journalists through the Minister of Information and a FAPLA commander. The visual footage that accompanies the report depicts news conferences and journalists taking down information from MPLA officials. The scene thus manifests the revolution's mandate to document and expose worldwide struggles against oppression, but also, in its reliance on visual footage and Portuguese without subtitles, points to documentary film's unique legibility to Cuban and international audiences. The scene is presented as intelligible both in the visual presentation and in the language of reporting, reinforcing the notion of a shared language of both oppression and resistance across the South Atlantic.

A photographer and documentarian character included among the Cuban contingency as part of the narrative structure of *Kangamba* represents this important area of the internationalist missions, whose images and footage are incorporated into *Kangamba*'s diegetic world. Although mostly shot in color, the film inserts black-and-white documentary-style footage to signal various key points of collaboration among the FAPLA and Cuban soldiers: in these shots, Cuban instructors teach FAPLA soldiers to use their weapons, soldiers construct a bread oven and water crops, and scouts discover grenades and signs that announce the borders of UNITA's territory. In each case, the presentation of seemingly rough footage, the whirring sound of the camera, and the vacillation between the documentarian's point of view and the extra-diegetic perspective clearly reference the styles of imperfect cinema that dominate Cuban filmmakers' interpretations of domestic and international issues. It underlines París's stated objective of using the fiction film medium to represent the real experiences of "men and women in war," where the men and women are not far-off others but part of a collective that includes the films' viewers ("Rogelio, aprendiz").

The "documentary" shots are concentrated in the first quarter of the film. This gesture augments a message of verisimilitude and reminds its viewers that the history of the Angolan intervention has played a fundamental role in the course of the political and social trajectory of the Cuban Revolution. In one scene that cuts back and forth between the documentary style and the fictional world depicted in the film, schoolchildren perform a patriotic play on a stage flanked by twin Angolan and Cuban flags. The documentarian's lens intercuts point-of-view shots of the performers and then the Cubans and Angolans in the audience watching the play. The technique enhances the impression of *Kangamba* as a celebratory patriotic war memorial to the veterans of the conflict but, by portraying multiple points of view, allows each group to alternately serve as viewers and the subjects of performances. This technique communicates a message that the Cuban and Angolan soldiers' resistance to global imperialism can be reproduced in a recognizable form by different actors and in different locations. The technique of a play-within-a-documentary-within-a-film allows each subject—the schoolchildren performers, the soldiers viewing the play, the documentarian, and implicitly, the directors and the viewers of *Kangamba*—to serve as both protagonist and audience. In positing this parallel among the three performances, *Kangamba* insists on the consistency of its message of horizontal solidarities across the Global South as an effective organization for military and ideological resistance to whatever external threat the larger geopolitical context may present. By suggesting the replication of resistance among different generations of participants, the scene also expands the relevance of this message to the early twenty-first-century moment of its production.

By contrast, in the scenes that depict interactions between the South African and UNITA leaders, visual and linguistic distinctions among the supposed allies create multiple modes of separation between the South Africans and UNITA soldiers. The South African officials and the UNITA general wear different colors of uniforms; while they rely on English as a common language of communication, the South Africans speak to one another in Afrikaans. The linguistic division reveals a power division as well. The South Africans use Afrikaans to discuss their concern over UNITA's failure to take Cangamba, but when the UNITA general asks them to return to English, their discussion ends and they order UNITA to take the city within forty-eight hours. The order, rather than the collaboration portrayed between Cuba and the MPLA, further establishes the separate realms in which South Africa and UNITA operate, as the film never portrays South African soldiers actively engaged in battle.[5] The exchange points to the fundamental incompatibility of an Angolan party born of the anticolonial struggle with the interests of the apartheid regime, coded in the film as a bridge between colonial and imperialist policies in Africa. The different military uniforms, the lack of mutually comprehensible languages, and uneven distribution of resources among UNITA and the South African commanders place the two camps on clearly opposing sides of the world ideological stage of the late Cold War. While Cuba is cast as a primary actor that draws other national and international communities in to revolutionary action through a mutual self-recognition with those it helps, UNITA's leadership reproduces old colonial relations and points to a new era in which the groundwork for neocolonial exploitation has already been established.

The communitarian aesthetic that marks the interactions between Cuban and FAPLA forces culminates in a melodramatic scene in which the exhausted soldiers receive a handwritten letter from the Comandante encouraging them to endure in their fight for the freedom of the Angolan people and the "libertad y dignidad de África" (liberty and dignity of Africa). João's question in Portuguese about the letter evokes the same wording in the affirmative answer in Spanish from Mayito—"para todos" (for everyone)—pointing once again to the politics of participation that arrives even at the highest levels of national and international leadership. As the letter ends with the Cuban Revolution's rallying cry of "Patria o muerte, ¡venceremos!" (Fatherland or death, we will triumph!), the scene reiterates a mutual recognition among the national and international communities contained under the banner of its collective first person, and the thesis that the defense of the "liberty and dignity of Africa" includes Cuba as an "Afro-Latino" nation. For Christine Hatzky, by insisting on the common African roots of Cubans and Angolans, Fidel Castro "invented a tradition in the sense of Eric Hobsbawm, in establishing a continuity with a suitable historical past as well as symbolizing the membership of a real or artificial community, and, in spatial terms, a 'Black Atlantic'—*avant la lettre*—at the same time" (11).

However, a comparison between *Kangamba*'s technique of a children's play-within-a-documentary-within-a-film and a similar technique deployed in the 2004 Angolan film *Na Cidade Vazia* (*Hollow City*) demonstrates how highlighting the now-conventional nature of the revolutionary poetics cited in *Kangamba* risks vacating them of their prior political effect. In the final sequence of Maria João Ganga's *Na Cidade Vazia*, as I have addressed in the introduction, the film cuts between scenes focused on the child protagonist N'dala as he is coerced into committing a home robbery and is himself shot and killed in the process, and those where his friend Zé performs the leading role in a didactic, revolutionary-era play based on Pepetela's children's novella *As Aventuras de Ngunga* (1972) (*The Adventures of Ngunga*). The film thus draws deliberate parallels between Ngunga's process of initiation into the then-developing revolutionary society and N'dala's brutal, opportunistic, and violent post-1992 present. *Na Cidade Vazia* accomplishes this parallel, as does *Kangamba*, by explicitly staging the scenarios and apparatus of mediation. An Angolan public familiar with Pepetela's work recognizes the lines that Zé rehearses throughout the film, as well as *As Aventuras de Nguga*'s call to replicate its revolutionary values in their everyday lives; by including Zé's performance as Ngunga, Ganga, therefore, also makes the mediated nature of the film itself an explicit focus. In drawing the viewer's attention to the differences in social contexts between the two scenarios, Na Cidade Vazia thus also implicates the viewers in the harsh reality that leads to N'dala's death.

Na Cidade Vazia and Kangamba thus use a similar technique of explicitly staging mediation to different effects. While in Na Cidade Vazia the disappointment is internal to the diegesis of the film—Angolan society is portrayed as having abandoned those values taught through Nguga's adventures—Kangamba's insistence on the ongoing coherence of the horizontal solidarities and sacrifice among the viewers and performers in the play, the documentary, and the fiction film ironically signals an extra-diegetic context in which this easy horizontal translation is no longer possible. Walter Benjamin's discussion of allegory points out that it is a figure that also makes its own constructedness explicit, and thus it is no accident that allegory dominates these films. As Hernández Salván discusses, allegory was a central figure in early revolutionary utopian thought in Cuba, less commonly used in the post-Soviet era: "Allegory, like the political message it conveyed, bore the form of a dialectical argumentation, whose synthetic moment would portray the liberating and redemptive goal of the nation" ("Out of History" 81). On a first level, Kangamba uses allegory in this way, as we have seen: the primary characters represent Cuba's leadership role and sacrifice to the cause of decolonization and third-world revolution. Benjamin, however, discusses allegory as a dominant device in times of historical crisis, regarding the seventeenth-century baroque repetition of familiar symbolic figures as a process of historicization of those very figures. In his reading of allegory, allegory is both "convention *and* expression . . . the allegory of the seventeenth century is not convention of expression, but expression of convention" (175). Allegory in Kangamba has a similar function.

Kangamba's repetition of familiar cinematic tropes, styles, and techniques drawn from the first decades of revolutionary film works to highlight the very familiarity and conventionality of these techniques. By being "revolutionary" in a historicizing sense, they have ceased to be "revolutionary" in another sense: that of shaking the viewers from their places of familiarity and spurring them to action. The very "conventionality" that these techniques communicate in their twenty-first-century context, rather, has a historicizing role, *implicitly* acknowledging the silence around the Angolan conflict in the decades after 1989, as well as the collective dismay at the revelations of the corruption of Cuban leadership and the after-effects of the violence on those who served in the mission. It is for this reason that I read these techniques as encoding the disappointment that dominates the post–Cold War environment.

Paulo Antonio Paranaguá notes that post–Cold War Cuban cinema has increasingly expressed internal social critiques of enforced conformity, labyrinthine bureaucracy, race- and gender-based social exclusion, and economic hardship. However, he argues that París's codirected 1990 Angolan war film *Caravana* embodies a "wait-and-see conservatism which simply advocates resistance against external threats and against the Wind from the East . . . even if that means supporting the corrupt rather than the cowardly, as the film does" (188). A similar notion undergirds *Kangamba*. Its references to the revolutionary film techniques that marked a new era in Latin American cinema are subsumed in the latter part of the film by a cinematic and political conservatism that returns to a traditional narrative structure guided by a voiceover narrator who reads the letter, cuts in clichéd images of African fauna, and wraps up neatly with a definitive victory for the heroes and Mayito's tragic death on the battlefield. Although *Kangamba* insists on a distinct contrast between the Cuba-MPLA collaboration and the exchanges from the South African leaders and their UNITA beneficiaries, the film's homage to the central role of the national patriarch in guiding the actions of the soldiers reveals a clear parallel between the two sides of the conflict.

International observers frequently expected the Cuban Revolution to collapse during or after the economic crisis precipitated by the fall of the Soviet Union, since the USSR had served as Cuba's largest trading partner and close political ally. However, as Esther Whitfield and others demonstrate, the crisis also sparked a period of increasing adaptation to a new economic and cultural climate in which Cuba's anti-imperial politics turned not on the divides of the Cold War but on a message of resistance to the dominance of market-based interactions with its neighbors in the Global South. Even as Cuba has shifted to a tourism-based economy with increased privatization and even as internationalist workers are now often contracted and paid by foreign governments, these workers continue to be seen in official discourse as building solidarity between Cuba and their destinations in Africa, Latin America, and South Asia (Blue 42). In the context of the 2000s, *Kangamba* insinuates that although Cuba sells its citizens' labor overseas, its human investment in south-south alliances continue to represent a model of engagement that resists market-driven exploitation and monetary and material investment. However, by highlighting the very conventionality of its visual poetics, the film repeats a message of third-world solidarity that made sense in the midst of global Cold War politics just as it references avant-garde documentary styles, without translating their radical nature in the twenty-first-century context. Both the anticolonial messaging and the citation of early revolutionary film serve as historical points of reference rather than proposing a new or even updated politics of engagement across the Global South. The film leaves uninterrogated an implied easy equivalence between the colonialists of the 1970s–'80s and a generalized global economic imperialism of the 2000s.

The Hero After the War

The postwar period appears in a very different form in the Angolan film *O Herói* (*The Hero*, 2004), the first full-length fiction film directed by Angolan filmmaker Zézé Gamboa (José Augusto Octávio Gamboa dos Passos). Rather than suggesting military and political victory as constitutive of the revolutionary decolonizing process, *O Herói* focuses on the gap between the official processes of the transition from colonialism to independence as well as from war to peace, and the lack of material change that such processes bring to the lives of the characters. *O Herói* takes place just after the end of the war, after the period of renewed and brutal violence that broke out after Angola's first multiparty elections in 1992 and continued until UNITA leader Jonas Savimbi's death in 2002. The film presents the story of the veteran Vitório, who ends up in Luanda after losing his leg in a mine explosion at the end of his twenty years as a FAPLA soldier. Rather than grandiose narratives of global solidarity, *O Herói* represents the disappointment and exhaustion with wartime factions and ideological divides that have dominated the postindependence era. As in the case of *Kangamba*, *O Herói*'s cinematic style references prior eras of revolutionary solidarity through form, by revealing its diegetic world largely through the visual perspective of the marginalized protagonists. However, Gamboa's film emphasizes the failures of these narratives of solidarity in the present, rather than *Kangamba*'s insistence on their continuity. The use of allegory is thus different in the two films. *O Herói*'s disappointment also registers within the diegesis of the film, rather than only as an extradiegetic effect of the now-conventional nature of the film techniques that it cites. Through Vitório—whose name, ironically, means "victory"—Gamboa's film indirectly alludes to both the euphoria and the purpose of the early postindependence period, and also suggests that the prolonged violence and loss have resulted in a national present very different from the one imagined in the early revolutionary years. The film's allegory of revolutionary solidarity is ironic, pointing to the idea of solidarity as vacuous linguistic convention that often fails to translate to social practice.

O Herói narrates Vitório's struggle to find employment and reintegrate into civilian society in parallel to the child Manu's difficulties navigating the rough-and-tumble environment of his *musseque* neighborhood as he mourns the disappearance of his parents to the war years before. Vitório's and Manu's analogous stories indicate not only the trauma of a youth lived entirely in the context of armed conflict, but also the problems of extensive unemployment, fractured families, crippled national infrastructure, and dependence on foreign investment that characterize early twenty-first-century Angola. Even after he obtains a prosthesis that allows him to walk, Vitório finds that his exemplary service to his country, his patriotic capital, does not help him secure a job or reintegrate into civil society. His prosthesis, representing the promise of reintegration and healing, belies his difficulties in contributing to a transitioning Angolan society that Vitório is unable to anticipate.

Rather than *Kangamba*'s explicit staging of mediation and evocation of imperfect cinema to place the viewer in a position of protagonism in worldwide decolonization and horizontal soliarity, *O Herói* more subtly incorporates visual cues that emphasize the vast differences between the perspectives of the privileged few and the marginalized characters who are the primary focus of the film. The film clearly references early revolutionary rhetoric and narrative styles focused on the common subject, through techniques such as point-of-view shots of the marginalized protagonists and explicit visual parallels between the older war veteran and the children living different kinds of battles for survival in the film's present. The plot emphasizes both small moments of camaraderie and kindness among individuals and the absence of broader notions of solidarity among social groups and classes. *O Herói* narrates Vitório's struggles on a thorny path to reconstituting a national family broken apart by wartime violence as he eventually forms a familial community of outcasts.[6] Vitório develops a relationship with the prostitute Maria Bárbara, who has lost her son; with Manu, the presumed orphan who now lives in a *musseque* with his grandmother, and with Joana, Manu's teacher who befriends Vitório and helps him eventually secure employment through her well-connected boyfriend. After Vitório's prosthesis is stolen as he sleeps on the street, he tells his story to Joana, who arranges for him to appear on the radio for an interview about his experience with a government minister. Manu, who has exchanged stolen goods for the prosthetic leg at a junk shop, hears the story, and returns the leg to Vitório. The film thus symbolically links the prosthesis to Vitório's recomposed surrogate family; it ends by showing Vitório working in a new job as a chauffeur who takes Manu for a ride, suggesting a paternal relationship with the child as the two literally and figuratively move forward in the car. Each of the characters in *O Herói* stands in for the lost relative of another, and they are thus able to reestablish a community despite the familial disintegration evidenced throughout the film.

However, unlike the brotherly relationships suggested among the soldiers in *Kangamba*, the family unit created by Vitório, Manu, Maria Bárbara, and Joana is not a symbolic extension of international and national solidarities; rather, it is a community that forms in the cracks of a semifunctional and undependable Angolan state. The solution to Vitório's unemployment—finding work as a driver for a government minister—is so localized that it provides no metonymic suggestion of systematic social change, and yet at the same time is the result of the webs of personal connections and mutual favors that, in the film, characterizes postwar notions of solidarity. In this way, *O Herói* clearly contributes to the debates about the legacies of the revolutionary past in the disappointed moment of the twenty-first-century present. As Mark Sabine astutely notes in his analysis of the film, *O Herói* undermines the straightforward thesis of an optimistic future symbolized in the reconstituted national family. For Sabine, the film comprises a subversive political allegory that critiques both the concentration of power in the hands of a ruling few and the lack of a collective spirit of mutual assistance among the populace, and calls for a return to the independence-era politics of solidarity. Sabine argues that this allegory is constructed around a number of hidden tropes that ironically refer to the ideals of independence-era revolutionary ideology. These tropes include the socialist New Man, ironically evoked in Vitório's broken body, the derailed national development project and the "prosthetic family"; the stalled and decaying construction projects that pervade the shots of the city as ironic evocations of national social construction; and the symbol of transport, privatized and unavailable to the vast majority of the public, signaling limited economic and social mobility for all but the political elite (209–12). Taken as a whole, the effect of these strategies is ambiguous:

> while in *The Hero*'s political allegory, Vitório may end up using his prosthesis to depress the accelerator pedal of the state-owned machine, the viewer cannot be certain whether the leg has come to represent an integral part of the organic body of the nation, or whether, conversely, it is the symbolic agent of Vitório's incorporation into the clientist and kleptocratic body of the state, which props up the hegemony of global capitalism. (215)

If, in fact, the film is advocating for a return to independence-era notions of solidarity, *O Herói*'s ambiguity arises in part from the question of whether this solidarity operates horizontally as well as vertically—between the populace and the leadership—or whether a new, postwar solidarity serves as a mechanism of collective opposition to the "clientist and kleptocratic state" that the former anticolonial leadership now represents. As in the case of *Kangamba*, the Angolan film's carefully constructed relationship with prior eras' cinematic and political grammar organizes its relationship to its contemporary postwar environment. The film systematically cites this grammar both visually and thematically, revealing how postwar feelings of disappointment register as an ironic gap between the imaginary of the past and the reality of the present.

Gamboa's prior work has addressed the origins of disappointment in the divisions among the MPLA's leadership and the broader civil conflict. The director's war documentary *Dissidence* (1998) for example, traces an eclectic group of Angolan intellectuals formerly allied to diverse political movements in the independence and post-independence era, each ousted for failing to comply with increasing measures of orthodoxy. As in the case of Cardoso's *Maio, Mês de Maria*, through its imprisoned, executed and/or exiled subjects, the film draws disturbing parallels between the practices of Portuguese colonial control and Angola's postcolonial governance, their parallel neglect of public institutions such as schools and universities, and the atmosphere of fear and violence that pervaded pre- and post-1975 Angola. While similar theses have been comprehensively theorized in canonical postcolonial works from Fanon's *The Wretched of the Earth* (1961) to Mbembe's *On the Postcolony* (2000), Gamboa's treatment of the colonial transition in *Dissidence*—in which Gamboa suggests that Angola's independence has only been partially achieved—can nonetheless shed light on how *O Herói* redeploys this critique in the context of the first treacherous postwar years.

In fact, rather than a nostalgia for early-independence-era notions of solidarity, *O Herói* points to the larger divisions of the civil war to signal the limits of practices of solidarity at a national level in the first place. The film's only use of flashback occurs when Vitório sleeps on the street, as he dreams of the landmine explosion in which he lost his leg; when he awakes, he discovers that his prosthesis has been stolen. The flashback scenes provide Vitório's visual perspective as he watches the enemy advance, steps on the mine, and see his damaged leg as his fellow soldiers load him onto a stretcher. By concentrating on Vitório's point of view, the film obliquely calls up the didactic use of cultural texts depicting the revolutionary hero to emphasize a chain of transmission from the revolutionary past to the present. However, what is transmitted to Vitório's present is not just the care of his fellow soldiers for the wounded, but the advance of enemy troops and the ongoing conflict that cost him the leg in the first place. The film vacillates between Manu and Vitório; the same point-of-view technique frequently opens the scenes that introduce these two characters. Breaking the possibility of continuity and solidarity among the social classes, however, by contrast, several of the scenes focused on members of the economic and social elite—Joana and her boyfriend Pedro—are introduced with high-angle shots, formally and visually emphasizing their relative privilege. Gamboa's use of similar techniques to develop Vitório's and Manu's parallel narratives and the emphasis he places on the gaps between their lived experience and that of the political elite suggest a broader relationship of transmission and inheritance of both the deep divides and the potential for reconciliation between the two.

This comparison between children and veterans is developed in a number of ways in *O Herói*. Early in the film, the doctor who finally secures Vitório's prosthesis after months of waiting warns him that he will have to learn to walk again, "como uma criança" (like a child). Vitório's incredulous response—"Eu, uma criança?" (Me, a child?)—points to Vitório's and his generation's childhood lost to war and violence; Vitório reveals that he had been conscripted into the armed forces at fifteen years of age. *O Herói* presents us with several child doubles of Vitório. Later in the film, as Vitório waits outside the hospital for help after he has lost his prosthesis, Joana and her boyfriend Pedro arrive with a street child whom Pedro has hit with his car. Pedro has attended college abroad on a government scholarship and returned home to a guaranteed job working for his uncle, a government minister, while Joana, a school teacher, is frustrated by the necessity for teacher strikes that close the school in protest of nonpayment of salaries and the lack of resources for education in general. To Pedro, they have done their duty by delivering the child to the hospital, but for Joana, who strikes up a conversation with Vitório and organizes the radio interview with Pedro's uncle that leads to the return of his leg, Vitório represents a small outlet for her frustrated efforts at assisting others, though one that is not generalizable to a larger populace. Vitório remains immobile and shadowed in the background as Joana and Pedro pass him going in and out of the hospital. To Pedro and those of his elite class, Vitório is a grown-up version of the street child, an uncomfortable part of the landscape that must be dealt with only when it physically (though also metaphorically) lands on the hood of his luxury car.

Manu, the primary child double or inheritor of Vitório's youth, is an ironic reflection of the veteran's sacrifice. He is shown playing in the decaying carcass of a bullet-riddled fighter plane, for example, a scene in which the camera shows us Manu's face as it pans through the bullet holes of the plane's windshield. Manu and his generation are only visible through the frame of the war's destruction, a technique that renders in the film's form the profound impact of the war on generations of young Angolans. However, this technique has additional vectors: on the one hand, it stages interpersonal relationships as constituted through the wartime political divides; it also signals to an international viewership the single lens of disaster and destruction through which Angola is discussed—if at all. The visual debris of the civil war reverberates in Manu's reproduction of conflicts over territory and resources: in the latter part of the scene, he steals the radio from a nearby parked car and refuses to share the profits with his friend who kept lookout. In another allegorical microcosm of the failed inheritances of the revolutionary ideas of the past, rather than dedicating himself to his studies and assisting his struggling grandmother, Manu engages in petty theft and falls on the wrong side of a more powerful bully and leader of a gang. The film clearly replicates Vitório's flashback to the war when the gang rushes out from behind decaying and inoperable train cars—additional wartime debris—to attack Manu.

If Vitório, and Manu as his double, can be taken here as representatives of the larger Angolan national body, the film also points to Angola's inexperience and difficulty moving beyond a violent, thwarted adolescence, despite its nearly thirty years of independence at the time of the film's production.

While micronarratives of everyday existence and frustrated national development dominate the film, O Herói, like Kangamba, takes on the history of international intervention in Angola. Whereas Kangamba insists on a recuperative gesture restoring Cuba to a central role of heroism in anticolonial resistance in the Global South, O Herói focuses on the international collaboration in the neoliberal turn of Angola's economic development in the twenty-first century. The film demonstrates this dynamic in a scene in which Vitório searches for work, passing a large painted sign proclaiming "Não há vagas" (No jobs). Insisting at a construction site that he is fit for labor despite his prosthetic leg, Vitório confronts the foreman's unexpected resistance to hiring him in recognition of his patriotic sacrifice; the supervisor insists he needs "homens normais" (normal men) rather than "heroes" for the physical demands of the job. The film's cynical commentary on the value of Vitório's sacrifice extends to the mechanism of national reconstruction. When Vitório mistakes the foreman for the building's owner, the camera cuts to a shot of the Portuguese man looking down through a second-story opening, maintaining the perspective of the two Angolans. By looking up at the Portuguese owner from below, the camera emphasizes the hierarchical relationship between the white owner and the black workers. The foreman corrects Vitório: "Eu o patrão? Eu sou só o encarregado. O patrão é português. Vais ver aquele gajo ali acima" (Me the boss? I'm just the supervisor. The boss is Portuguese. Go see that guy up there). The trope of construction here does not solely reference stunted national reconstruction, however. Sambizanga (1972) is one of Angola's best-known anti-colonial films, directed by French filmmaker Sarah Maldoror. It retells the story of the torture and murder of an anti-colonial hero at the hands of the colonial police drawn from Luandino Vieira's classic novella A Vida Verdadeira de Domingos Xavier (1971).[7] Sambizanga opens with a long sequence portraying colonial subjects performing manual labor at a construction site for the benefit of the white overseer. The visual reverberations in similar scenes of colonial exploitation in Sambizanga and the privatized construction for the benefit of a foreign investor in O Herói emphasize that a new era of globalized economic development has done little to interrupt the model of colonial dependency in place prior to 1975.

The government minister who eventually interviews Vitório and secures him a job as a car driver reveals the film's ultimately cynical view of the possibilities for a vertically-integrated notion of solidarity in the neoliberal twenty-first-century moment. While the film portrays diverse groups of sympathetic listeners to Vitório's appeal for the return of his prosthesis (as well as the gang leader mocking him), when the minister himself calls for the reestablishment of national solidarity, Manu's grandmother snaps off the radio in disgust at the words of yet "another politician." His words reveal how the repetition of the vocabulary of revolutionary transformation in the context of clientelist privilege are vacated of prior meaning: as the minister pulls away from the radio station, a quiet group of veterans waits outside the gates. The minister, promising to help them, closes his window as he instructs his driver to push carefully through the group; within the film, however, only Vitório receives the minister's assistance. Similarly to Pedro's interaction with the street child, the film presents the minister as both neglectful and willfully blind to the dire situation in which the rest of the characters live, until political opportunism forces him to act in a limited way.

Both Kenneth Harrow's and Connor Ryan's readings of O Herói focus on the exchange value of the physical and figurative detritus of the protracted period of war and subsequent postcolonial transition in the construction of a new economic and political order. As Harrow signals, the very unavoidability of trash throughout the film reveals its value: "The prevalence of trash on all levels prevents us from evaluating the people and the objects as being permanently worthless because the motility of trash lies in its being ensconced in systems where objects lose value over time and at the same time enter into differing regimes of value" (Harrow 217). As living incarnations of this debris, the veterans prove to provide passing political capital to the minister: Pedro convinces him to do the radio interview with the promise that it will help him come reelection time. The human casualties of the war who remain outside the world of O Herói, however, are even more significant. The film depicts the lines of people who come out to speak on the weekly television program *Ponto de Reencontro*, where Angolans announce their missing family members, sometimes with photos and other identifying information. As Ryan suggests, there is little hope for systemic change for Angola without both reckoning with and incorporating the war's living debris into a new transformed order (Ryan 66). Similarly, O Herói's opening and closing long aerial shots of Luanda's extensive shantytowns interrupted by occasional high-rises and well-groomed luxury homes contrasts with the intimate perspectives that dominate our access to Vitório's and Manu's realities. With the aerial shots, the film's characters become anonymized among the large populations of *musseque*-dwellers. The technique thus generalizes the characters' experiences and implicates a global viewership in the distance from which the scope of the shantytowns is perceivable but the individual inhabitants, with their struggles and triumphs, remain impossible to discern.

Transnational Context and Production in the Post-Cold War Era

In the first years following independence in Angola, as in Cuba after the revolution, film was an integral area for cultural development and an important medium for the dissemination of revolutionary ideals. Marissa Moorman's comprehensive study of Angolan cinema summarizes its place in the anticolonial and post-independence cultural order:

> During the [anticolonial] struggle, film was used as a means of propaganda, of mobilizing political support for an exiled nationalist leadership and the guerrilla war they were waging in the country. In the postindependence period, film was taken up by the state as part of the project of forging the nation and national unity through the documentation of local events and endowed with national significance and diffused, primarily, through television. (Moorman 119)

While Cuba developed a cinema at the vanguard of both theory and practice in the Global South, developed a robust domestic film industry, engaged in transnational coproductions, and trained generations of international filmmakers through the ICAIC, the promising beginnings of an Angolan national cinema were stymied by reduced state support as the war dragged on until the release of three feature films, including *O Herói*, in 2004. The temporal gap between early post-independence film and the 2004 re-initiation of Angolan film appropriately figures *O Herói*'s formal and thematic focus on the breaches between the everyday existence of the *musseque*-dweller protagonists and the political elite as part of the poetics of disappointment. However, *Kangamba*'s interpellation of the ideal revolutionary viewer and its focus on the act of filmmaking and representation as a metaphorical parallel to the construction of the relationship of solidarity, nonetheless, reveals how disappointment is also encoded in these very poetics. The urban decay, war debris, and physical barriers between the marginalized and the privileged that dominate *O Herói*'s visual landscape communicate a similar message about mediation to *Kangamba*'s. Rather than the revolutionary hero who participates in the literal and metaphorical construction of the new society, Vitório and his child doubles, as well as the viewers, negotiate landscapes that register the palimpsestic ruins of war, colonial and neocolonial incursion, and precarious infrastructure that they have a limited capacity to remake.

While both films present a nostalgia for the solidarities of the past, *Kangamba* ultimately constructs a vertical hierarchy of power/right that privileges a single mode—heroic nostalgia—embodied in the national patriarch, where the will of the people is aligned with the Cuban and MPLA leadership and the military forces. And yet, in the early twenty-first-century context of its production, the allegiance no longer functions as it did in the 1970s and 1980s. Neat divisions between Cold War superpowers and the Third World, between imperialists and anti-colonialists, no longer so easily organize the geopolitical context of the early twenty-first century, and Cuba's internationalist missions are increasingly seen as opportunistic economic enterprises necessary to the country after the economic crisis of the 1990s. The conviction and execution of General Arnaldo Ochoa in 1989, accused of drug trafficking and diamond smuggling during his service in Angola, marked a definitive break with the collective utopian imaginary, as both Padura and Jorge Fornet note. Both Hatzky's research on Cuban veterans and the French documentary *Cuba: une odyssée africaine* (2007) (*Cuba: An African Odyssey*) undermine the official state position of racial equality by pointing to how exoticist and prejudiced racial views of Africa and Angolans persisted among some of the Cuban contingency. Finally, the national trauma of a generation of youths marked by the loss of friends and family in internationalist missions further complicates *Kangamba*'s portrayal of heroic revolutionary sacrifice. While there continues to be a significant national reticence around the Angolan missions, literary portrayals of veterans such as Carlos, Mario Conde's wheelchair-bound friend in Padura's detective novels, capture the ambiguous collective memory of the Angolan mission. It is for this reason that I argue that the disappointment that does not appear as part of the film's revival of characteristic messages and techniques of revolutionary cinema is nonetheless detectable in the jarring incompatibility of the film and its context. *O Herói*, which uses revolutionary convention to ironize and criticize post-revolutionary neocolonial exploitation and three decades of destructive civil divides, serves to put into relief how *Kangamba*'s citation of convention reveals that the possibility of this ideological collaboration remains buried in the past. The disappointment and ideological exhaustion depicted as a structure of communal feeling in *O Herói* therefore become part of the film's critical apparatus. Considered in this way, *O Herói* partially returns to revolutionary cinema's demand for critical participation from the audience.

The respective conditions of production of *Kangamba* and *O Herói* offer an additional commentary on their place in negotiating postwar memorializations of the internationalist collaboration and the legacies of civil conflict. While París's 1990 film *Caravana* was coproduced with the Angolan state entity Laboratório Nacional do Cinema and employed Angolan actors alongside Cubans, *Kangamba* is a national collaboration between the ICAIC and MINFAR, Cuba's Ministry of the Revolutionary Armed Forces, and was filmed in Camagüey with Cuban actors playing Angolans (de la Hoz n/p). Cuba's internationalist support largely limited to humanitarian assistance and programs of paid, limited-term, highly skilled employment under the auspices of foreign government sponsorship have replaced the era of military intervention. By contrast, Gamboa has expressed frustration with the Angolan state and private entities' lack of investment in cinematic production and discussed how his own productions are dependent upon, for example, European investors, particularly from France ("Entrevista" 233–34; "Como Angola"). Sabine highlights this situation as analogous to the neocolonial development critiqued within the film (215). Ferreira has analyzed the complications that coproductions with former colonial powers can introduce, calling transnational productions "ambivalent" for their neocolonizing potential, though they also offer a vital platform for both national and international distribution (225). Gamboa notes that despite its excellent reception at international film festivals, winning the 2005 Sundance Grand Jury prize and enjoying a successful premier in Portugal, *O Herói* at the time was not available in Angola; it was later distributed on DVD ("Como Angola"). The economy of internal production and consumption of a film like *Kangamba* no longer has to make the case for internationalist intervention that it did even at the end of the Angolan collaboration in the late 1980s. The limitations with national production and consumption for a film like *O Herói*—Gamboa's 2012 film *O Grande Kilapy* was filmed entirely in Brazil and, like *O Herói*, employed a number of Brazilian actors—suggest that the cultural packaging of grappling with the wartime legacy is as contested as its method. The disappointment that pervades the post–Cold War era is a product, in part, of Angola's and Cuba's rapid initiation into a new global economic order, which places into crisis the relationship between the past and the present. The material conditions of production and consumption of these two films evidence this crisis.

The two films together emphasize the importance of the Angolan war and the Cuba-Angola allegiance as a definitive example of anticolonial solidarity in the South Atlantic. As Hatzky points out, the overwhelming focus on the Cold War superpowers as the only independent actors in the limited historiography of this interaction obscures the radical nature of third-world allegiance in the mid-twentieth century (7). The two films nonetheless represent divergent viewpoints on how to negotiate the legacy of south-south alliances once the global enthusiasm for utopian idealism founded in revolutionary orthodoxy has faded away. It cannot be ignored that *Kangamba*'s defense of Cuba's ongoing internationalist collaboration is advanced via allegiance to one side of a violent civil conflict, and produced at a moment when concerns over postwar reconciliation have saturated the public sphere in twenty-first-century Angola. While *Kangamba*'s investment in a narrative of continuity between

Cuba's twentieth- and twenty-first-century forms of international assistance might imply an ongoing criticism of the neoliberal and exploitive models of engagement and "development" that so often guide relationships between sites in the Global North and South, the film fails to interrogate these two conflicting contexts. *O Herói*'s complex engagement with the larger national and international narratives that so thoroughly occupy intellectual debates in and about Angola in film and literature posits localized mini-narratives as a method for grappling with the inheritances of the war that have relevance because they are so divorced from the unrealized promises of the revolutionary period. This example of post–Cold War disappointment, therefore, provides an important representation of nodes of personal contact and ironic distancing from broad ideological framing of international relations that are lost in the orthodox point of view of which *Kangamba* is an example, and thus provide a necessary perspective on how historical ideas of solidarity demand both critique and revision as the global context in which they are embedded changes.

Part II

The Mobility of Form

3

The War Abroad and the War at Home
Eliseo Alberto's *Caracol Beach*

Popular knowledge asserts that Fidel Castro never appeared publicly in anything other than military fatigues from 1959 until 1994, when he was famously photographed in a guayabera at the Ibero-American Summit. Nonetheless, fatigues continued to be Fidel's preferred public dress until he stepped down from the presidency in 2006. The November 27, 2016 issue of the Cuban state newspaper *Granma*, one of the multiple issues dedicated to his memory in the days after his death, contains photos of Fidel from throughout his long political life: chatting with school children, visiting a science laboratory, playing baseball, greeting world leaders, and speaking from podiums, all the while dressed in the military uniform that provided him visual continuity over the decades of his leadership. The cover page graphic from the same issue, a black-and-white stylized image of dozens of identical, armed, soldier Fidels filling the frame, emphasizes both the saturation of images of the iconic leader inside and outside of Cuba, and communicates the idea of the soldier-cum-everyman in the headline that accompanies the image: "Cuba es Fidel" (Cuba is Fidel).

Visual "fidelity" to these consistently militarized images has extended throughout public spaces in revolutionary Cuba. A street mural promoting the Unión de Jóvenes Comunistas de Cuba (the Young Communist League of Cuba) that I photographed in Havana in 2010 displays a row of marching legs and feet, headed by pairs of fatigue- and boot-clad legs preparing to stomp on the word "bloqueo" (embargo), surrounded by the conceptual associations with the US trade embargo that the soldiers are prepared to combat: "guerra, genocidio, terrorismo" (war, genocide, terrorism).

Figure 3.1. Public mural in Havana, Cuba. Photo by the author.

The UJC contingent at that year's May 1st parade presents a similar sense of visual continuity and proliferation of soldiers prepared for battle. Depending on the audience's visual, rhetorical, or political vantage point, these types of images suggest that the viewer is incorporated into the multitude, replicating Fidel's march toward the future of the revolution. Alternatively, the viewers of these images might be face-to-face with an army of infinitely reproducing opposing forces, perhaps even about to be overcome. In their visual rhetoric, these types of militarized images capture the starkly divisive ways in which the history of the Cuban Revolution has been read by its defenders and by its critics: the viewer is either one among the masses or facing off against an ever-multiplying adversary. However, the notions of what these adversarial positions consist of in the context of Cuba's post-1959 history is hardly consistent through the twentieth century, even as Fidel's symbolic weight remains at Cuba's political center. In fact, we may extend the replication of these soldier figures even further: they could, in fact, demonstrate that the ways that the Cuban community has often been partitioned into opposing groups defined by the politics of the moment. These partitions themselves seem to divide

Figure 3.2. Unión de Jóvenes Comunistas de Cuba (the Young Communist League of Cuba) at the 1st of May parade in 2010. Photo by the author.

and multiply over the course of the revolutionary era, producing dozens of different iterations.

The opposing, polarized readings I have hypothesized for these images, to which I will return later in the chapter, are emblematic of the cultural landscape that post–Cold War writers such as Eliseo Alberto de Diego García Marruz (1951–2011) describe as inhabited by a Cuban community divided against itself. In his prizewinning 1998 novel *Caracol Beach*, Eliseo Alberto reflects on how the revolution's divisive rhetorical inheritances have overdetermined the representational charge to Cuban artists and writers, particularly regarding the political meaning assigned to their places of residence: either on or off the island.[1] The Cuban Revolution's saturation of images, slogans, and language of militarization and Manichean divides is one of the effects of a national leadership that saw itself as under constant threat, or even attack, by the larger forces—often symbolized by the United States—that threatened to undo the course of its history since 1959. Alberto's novel addresses the extension of the sense of threat from without through reference to two phenomena that mark the configuration of the Cuban community in the latter decades of the twentieth century: internationalist missions abroad, extensions of revolutionary enthusiasm and solidarity on foreign ground, and divisions among the Cuban community, especially as imposed through exile. In *Caracol Beach*, the techniques of disappointment shape a text saturated with media and other textual and cultural references associated with this idealized revolutionary and a state of perpetual war. The novel, however, also expands its range of referents to include a diverse array of other artists, works, and genres to argue for "clemency," or textual generosity, as a response to the generalized disappointment for a community that has lived through many real and figurative battles.

Caracol Beach's protagonist Beto Milanés, a Cuban veteran of the Angolan war, is desperate to rid himself of the war flashbacks and visions that have haunted him for the seventeen years he has lived in a small Florida community; the novel traces the night he kidnaps three teenagers in order to commit suicide by police. Beto's suffering stems from two linked traumas: the loss of his comrades in the war abroad, and the loss of his home and community through self-imposed exile, even as he is surrounded by a group of eclectic displaced and marginalized exiles and outcasts who together comprise glimpses of the complex, entangled histories of the greater Caribbean. Among them are a descendant of white Haitians who fled the island after the 1804 Revolution, a Puerto Rican war veteran turned sheriff and his estranged transgender daughter, a Mexican sex worker, and the teenage daughter of a Cuban mother and Spanish father exiled after the Spanish Civil War. The novel's portrayal of these overlapping historical and social networks place Cubans living outside of the island into a longer history of displaced and dispersed communities, offering an implicit corrective to the permeation of public discourse on Cuba that reinforce the idea that its insular community was cut off from the outside world, or that it needed to remain on guard against outside influence. The form of the novel, too, reflects this eclectic intersection of communities and histories: the narrative incorporates song lyrics, verses of poetry, and references to a diverse array of other texts. However, film is the artistic medium that most pervasively penetrates *Caracol Beach*, and in the novel, film is associated with the construction of the idealized revolution and its subjects, Socialist New Men. This chapter argues that the eclectic form and the transmediatic texture of the novel—by which I mean not just references to other media, but formal intrusions of their style and characteristics—signal disappointment as encoded in how visual, political, and artistic rhetoric intended to create social unity and coordination fail in this goal. Rather, *Caracol Beach*'s eclectic form enacts a textually embodied call for clemency across the divides imposed by the accumulated weight of the divisive rhetoric surrounding Cuba's internationalist missions in particular and revolutionary politics more generally on and off the island.

Caracol Beach as Cinematic Novel

Eliseo Alberto, a member of one of the most prominent intellectual families in twentieth-century Cuba, was a diverse and prolific writer. He was a young child when the revolution triumphed, and was educated and came of age during its first two turbulent decades. He established his reputation in journalism, film, and eventually television script writing, co-authoring the script of 1997's *Guantanamera*, directed by the famed Tomás Gutiérrez Alea, among other films. Alberto also directed the cultural review *Caimán barbudo* and was associate director of the journal *Cine cubano*, and throughout his life published chronicles, essays, poetry, and novels. He moved to Mexico in 1988; unlike prior generations of emigrants, he was able to return to the island. *Caracol Beach*, in fact, is not Alberto's first work to deal with Cuba's internationalist missions: he wrote the script for the film *El corazón sobre la tierra* (1982) (*Heart Above the Land*), directed by his brother Rapi (Constante Alejandro de Diego García Marruz). *Corazón sobre la tierra* deals with a father's attempt to establish a farming collective in memory of his son's death during a mission in Ethiopia. As in *Caracol Beach*, in *El corazón sobre la tierra* the faraway locales of internationalist missions and the local space of the island are mapped as geographic analogies. However, while in *El corazón sobre la tierra* the collective sacrifice of the protagonist's son elsewhere is compared to collective solidarity-building at home, in *Caracol Beach* the violence and tedium of war are absolutely divorced from the political narratives that justify it: the links between those abroad and those at home are representative of an almost insurmountable disunion. In this sense, *Caracol Beach* shares many similarities with Emilio Alcalde's critical portrayal of the effects of the internationalist missions on those family members left behind on the island in his never-distributed film *El encanto del regreso*. Alberto's experience with cinema and the breadth of his areas of production are evident in all of the author's work, but particularly in his novels. In addition to a vast array of cultural reference points drawn from music, literature, and film, *Caracol Beach* frequently lapses into extradiegetic commentary that reads at times like a film voiceover, stage directions, or director's commentary on the action taking place in the background. Central scenes in *Caracol Beach*, including Beto's imagined suicide and the final scene of his actual death, are narrated as if in movie scripts, with action sequences, details drawn from a cinematic history of revolutionary heroes' deaths, soundtracks, and director's notes.

Beyond a quirk of the individual author's range of talents and interest, however, this technique points to a broader context: the mediatic texture of the novel also signals to its readers a history of the ongoing, participatory construction of the Cuban Revolution and its lived realities via visual and linguistic representation. Yamile Regalado Someillan, for example, has analyzed the impact of mass-produced visual art such as cartoons distributed in posters and print media, arguing that between 1959 and 1963, visual propaganda was a central force in creating a feeling of civic responsibility, by assigning concrete tasks that each member of the community should undertake to build the revolution. In this sense, the masses, the political leadership, and the intellectual class should work in tandem. Famously, the first cultural institution established after the triumph of the revolution was the ICAIC, the state film institute. Similarly, the UNEAC, the Cuban writers' union, was founded mere days after Castro's infamous 1961 speech at the close of the Meeting of Cuban Intellectuals, in which the revolutionary leader declared "dentro de la Revolución, todo; contra la Revolución, nada" (within the Revolution, everything; against the Revolution, nothing) (Castro 1961 n/p).

The extent to which slogans, images, film, and literature associated with the revolution saturate *Caracol Beach* offers evidence of what Lillian Guerra has analyzed as the revolution's construction of a "hyper-real" futurity in media. Guerra's analysis examines how the future of the revolution was brought into being through television, photography, and film's portrayal of social mechanisms like mass rallies, voluntary labor, and military service. In postmodern theory and media studies, the hyper-real refers to a displacement or disappearance of external reality in favor of a reality experienced through simulation, image, and/or representation.[2] Such representations result in the erasure of a sense of temporality—the hyper-real is experienced as an eternal present in the process of becoming. While the hyper-real is often theorized as part of postmodernism's critique of mass consumer culture, in Guerra's analysis, the hyper-real revolution was built via the collective consumption of images and rhetoric that framed and interpreted for the populace the collective action on which the revolution's future would depend:

> Critical to explaining the imagery's importance to struggles over the grand narrative is the idea that images—photographic, imaginary, personal—played a central role in placing Cubans outside the mundane circumstances of their daily lives and into the "hyper-reality" of the Revolution—that is, a utopia caught in the process of becoming. Like hyper-real spaces in any society, hyper-realities of state orchestrated mass rallies and routinized volunteer labor projects convinced participants that the euphoria, the happiness, the sense of justice, the pride of unity and self-righteousness that the experience generated were emblematic of reality—that is, the rest of society external to the hyper-real experience. One

authenticated the other, even though they were not the same; that authentication showed that the values of the hyper-real experience should not be contested. (269)

For Guerra, one of the central functions of film in the early years of revolution therefore constituted a paradox: on the one hand, its role was to train common citizens in the construction of the revolution. On the other, it had, at least partially, to deny the gap between lived conditions and the idealized revolutionary society they did not yet inhabit, and to deny the existence of conflicts in the construction of that society: "not only did 'authentic' filmic representations of the Revolution *require the denial of all local conflict* but they also required a *denial of the need to deny conflict* as foundational to the building of a truly classless society" (271; emphasis in the original). This is, of course, not an interpretation of early revolutionary cinema that all critics share. Juan Antonio García Borrero argues that during the 1960s, Cuban film sought to provoke discussion, rather than impose a single point of view, and that the ICAIC's iconic first director Alfredo Guevara explicitly distinguished cinematic art from propaganda (9). However, the concept of the hyper-real revolution is helpful in understanding the filmmaking that surrounded the Angolan conflict. As chapter 2 has explored, the first Cuban documentaries that recorded the mission—for example, Miguel Fleitas's *La guerra en Angola* (1976) (*The War in Angola*) or José Massip's brief history of the anti-colonial struggle *Angola: victoria de la esperanza* (1976) (*Angola: Victory of Hope*)—were produced simultaneously with the wartime experience. They served as the record of the history-in-becoming in which the Cuban soldiers should see themselves as the co-authors in real time.

In *Caracol Beach*, the vestiges of revolutionary hyper-reality show up most frequently in the protagonist's flashbacks and memories of both his prewar life and his experience in Angola. However, throughout the novel, these memories lose their integration with Beto's external reality, and are just as frequently challenged by other media and literary references associated with artists exiled or marginalized by the revolution. Guerra's analysis focuses on revolutionary temporality—the mediatic creation of the future of the revolution—while Beto's tortured isolation also points to another mediated projection of reality not just through time but through geography: the island always out of reach, but to which he longs to return.

In the preface to the novel, Alberto recounts the process that led him to write *Caracol Beach*, in a screenwriting workshop directed by Gabriel García Márquez (to whom the novel is dedicated), in which the exercise was to imagine a plot around which four youngsters are harassed all night by a carjacker. Incorporating the varied suggestions from the workshop participants that the carjacker should be a suicidal, psychopathic war veteran, hunted by a Bengal tiger, Alberto proposes a series of possible biographies for the character:

> pasó a ser un veterano de California en la Guerra de Vietnam, un marinero argentino en la guerra de las Malvinas, un combatiente Sandinista en la guerrilla nicaragüense, un terrorista palestino en la guerra del Medio Oriente, un artillero soviético en la guerra de Afganistán, un piloto inglés en la guerra de Irak, un miliciano croata en la guerra de Bosnia, hasta que terminó convertido en un soldado cubano en la guerra de Angola, 1975–1985. Guerras no faltan. La posible película nunca se realizó . . . Entonces me senté a escribir esta novela sobre el miedo, la locura, la inocencia, el perdón y la muerte. (10)[3]

> (he was transformed into a Californian in the Vietnam War, an Argentine sailor in the Malvinas War, a Sandinista guerilla fighter in the Nicaragua war, a Palestinian terrorist in the Middle East war, a Soviet artilleryman in the Afghanistan war, an English pilot in the Iraq war, a Croatian militiaman in the Bosnian war, until he finally became a Cuban soldier in the Angolan War, 1975–1985. There's no lack of wars. The film was never made . . . Then I sat down to write this novel about fear, madness, innocence, forgiveness and death. [viii])

From its preface, *Caracol Beach* explicitly imagines itself as a novelized film, or perhaps a novel that encompasses two competing film genres: war epic and thriller. The plot of the novel revolves around one night on which the soldier, who lives and works in an old circus trailer at a car salvage yard, kidnaps three teenagers and forces them to help him commit suicide. Alberto's novel records the interior dimensions of several characters, primarily focusing on Beto Milanés both in the present of the novel and in his diary from the war, the group of teenagers celebrating their high school graduation, and the sheriff who eventually discovers the soldier's kidnapping and the deaths of two of the teenagers as they attempt to rescue their shared love interest, Laura, from Beto. Throughout, a vision of a winged Bengal tiger haunts Beto, appearing at his moments of greatest fear, while its specter—in the form of a few floating feathers, a breath or the touch of a rough tongue—appears to those whom his violence affects throughout the evening of his suicide. The winged tiger, perhaps, is a direct homage to the magical realism that marked the style of Alberto's mentor, García Márquez. *Caracol Beach* largely depends on portraying representation itself, especially of violence, to link the various subplots: the soldier frames his expectations for war through films he has seen, especially Akira Kurasawa's *Seven Samurai* (1954), while, like a film director, he orchestrates the teenagers' forced performances of violent acts on the way to their eventual deaths and his own suicide.

Caracol Beach has two foundational traumatic events that allude to the film genres of epic and thriller. In the novel's present, the plot device wherein the soldier kidnaps the teenagers and then holds Laura hostage while the boys plot to rescue her, calls up the familiar Hollywood cinematic convention of the woman in peril, perhaps even as a direct reference to Otto Preminger's classic 1944 noir film *Laura*.[4] But the genre that dominates is the war film. Central to the novel is how the war in Angola, in particular the surprise ambush that kills Beto's fellow soldiers and his lieutenant, the Afro-Cuban *santero* Lázaro Samá, fails to reproduce the conventions of a heroic war epic, through which Beto has been trained in what to expect. Confused by the *décalage*, he turns repeatedly instead to comparisons between his experience and the fallen samurai in Kurosawa's classic film. The vast majority of the novel's cinematic references are to international films, indicating Alberto's investment in film as a global medium. Yet this trend runs up against Beto's particular mode of framing world events through the commitments of the Cuban Revolution, a mode that draws upon the history of forms disseminated through the medium of revolutionary filmmaking.

Alberto's *Informe contra mí mismo* (1996) (*Dossier Against Myself*), published two years prior to *Caracol Beach*, is ironically titled as a caustic response to the request from Cuban authorities that he spy and report on the literary *salons* run by his poet father in the 1970s. In the *Informe* Alberto characterizes the Angolan war specifically as an extension of the ideological battle against the imperialist-capitalist enemy of the United States: "El frente de batalla en la contienda Cuba-Estados Unidos se había desplazado a tiro limpio hasta las costas de África, y los hombres y mujeres del primer territorio libre de América Latina estábamos dispuestos a pagar con sangre solidaria nuestra deuda con la humanidad" (11) (The battlefront between Cuba and the United States had been displaced with a clean shot to the coast of Africa, and the men and women of the first free territory of Latin America were willing to pay our debt to humanity with the blood of solidarity). Later in the same text, Alberto calls the internationalist mission in Angola "la campaña más larga y sin sentido en quinientos años de historia insular" (the longest and most senseless campaign in five hundred years of island history) (164). However, similarly to Cardoso's novels discussed in chapter 1, *Caracol Beach* fails to offer historical context of the war in Angola, or to explain the broader political framework of Cuba's missions abroad. This technique universalizes the tedium and overwhelming violence of the soldier's involvement in the war, suggesting the soldier's experience as malleable or adaptable to a broad array of shared wartime circumstances—that is, plotable in a variety of different contexts.

The war is recalled primarily in the chapters drawn from Beto's diaries; rather than a heroic adventure, the novel presents the war as, fundamentally, a conflict between the tedium and boredom of repetitive day-to-day operations, and the fractured, impressionistic narrative of the violent death of Beto's fellow soldiers. The result of this conflict is Beto's descent into madness. From his first diary entry, the war is presented through the soldier's saturation in both revolutionary and global media, establishing the cinematic themes to which he returns throughout the novel: "Estoy medio loco, igual que aquel samurai quendy que acompaña a sus maestros a la guerra (yo) y que aparece en la película *Los siete samuráis*, la que nos pasaron en el barco cuando atravesábamos el Atlántico" (37). ("I'm half crazy, just like that loony samurai (me) who goes to war with his teachers in *The Seven Samurai*, the movie they showed us on the ship when we crossed the Atlantic" [20]). The reality of war versus its cinematic depiction continues to cause conflicts for the soldier, as he recounts in a later entry:

> Lo que pasa es que no pasa nada. En los entrenamientos, allá en Cuba, nos proyectaban películas sobre la Gran Guerra Patria y, claro, la defensa de Leningrado, que duró un montón de meses, estaba condensada en dos horas de función, a color, con música de fondo, de manera que los combates resultaban emocionantes, pero en la cruda realidad uno descubre que las guerras están llenas de tiempos muertos, de rutinas, de tedio espantoso, abre y cierra trincheras, súbete a un árbol, busca agua en el río, y los tiros no se ven por ninguna parte, o se escuchan como truenos de un aguacero que está cayendo en casa del Diablo, hasta que, supongo, llegará el día en que a uno le toque mojarse con la lluvia de plomos y sean otros los que vean nuestros relámpagos a la distancia, mientras abren y cierran sus trincheras. Dice Panetela que nosotros sí somos los siete samuráis (el loco soy yo), porque por techo y sardinas venimos a defender el destino de un pueblo del cual nunca habíamos oído hablar. (127)

> (What's happening is that nothing's happening. In training, back in Cuba, they showed us movies about the Great Patriotic War, and naturally the defense of Stalingrad [sic] that lasted months

and months, was condensed into two hours, in color, with music in the background, and so the battles were exciting, but in real life you learn that wars are full of dead time, routine, the worst boredom, you dig trenches and fill them in, climb a tree, get water from the river, and you don't see shooting anywhere, or you hear it like thunder in a rainstorm falling in hell, until I guess the day comes when it's your turn to get wet in the shower of lead and others see our lightning in the distance, while they're digging and filling their trenches. Poundcake says we really are the seven samurai (I'm the crazy one), because just for a roof over our head and a few sardines we've come to defend the future of a people we never even heard of. [96])[5]

As Beto's recurring identification with the "loco" warrior in *Seven Samurai* indicates, the soldier repeatedly uses the epithet of "the crazy one" to bridge the gaps in comprehension between experience and image: what defies logic for him can be accommodated only by searching for a psychological state that allows simultaneous, contradictory representations.

In Guerra's analysis of the hyper-real revolution, she uses the example of the documentary filmmaker Nicolás Guillén Landrián as the author of multiple cinematic "countertexts" to the official revolutionary images, arguing that the filmmaker's highly innovative works seemed unable to accommodate the political party-line either technically or narratively.[6] The relationship between scripting revolutionary action and madness as the marker of a failure or inability to do so provides a striking parallel between Guerra's discussion of Guillén Landrián and Alberto's portrayal of Beto. The political consequences for Guillén Landrián's "subversive" films went beyond the censorship of his works: as Guerra recounts, after the ICAIC refused to release Guillén Landrián's *Desde la Habana: ¡1969!* (1971) (*From Havana: 1969!*) as "incoherente con el contexto [clashing with the context]," the filmmaker was repeatedly interned in mental hospitals and subjected to shock treatments:

> Until he was finally allowed, in 1988, to leave Cuba for Miami, where he became a visual artist, Guillén Landrián reportedly lived for many years as a part-time vagrant who wandered Havana's streets, hallucinating, paranoid, and alone . . . his work demonstrated how the power of documentary film, like the power of the state, lay in framing reality as a dramatic spectacle in which citizens were invited to participate and observe but not direct or control. (285)

Here, Guerra points to a critical intersection between state power and the artist's power to create the lived reality of the audience via the work of art. Guerra's characterization of Guillén Landrián casts the filmmaker's "madness" as the result of the failure of the artist to accommodate the work of art to the idealized experience of the people: being out of "coherence with the context" is equivalent to being "out of one's mind."

Guerra's analysis portrays the role of the revolution's functionaries in art-making as, fundamentally, ideological direction orchestrated from above. Using Guillén Landrián as a synecdoche for the entire artistic community, Guerra argues that artists in Cuba must accommodate their work to political direction or lose their public space to practice their art. This is a common criticism levied against the revolution from both within and without. However, as Doreen Weppler-Grogan points out, the revolution enacted changing policies at different phases: Guillén Landrián suffered under the escalating rigidity of a program of enforced orthodoxy that reached its peak in the *quinquenio gris* (gray five years) between 1971 and 1976. Weppler-Grogan also signals the range of positions among the cultural leadership, some of whom worked to protect space for artists, and external events, such as the internationalist missions in Angola, that "decreas[ed] the sense of isolation and in turn opened up cultural space on the island" (Weppler-Grogan 146). Christabelle Peters makes a similar argument about the de-isolating effect of the Angolan experience in Cuba, showing that the Angolan missions offered Cubans the first "essential collective encounter with Africa outside of the historical, and problematic, context of slavery . . . [giving] birth to a new idealized image of what it meant to be Cuban" (7).

Alberto presents the explosion of artistic creativity in the first decades after 1959 through a similarly nuanced lens. While refusing to acquiesce to the notion that Cuban art was born with the revolution or to shy away from criticizing the censure of artists and writers, he argues that "Lo que no puede negarse es que, a finales de los sesenta y principios de los setenta la cultura cubana llegó a alcanzar una vitalidad nunca antes conseguida en setenta años de vida republicana" (*Informe* 152) (What is undeniable is that at the end of the sixties and beginning of the seventies, Cuban culture achieved a vitality it had never seen in the prior seventy years of republican life). Outlining the early battles between an artistic inheritance built on Hispanic heritage and one drawn from allegiance to the socialist bloc, Alberto fiercely criticizes the implementation of a bureaucracy intended to mediate what works and texts circulated among the populace, but lists among the outstanding artistic achievements of writers, filmmakers, and visual artists works by figures who were embraced and promoted on the island, others who were ignored or censored (he mentions Guillén Landrián), as well as those who ended up in exile (*Informe* 153–59). Where Guerra sees state institutions as consisting primarily in their functions of disciplining the artistic scene, Alberto centers on the triumph of artistic creativity both inside and outside of cultural institutions as a fundamental challenge to the worst phases of the strictures of bureaucratic control. He argues that by the end of the twentieth century, "En la isla, el arte y la literatura habían vencido el reto. Hoy nadie recuerda los nombres de los funcionarios. Se hizo justicia. Los condenó el olvido" (*Informe* 159) (On the island, art and literature had met the challenge. Today nobody remembers the names of the bureaucrats. Justice was served. They were condemned to oblivion).

Caracol Beach repeatedly dramatizes the tension between the "scripting" of the work of art to reflect the projected reality that its observers should experience and art as the product of an imaginative engagement with the world. This tension is most evident in the protagonist's constant return not just to imagining his own death, but to *how* his death should be formulated to comply with the cinematic tropes that have guided his expectations of war. A flashback passage brings together the script—in this case, literally a letter—and scene, revealing how Beto imagines his death in a letter to Sam Ramos, the sheriff of Caracol Beach who in his past as a soldier in the American army rescued Beto after the devastation of his company. Sam is thus associated both with Beto's survival and with the loss of Beto's community: rescue by American forces also ironically underlines Beto's certainty that he will be seen as a traitor in Cuba, and that his service in Angola would be seen as treason by the Cuban exile community in Florida. In the letter/script, Beto imagines taking back the biopolitical power exercised by the state over its soldiers and its directorial power to script his reality. Although he invites Sam to author the crime by coming to Caracol Beach, Beto nonetheless stages how it should happen:

> Aproveche algún descuido mío para pegarme un tiro . . . Traiga a su hijo. El muchacho presenciará una escena maravillosa. Como en las películas. Caeré desplomado sobre la arena. En cámara lenta. Música del fondo. Una armónica. La arena se teñirá de sangre, poco a poco. No voltee mi cuerpo. Déjeme así. Con los brazos en cruz. Un puñado de arena en la mano derecha. Los dedos de la izquierda abiertos en abanico. Bárbaro. Traiga a su hijo. (264–65)

> (Watch for any carelessness on my part and shoot me . . . Bring your son. The boy will witness a wonderful scene. Like in the movies. I'll fall on the sand. In slow motion. Background music. A harmonica. The sand will gradually turn red with blood. Don't

turn my body over. Leave me like that. With my arms outstretched. A fistful of sand in my right hand. The fingers of my left hand spread open in a fan. Fabulous. Bring your son. [207–08])

The scene Beto describes is a common cinematic trope—the sacrifice of the revolutionary for the good of the community—that appears repeatedly in Cuban film, especially those about collective resistance and international missions.[7] The details the soldier mentions—the background music, the slow spreading of the blood, the position of the hands, even the perspective of the spectators—fulfill the cinematic particulars that were missing from the tedium and boredom of Beto's "dead time" in combat. They produce via simulated image the sacrifice that would allow him to comply with the projected course of the revolutionary soldier. More importantly, however, their cinematic staging transmits that message of sacrifice to the spectators, whom he has included in his staging of the scene.

The ultimate danger, however, of the kind of aestheticized and scripted violence that the soldier imagines is not just individual suicide, but the reproducibility and actual reproduction of the violent scene, which results, Alberto warns, in a kind of collective annihilation. The novel contains multiple parallel scenes of wartime death. Not only do we hear of the deaths of Beto's fellow soldiers in Angola, but in another flashback, Lázaro Samá, Beto's lieutenant, recounts how his own son died in a landmine explosion as he attempted to cross the area between Cuban territory and the US military base at Guantánamo Bay (185). When Beto, after taking the teenagers hostage, tells the young people that his name is Lázaro, he is effectively usurping Lázaro Samá's identity to assume the leadership role of the lieutenant/director, another doubling. Again, he stages the scene by intensifying experiences drawn from the army: while he holds Laura hostage, Beto orders Tom and Martin to destroy an abusive fellow bar patron's car, to kill a passerby's pet dog, and to rob a nearby sex worker. This vicarious violence transports the soldier back to his prewar training: "el soldado se sentía eufórico y esa sensación de peligro le recordaba situaciones anteriores, en particular los días de los entrenamientos militares en los polígonos de la escuela provincial de milicias" (151). ("The soldier felt euphoric: the sense of danger reminded him of earlier situations, in particular the days of basic training in the fields of the provincial militia school" [114]). In their turn, Tom and Martin echo back the soldier's jubilation: as they begin to destroy the car, "Laura los oyó resoplar, ahogados en adrenalina. Martin dejó escapar un contraproducente chillido de júbilo" (153) ("Laura heard them pant, drowning in adrenaline. Martin let out a counterproductive whoop" [116]), while the soldier orders Laura to applaud the violent scene. In these echoes, or doublings, a chain of actors transmits and spreads the destruction associated with the performances of war, including bodily annihilation and the feelings of pleasure and excitement associated with violent acts. Each violent scene becomes a sort of rehearsal for the next, while the pairing of training and rehearsal, each implying repetition and reproduction of the scene, culminates in the final climactic performance in the car salvage yard.

In their attempt to rescue Laura in the salvage yard where Beto lives in his trailer, Tom and Martin scuffle over their shared attraction to their classmate. As a result Tom is accidentally impaled by scrap metal—a clear reference to wartime paraphernalia, a bayonet or shrapnel—while Martin is shot by a an eighteen-year-old trigger-happy new police officer, himself an aspiring young soldier. The novel clearly implicates Beto in the deaths of the teenagers, through the soldier's allegorical role as director of the scene and commander of the war within the diegetic action of the novel. However, in the scene narrating Tom's death, the novel's narrator steps outside in a kind of "voiceover" to incriminate himself and the readers of his chosen medium as well:

> Cómo describir ese momento terrible si ninguno de los dos vivió para contarlo . . . ¿Sería mejor aprovechar esta página para hacer una reflexión sobre lo impúdico de las guerras, que no terminan cuando los políticos firman las paces sino que se perpetúan en los sobrevivientes, víctimas de una cruzada desigual que sigue aconteciendo dentro de cada uno, entre las tripas y el corazón? Y mientras Tom y Martin se empujan entre los coches, se abrazan, forcejean, se debilitan y enloquecen, decir a voz en cuello que los verdaderos culpables de la masacre no aparecen en esta novela porque antes se las ingeniaron para mandar a otros a las primeras líneas de fuego, a la batalla estúpida de la política, para que vuelen en pedazos y ellos puedan decir en las tribunas que el pueblo ha cumplido su glorioso deber con la historia. ¿Pero tendrá sentido? ¿De qué sirve? Tom y Martin no leerán este libro: si existe el documento, la ficción de los hechos, es porque ellos no contaron con el escudo de las letras, oraciones, párrafos, parapetos de palabras. La única manera de cambiar el destino sería mintiendo y ni la mentira podría ampararlos: la muerte también es una dictadora. ¡Con qué paciencia va cosiendo la mortaja! La vida es una suma de casualidades. De equívocos. (284–85)

> (How can that terrible moment be described if neither of them lived to tell about it? . . . Would it be better to use this page to

reflect on the indecency of wars, which do not end when the politicians sign their peace treaties but live on in the survivors, the victims of an arduous campaign that still goes on inside each one of them, between their guts and their hearts? As Tom and Martin struggle among the cars and embrace, push, weaken and go mad, would it be better to say at the top of one's voice that those truly responsible for the massacre do not appear in this novel because they first arranged to send others to the front lines, to the mindless battle of politics, so that others would be blown to pieces and they could say in public forums that the people fulfilled their glorious obligation to history? But does that make sense? What good would it do? Tom and Martin won't read this book: if the document exists, this fiction about the facts, it is because they could not rely on the shield of letters, sentences, paragraphs, parapets of words. The only way to change destiny would be to lie, and not even a lie, would save them: death, too, is a tyrant. How patiently she weaves the cloth and sews the winding sheet! Life is a totality of coincidences. And accidents. [224])

In this passage, the narrator exploits the plasticity of the novel and its intradiegetic analogue, the soldier's diary, in order to insert another type of mediatic intrusion in between the lived experience of the soldiers, and the hyper-reality of the wars being fought on foreign soil and among the citizens at home. As an observer of the revolutionary event, the narrator both condemns the distance the novelistic form provides him from the violence through its "letters, sentences, paragraphs, parapets of words" while also asserting that the novel, in its plurivocal potential and its ability to absorb other genres, can also undermine the authorial position of those authorities who "send others to the front lines": authorities appear in the novel through their simulations—Beto as director—but not as either authors or authorizers of the text.

This crucial moment in the novel signals to the reader that the true subject of the novel is another iteration of what Rafael Rojas calls "a war to the death among brothers" ("Anatomía del entusiasmo" 8), in reference to playwright Antón Arrufat's censored *Los siete contra Tebas* (1968) (*Seven Against Thebes*), a rewriting of Aeschylus's play of the same title. Tom and Martin's struggle to the death is made all the more absurd by their distance from the political discourse that serves as the "original conflict" passed along the chain of violence from the revolution to the internationalist missions to the fight over teenage love, while in parallel form, the protagonists of each stage of the chain become increasingly distanced from what Alberto calls the "mindless battle of politics." And yet, the novel refuses to reify the originary status of a narrow, politicized interpretation of Cuban history as a sort of lost authenticity.

Textual Intrusion

There is a clear correlation between the novel presented as the fiction of those "sent to the front lines" and the names of his fallen fellow soldiers that Beto has tattooed on his arm, which Beto tells the teenagers are the names of those he has killed. The tattoos, in fact, are one of the details that Alberto uses to link Beto to one of his teenager soldier-doubles. As one of the boys, Martin, assaults a milk delivery truck driver in order to carjack his vehicle and chase down Beto and Laura, Martin realizes that he has become like the soldier: "De lo que se trataba ahora, ahora que la cobardía acababa de proporcionarle un nombre para grabar en el panteón de su antebrazo, era conseguir que alguien le afileteara en la camisa una última medalla: la de una bala" (288) ("The question now, now that cowardice had just given him a name to engrave in the pantheon of his arm, was who would pin a final decoration on his shirt: the medal of a bullet" [227]). Cuban writer and literary theorist Severo Sarduy contemplates the tattoo as a figure for writing itself. In *Escrito sobre un cuerpo* (1969) (*Written on a Body* [1989]), Sarduy's analysis of Maurice Roche's *Compact* (1966) exalts the textual excesses that separate literary texts from "informative communication," figuring "literariness" through the comparison between text and tattoo:

> La literatura es . . . un arte del tatuaje: inscribe, cifra en la masa amorfa del lenguaje informativo los verdaderos signos de la significación. Pero esta inscripción no es posible sin herida, sin pérdida. Para que la masa informativa se convierta en texto, para que la palabra comunique, el escritor tiene que tatuarla, que insertar en ella sus pictogramas. La escritura sería el arte de esos *grafos*, de lo pictural asumido por el discurso, pero también el arte de la proliferación. La plasticidad del signo escrito y su carácter barroco están presentes en toda literatura que no olvide su naturaleza de *inscripción*, eso que podía llamarse *escripturalidad*. (52)

> (Literature is an art of tattooing; within the amorphous mass of informational language it inscribes, encodes the true signs of signification. But this inscription is not possible without wounding, without loss. In order for informational mass to become text, for words to communicate, the writer must tattoo that mass, insert

his pictograms in it. Writing could be the art of these *graphies* of discourse appropriating the pictorial, but also the art of proliferation. The bonds between the plastic arts and the written sign as well as its baroque character are present in all literature that retains its *inscriptive* nature, what we could call its *scripturality*. [41])

In a very literal way, the tattooed names on Beto's arm—and the name imagined for Martin's arm—become the text of the novel. It is Beto's own tortured reading and writing of the mission, the violent deaths of his companions, and the proliferation of that violence on the night of the teenagers' kidnapping that structure the plot of the novel. The process of tattooing and its associated wounding and loss in *Caracol Beach* is not solely the corporal inscription of Beto's lost companions, or his presumed autobiography as the "murderer" of those whose deaths he witnessed and survived. By inscribing the pantheon of names on his arm, Beto composes a list that takes on the allegorical function of a generation wounded and lost in missions abroad. Similarly, at various points in the narrative, Beto erases himself from his own history by telling the teenagers that he is, in fact, his lieutenant Lázaro Samá; in this erasure, Beto creates a textual space for those who, the narrator has told us, are responsible for the violence, and yet do not appear in the pages of the text.

In Sarduy's formulation, a text's literariness resides in its textual "proliferation" and "baroque" character. These same elements enter *Caracol Beach* via the multiplying of genres, cinematic doubling, and the proliferation of representations and simulation—for example, Martin's assumption of Beto's soldier role, with its concomitant textual charge to "tattoo" the name of the man he has harmed on his own arm. The historical and political disappointment that surrounds the internationalist missions and Beto's subsequent exile is literally visible in the text that according to orthodox positions *should* describe a simplified and unified narrative of heroic sacrifice, and yet opens itself to a multiplicity of literary incarnations and interpretations. Though Alberto ostentatiously draws attention to the "plasticity" and "proliferation" of cinematic elements, he also incorporates a diverse range of other referents, a technique evident in other works, but most famously in the *Informe*.

In some ways, the *Informe* and *Caracol Beach* are complementary archives focused, in the case of the *Informe*, on the cultural conflicts before and after 1959 on the island, and in the case of *Caracol Beach*, on a broader range of referents, including pre-revolutionary cultural figures, exiles, and artists who at one time or another fall on the wrong side of the cultural authorities. In the *Informe*, the notion of artistic unity within the work and between the work of art and external sociopolitical reality is explicitly subverted through the author's techniques of combining an array of narrative genres that are both fictional and autobiographical. In the *Informe*, the disjointed effect of the personal memoires that recap particular episodes of the author's life, beginning with the request by Cuban authorities to report on his father, are joined with "letters" from friends (of his own authorship, the narrator tells us). The text also includes reflections on Cuba's history, marked at times by repetitions of phrases and slogans popular after the triumph of the revolution, such as "La guerra es la guerra" (War is war), a phrase which the authorities use to authorize his spying on his father to support the perceived "war" at home. This particular technique of interrupting the text with slogans bridges the *Informe* and *Caracol Beach*, and exemplifies how Alberto mocks the linguistic dimension of the hyper-real construction of the revolution that Guerra explores through images.

In the *Informe*, Alberto's repetition of slogans extends into lists several pages long, which take over the narrative:

> El ejército es el pueblo uniformado. La Reforma Agraria Va. Estudio, trabajo y fusil. Cuba: primer Territorio Libre de Analfabetismo. Cuba: primer Territorio Libre de América. Cuba: faro de América Latina. Te queremos, Fidel. Fidel o Muerte. Alfabetizar, alfabetizar, venceremos. Para lo que sea, como sea y donde sea: Comandante en Jefe, ordene. Abajo la explotación del hombre por el hombre. Abajo el imperialismo. Cinco picos para la juventud cubana. Proletarios de todos los países: uníos . . . (33)

> (The army is the people in uniform. The Agrarian Reform Advances. Study, work and rifle. Cuba: first Territory Free of Illiteracy. Cuba: first Free Territory of America. Cuba: lighthouse of Latin America. We love you, Fidel. Fidel or Death. By Teaching Literacy, Teaching Literacy, We Will Overcome. For whatever, however and wherever: Commander in Chief, command. Down with the exploitation of man by man. Down with imperialism. Five trips up the Pico for the Cuban youth. Proletariat of all countries, unite . . .)[8]

The playful, mocking irruption of slogans in the text creates a kind of absurdist poetry, turning into literature the part of the everyday existence of those Cubans who experience the slogans reproduced in public fora and chanted at mass meetings. By listing them in this way, however, the text also displaces their ostensibly didactic purpose: the accumulation and arrangement of the slogans strips them of their context, and invites the reader to focus instead on their very multiplicity and excess. This technique reappears in *Caracol Beach* as part of the marker of Beto's "mad" mind, a symptom of his position "out of context" by virtue of his exile.

The repetition of slogans and phrases associated with the revolution echoes throughout *Caracol Beach*, albeit less prominently than in the *Informe*. Beto's lieutenant Lázaro Samá rallies the troops with "Patria o Muerte" (129) (Fatherland or Death), for instance, while Beto claims to be from "Cuba, primer territorio libre de América, Faro Continental" (159) ("First Liberated Territory in America" [122]). But repeated phrases from other sources predominate in the novel, displacing in Beto's experience the revolution's rhetorical dominance of public space and its associated metonymic signification of Cuba. The most frequent of these is a verse from Cuban-American musician José Curbelo's 1952 popular song about Cuba's unique hummingbird, the "zun-zún" or colibrí, which Beto repeats and which indicates the protagonist's "locura": "zun zun zun, zun zun-dambaé, pájaro lindo de la madrugada" ("zun zun zun, zun zun-dambaé, pretty bird at the break of day"); Beto calls the verses "nuestro particularísimo himno de guerra" (33) ("our own special marching song" [17]). The irruption of the verses in the novel's dialogue and narrative apparatus provides a musical theme and anchors a soundtrack for the novel. That soundtrack also includes exiled Cuban singer Albita Rodríguez, whose songs play at the party where the teenagers celebrate their graduation; Cuban musicians Silvio Rodríguez and Pablo Milanés, symbols of the politically-engaged *nueva trova* movement of the 1970s and whose song "Yolanda" Beto chooses to accompany his suicide (234); and Sting, whom the teenagers listen to in their car as their search for beer leads to the fateful encounter with Beto that ends in Beto's, Tom's, and Martin's deaths.

The repetition of verses and slogans in the novel serves multiple functions. One is certainly as a popular, international counterpoint to the ritual recitation of prayers to the Santería *orishas* that I will discuss in the final section of this chapter. However, another function of the combination of artistic and political refrains is to draw attention to a broader canon of Cuban artists than those recognized and embraced by authorities on the island. In the *Informe*, the list of slogans interrupts Alberto's observations about José Martí, Cuba's national poet-martyr who, the novelist argues, constructed Cuba both poetically and politically from his long periods of exile: "Martí no vivió en Cuba, no vivió la isla. La padeció, eso sí. La dignificó. La escribió. La poetizó. La defendió. La amó más que nadie en cuatro siglos. Hizo la suya, ya para siempre exacta a la nuestra. 'Verso (patria pudo decir) o nos condenan juntos o nos salvamos los dos'" (*Informe* 32) (Martí did not live in Cuba, he did not experience the island. He suffered it, for certain. He dignified it. He wrote it. He poeticized it. He defended it. He loved it more than anyone in four centuries. He did things his own way, always exactly like our way.

'Verses (fatherland he could have said) either condemn us together or save us both').[9] The *Informe* here points to one of the central paradoxes of Cuban national revolutionary mythology: that Cuba's national patriarch spent much of his adult life, and wrote the majority of his vast canon, outside the island.

The example of the juxtaposition of Alberto's examination of Martí, the pages of slogans, and a long discussion of Cuba's other national patriarch, Fidel Castro, points to what James Buckwalter-Arias sees as the *Informe*'s central thesis. Buckwalter-Arias argues that while the *Informe*'s techniques might otherwise be seen as a postmodern rejection of metanarratives, Alberto preserves a "utopian impulse" that imagines a "society responsive to the needs of diverse subgroups. The anticipated society is implicitly articulable or narrable, and literature is a major player in the anticipated politico-cultural transformation; it is the artists, after all, who have triumphed over the bureaucrats" (30). By juxtaposing Martí's invocation of poetry with the poeticized sloganeering, Alberto inextricably links the salvation offered through art to the bridging of multiple categories of social and political divides. Alberto's passage on Martí points to how Alberto privileges artists writing from exile as legitimate authors in and of the *patria*. In *Caracol Beach*, the layering of artistic genres, especially novel, music, and film, encodes in the novel's form the kind of bridge-building that serves as the ethical core of Alberto's works. This technique also points to the central alienation between the "scripted" revolution as seen from a position limited to strict revolutionary orthodoxy, and two different types of textual proliferation. On one hand, as Alberto signals, the layering of genres points to the proliferation of artistic creativity that took place within and parallel to the revolution's first decades. On the other hand, it points to the multiplicity and replication of unseen and unacknowledged consequences that reverberate in ever-widening circles beyond the island's limits.

In *Caracol Beach*, Alberto revisits the proliferation of simulations and repetition of the island elsewhere through settings as well. The majority of the novel takes place in Florida and Angola, even as the spaces through which the characters move are frequently described as duplications or recreations of somewhere else. The resort town of Caracol Beach and the larger South Florida Cuban community both function as what Adriana Méndez Rodenas, reflecting Antonio Benítez Rojo's seminal analyis of the Caribbean as a "meta-archipelago," calls "meta-island[s] or simulacr[a]," the spatial incarnations of "a series of images or recurring tropes of an alternative island—an island of the imagination set in an imagined seascape that functions as artistic equivalent for the process of psychic compensation" that is the ineluctable result of exilic and diasporic consciousness (151). In fact, *Caracol Beach* adapts the hyper-real effect that Guerra associates with the construction of the revolution's future in visual media to the space of the meta-island (or meta-archipelago). The geographical "meta-islands" of Méndez Rodenas's analysis themselves produce the hyper-reality of the "original" island that the diasporic or exiled subject imagines as irrecoverably lost to time or distance. This recreative impulse manifests itself in different ways in the novel: at times, via the faithful reconstruction of scenes and cityscapes the diasporic subjects have left behind; and in other instances, via the creative manifestation of *what could have been*, or what was left incomplete, in the place of origin. However, as Benítez Rojo's analysis reveals, such imagined origins fail to produce the fixity of meaning that they search for; the meta-island (or the meta-archipelago) is always illusory, remaining permanently out of reach.

In one example drawn from the soldier's memories of his initial arrival in Florida, Beto seeks out the Cuban community after he decides that returning to Cuba after all of his companions died puts him in danger of being punished for treason. Overcome with nostalgia for the island left behind, he immerses himself in the community of Cuban exiles who, in the narrator's description, engage in the task of constructing their "set" of the island with the visual and auditory details that lend it verisimilitude: "conoció a hombres y mujeres azotados por el recuerdo de un país que habían decidido reinventar calle a calle, ancianos en guayabera que apostaban sus propiedades en La Habana o en Bayamo ante una mesa de dominó, señoras que intercambiaban recetas de concina para impedir a tiempo que se les olvidaran las proporciones" (54–55) ("He met men and women flogged by their recollection of a country that they were determined to reinvent street by street, old men in guayaberas who wagered their properties in Havana or Bayamo at the domino table, matrons who exchanged recipes in an effort to keep the proportions from being forgotten" [36]). The recreation of a setting of Havana is sufficiently effective, in fact, that it produces for the Cuban exile community an extension of the community surveillance, tests of orthodoxy, and threat of expulsion that marked the most difficult years of revolutionary fervor: "al soldado no le gustaba hablar de política y esa apatía por lo que sus compatriotas llamaban el futuro de la nación acabó por excomulgarlo de la colmena . . . el soldado se atrevió a criticar en público a uno de los líderes del exilio . . . y sus comentarios le merecieron para siempre una cruz en la lista de confiables" (55) ("the soldier . . . did not like to talk about politics, and his apathy regarding what his compatriots called the nation's future ended up excommunicating him from the hive . . . the soldier dared to publicly criticize one of the expatriate leaders . . . and his remarks earned him a permanent cross next to his name on the list of those who could be trusted" [36]). The details that the narrator describes would accompany any cinematic or television recreation of a "typical" Cuban street scene—guayaberas and dominos, neighbors exchanging recipes. However, in Beto's experience, the meta-island is inseparable from the hyper-real counter-revolution, experienced through the Florida Cuban community's own enforcement of orthodoxy. Iván de la Nuez sees this tendency as a "negative utopia" accomplished through a retrograde idealization of the past that castrates an imagination for the future: "la prolongación en el espacio de un país en otro (Cuba dentro de Estados Unidos), y la prolongación en el tiempo del pasado en el presente" (169). The spatial metonymy results in two "closed sets": one on the island where the revolution is being staged, and an alternative double in Florida where the same characters, scripts, and props are used in the creation of a past-oriented counter-revolution. In both cases, Beto finds himself outside the community.

Beto eschews the Florida Cuban community for its rigidity precisely because he finds that its members prefer a carefully constructed, scripted space that produces a notion of Cuban authenticity and orthodoxy that its defenders fear has been erased or changed by the revolution. Svetlana Boym, arguing that nostalgia is the dominant mode of the late twentieth century, calls this reconstructive tendency "restorative nostalgia," or the paradoxical attempt to reconstruct lost traditions and histories via a radically selective vision of the past and an enforced orthodoxy in defending them. This type of nostalgia "builds on the sense of loss of community and cohesion and offers a comforting collective script for individual longing" (14). However, at other moments in the novel, cinematic and theatrical language point to the plastic possibilities of urban spaces as the site of recuperating creative potential made invisible or impossible by politics of silencing on the island or the erasure of artists who leave it, a potentiality that Boym refers to as "reflective nostalgia" as an aesthetic mode that "cherishes shattered fragments of memory and temporalizes space" (15). Cuban writers and artists who lived outside of the island appear repeatedly throughout the novel, a technique that places *Caracol Beach* among a group of novels that explore the more expansive imaginative possibilities opened up by envisaging a Cuban cultural fabric that explicitly bridges the island-diaspora divide. Beto lives in an abandoned circus trailer in the car junkyard; we can read in the decaying circus car the cinematic tradition of the sad clown. For example, Beto shares with Gelsomina, the protagonist of Fellini's *La Strada* (1954), a destructive and deadly horror at witnessing the death of another. The circus car may also represent, however, an oblique reference to Cuban poet Heberto Padilla's poem "Fuera del juego," (1968) which cynically compares the revolution's apologists to clowns in a circus in which the poet refuses to participate.[10] Beto's slowly consuming madness also recalls exiled Cuban novelist Guillermo Rosales's 1987 *La casa de los náufragos* (*Halfway House*), in which the main character cannot escape the Florida mental institution where he has landed upon leaving Cuba; the novel ultimately posits his inescapable madness as the product of the irredeemable fracturing of the national body. Like Rosales and his compatriot Reinaldo Arenas, also a victim of censorship and exile, Beto sees suicide as the only possible escape from his suffering.

At the same time, however, the novel draws other parallels among figures who are distanced or exiled from their homes and who break with a model of self-flagellating national insularity. Francisco Brignole sees in *Caracol Beach* a system in which the binaries of the island-exile community are broken down through the use of hyperbole and magical realism, the latter as an homage to Alberto's mentor García Márquez (78). For Brignole, Beto's eclectic community manifests a "global imaginary" in its composition of other political outcasts, misfits, and surprising allies, like the Puerto Rican Ramos himself, who, despite representing the other side of the Angolan conflict from Cuba's allies, is assigned to watch over Beto after his rescue because of their Caribbean affinity. However, a closer examination of Alberto's use of "magical realist" elements reveals functions that go beyond an homage to the technique's most globally recognized practitioner. In Brignole's analysis, magical realist elements are associated with the "global imaginary" of the liminal geographic space of encounter, the Florida coastal town of Caracol Beach. In this sense, his analysis is in line with Alicia Llarena's examination of the primacy of space in effecting the verisimilitude of the extraordinary in works of magical realism and the marvelous real (33–38). However, *Caracol Beach*'s extraordinary elements—the central one is the winged Bengal tiger that haunts Beto—are also associated with Beto's madness, with his inability to assimilate the violence of the war and his separation from the island community into a rational, narrable form. These two uses of magical realism coexist in *Caracol Beach*. An otherwise marginal and somewhat stereotyped figure in the novel—the gym teacher Agnes, both an aging single woman longing for a partner and the object of the teenage boys' sexual desire—provides a surprising window into the novel's presentation of strange and imaginative possibilities as a counterpoint to Beto's paralyzing disappointment.

The way the novel uses space as a stage to bridge divides is explicitly on display in a scene when two of the teenagers' high school teachers attend a tribute to Reinaldo Arenas at a club called "Dos Gatos Tuertos." The name of the club is a clear reference to Havana's famed bar and gallery space "El Gato Tuerto," itself a gathering place for Cuba's most important intellectuals, artists, musicians, and writers in the latter half of the twentieth century. The invocation of a figure such as Arenas, who wrote extensively about homosexuality as both the reason for his oppression and a source of artistic creativity, therefore serves as an important signal in the novel. *Caracol Beach* is virtually entirely populated by men, many of them hyper-masculine soldiers, ex-soldiers, or soldier-proxies; the few exceptions—Laura, the kidnapped teenager, and Agnes, the school's gymnastics teacher, as well as Sherriff Ramos's transgender daughter Mandy—are relatively underdeveloped characters. The panoply of artists, writers, and filmmakers that are invoked throughout the novel are almost all men, whether seen as a reflection of the entrenched gender politics of the twentieth century or as a deliberate technique that links the masculine characters to the masculine-dominated canon. And yet, alternatives to the hyper-masculinity of the soldier/socialist New Man is, fundamentally, a primary locus of the novel's calls to artistic creativity. In fact, the way that the soldiers' violence and madness spreads among other characters, such as in Beto's "training" of Tom and Martin, makes the interruption of alternative modes of seeing all the more surprising, especially through the eyes of otherwise minor characters.

In a central example, upon leaving the "Dos Gatos Tuertos," Agnes sees the city transformed into a place where every element contains two possibilities:

> Agnes se fijó. No había nada extraño. ¿O sí? Las constelaciones estaban alineadas en el firmamento. También la luna. La ciudad olía a pueblo, la calle de comercios a huerto roturado, el aire a agua, el agua a tierra, el asfalto a cedro, el domingo a jueves, el mar a campo, lo antiguo a nuevo. Se respiraba un aire de mañana. De rocío. De estrenos. Hasta volaban tontas mariposas alrededor de los faroles, convencidas de que eran salvajes tulipanes, y los perros daltónicos cruzaban de esquina a esquina al cambio de luz en los semáforos. Como había estado lloviendo, las centellas de los anuncios de neón se reflejaban en los cristales del pavimento y producían un efecto teatral muy convincente, de espejos telegrafiados. (97–98)

> (Agnes paid attention. There was nothing unusual. Or was there? The constellations were in place in the firmament. And the moon. The city smelled like a village, the business street like a tilled garden, the air like water, the water like earth, the asphalt like cedar, Sunday like Thursday, the sea like the countryside, the old like the new. She inhaled the morning air. Dew. Beginnings. Even the foolish butterflies were fluttering around the streetlights, convinced they were wild tulips, and color-blind dogs crossed from one corner to the other each time the traffic lights changed. Since it had been raining, the flashing neon lights were reflected in glassy pavements, creating a very convincing theatrical effect, of telegraphed mirrors. [72])

The "Dos Gatos Tuertos"—the two one-eyed cats—suggests an additive, a doubling of visual possibilities, though not necessarily the recuperation of a whole. In Agnes's observations, this doubling generates multiple imaginative potentials, where each element—the butterflies, the city, the asphalt—assumes properties of some other reality, where both appear on the stage marked by the theatrical reflections of the neon lights. In this sense, Agnes's perception offers a different interpretation of mediatic doubling from Beto's. The novel presents Beto as caught between the Cuba that remains at an irretrievable distance, and a perceived reality that remains out of reach, whether seen in the gap between his lived wartime experience and the hyper-real model of the soldier or the "meta-island" of the Cuban exile community in Florida. In both these configurations, the "real" and the "simulated" remain irrecoverably distinct, and it is in these gaps that the novel registers the feelings of social and political disappointment stemming from the internationalist missions and the experience of loss and exile. Yet, Agnes's intoxicated vision perceives two, at times discordant, possibilities that coexist in the theatrical/mediated space of the street's eclectic illuminations and reflections. Her ability to perceive both contrasts with Beto's perception of his reality as "incoherent with the context," begging for a kind of reconciliation of his various lived realities that would give him relief from his debilitating madness. In this sense, *Caracol Beach* proposes Agnes's more expansive vision as a means of addressing disappointment.

Santería as Alternative Medium

The mechanism of that attempted reconciliation for Beto comes via rituals drawn from the Afro-Cuban religion *Regla de Ocha* (Cuban Santería) particularly in the rites invoking the *orishas* (saints/deities) Yemayá and Babalú Ayé. Yemayá represents both maternity and waters, the substance that connects Cuba to Africa and well as the island to its exile communities; Babalú Ayé, syncretized with the Catholic Saint Lazarus, both causes and cures illness. In Santería, both the orishas and the dead have material manifestations and interactions in the world of the living, what Aisha Beliso-De Jesús calls "copresences" (10). In her analysis, Beliso-De Jesús examines how "copresences" manifest themselves somatically, not only through possessions of the practitioner's body, but through "messages from oricha and dead spirits heard in one's ear, or seen in visions, dreams or other forms of spiritual communications . . . The *corriente espiritual* is a 'charge' to the ambient power of a ritual space, and it connects practitioners and copresences to each other with bodily tingles, sounds, sensations and possessions" (42). Throughout the novel,

Beto's character gestures toward the importance of Santería in both explicit and more opaque ways: when he first meets Lázaro Samá, his army lieutenant, he is ignorant of and resistant to Afro-Cuban religions, but eventually allows Lázaro to initiate him into Santería. Beto subsequently prays to both Yemayá and Babalú Ayé, and he manifests the names of his seven dead companions-in-arms literally on his body by tattooing their names below the symbols for the two orishas. The tattoos serve as a kind of conduit to call up their presence: over the twenty-four hours of the novel's present, Beto "escucharía las voces de los amigos, ocultos bajo la piel en las tumbas del brazo" (57) ("would listen to the voices of his friends hidden under his skin in the graves on his arm" [38]). The sensations associated with the presence of the Bengal tiger that stalks Beto as a symbol of his fear is passed through bodily sensations to other characters whom he infects with the same terror: Gigi Col, the sex worker whom Tom and Martin rob at the soldier's orders, feels "que el invisible felino se rascaba el lomo en su falda de cuero, a la altura de la cadera . . . Y olía a rata" (158) ("the invisible feline rubbing its back along her leather skirt, at the height of her hips . . . it smelled of rat" [120]), while Laura, after she is rescued, reports to Sam Ramos that she dreams of the tiger. Beto assumes the identity of his lieutenant Lázaro Samá in his interactions with the teenagers, referencing how the dead accompany him in his quest to join them, and even calls out to the Lieutenant not to abandon him in the moments before he dies (302). In this way, Beto's initiation into Santería also serves as another method of bridging divides, this time between the licit and the illicit, and between the past and the present. As Peters argues, post-revolutionary bans on practicing Santería relegated Afro-Cuban religions to folkloric "repositories of the past" (56). In *Caracol Beach*, Lázaro is prevented from joining the Communist Party because he continues to practice Santería (106). However, Beto's time in on the African continent and his contact with the Afro-Cuban Lázaro counter this narrative, asserting the lived importance of Santería ritual to his relief from his madness. *Caracol Beach* thus positions praying to the orishas as a way of contending with disappointment: it can bridge communities, the realms of the living and the dead, and the spaces of exile with the island.

In participating in Santería, Beto places himself as an inheritor of diverse and often overlapping communities—national, racial, political, etc.—which Beliso-De Jesús conceives through Deleuzian "assemblages": she argues that assemblages can be "landscapes, diasporas, racial, sexual and national scapes" which permit the interrogation of "the intensities and affective economies of religious feeling through copresences" (13). Beliso-De Jesús's analysis focuses specifically on trans-national practitioners of Santería's participation in rituals and access to copresences through video and Internet media, which she notes explodes in the 1990s with the legalization of the practice and introduction of Santería tourism to Cuba. Indeed, the scene of Beto's death at the end of the novel brings together both the mediatic presentation of Beto's scripted death scene and his ritual invocation of the orisha Yemayá. A number of the cinematic details that Beto has imagined in the letter he sends to Sam Ramos years before take place when he finally dies: his exhortation to Sam to "bring your son," for example, as Mandy is one of the many spectators who witness the final scene. Beto, as he scripted, is shot to death in a "balacera," a shoot-out among the various police officers and armed teenagers; the final scene, described as a "cerco," a siege, equally recalls the ambush that killed Beto's comrades-in-arms as a final, explosive scene that caps an exciting war film (326; 328). Even the soundtrack returns to Beto, as in his final moments he imagines his friend José Lonoño singing Silvio Rodríguez and Pablo Milanés's "Yolanda."

However, Beto's cinematic death also turns out to be the ritual space where Yemayá first possesses Beto's body, following the "script" and directing the actions of Beto's body "al ritmo de un secreto melodía" (309) ("following the rhythm of a secret melody" [244]). The perpetrators of the siege are also the ritual observers who witness Yemayá's final intervention: "Yemayá le tiró del cabello para que alzara la cabeza y recibiera la muerte con dignidad" (325) ("Yemayá pulled his hair so he would raise his head and receive death with dignity" [256]). Rosa María Lahaye Guerra uses, in fact, the vocabulary of the medium/media to describe the process of the orisha's possession: "[la] oricha . . . se apodera de su cuerpo y lo convierte en instrumento, vehículo, medio" (84–85) (the orisha . . . takes over their body and converts it into an instrument, vehicle, medium). The concern in *Caracol Beach*, however, is not in the generalized sense of "medium" but rather in its mass-communications manifestations. Like in Agnes's double vision, the final scene of Beto's death brings together multiple mediatic incarnations: a film script for a melodramatic death scene and an action sequence, a fictionalized, novelized memory of the war in Angola that answers the soldier's claim that "La guerra nos cortó la lengua" (279) ("the war cut out our tongues" [219]), and a ritual invocation of an orisha, accomplished *with and through* the alternative mediatic stagings and interpretations.

However, there is another available reading of Santería ritual in the novel. Beto's assumption of Lázaro's name signals not only his devotion to the orisha to whom practitioners promise all manner of self-inflicted bodily suffering in exchange for particular requests, but positions Beto as a representative member of a larger Cuban community composed of the marginalized, outcasts, and others who exist "out of coherence with the context." Describing to Laura El Rincón, the Cuban birthplace of Laura's mother and the site of yearly devotions to Babalú Ayé, Beto recounts his recurring dream of crawling on his knees, chained with a seven-link chain to a log (he also has the seven names on his arm), across the ocean floor that separates Caracol Beach from Cuba. His purpose is to participate in the processions to Babalú Ayé/San Lázaro to pay his bodily penance for one last chance to hug his mother—cast here as both his literal mother and the *madre patria*. The ritual practice serves as a counterpoint to the revolution's mediatic representation, but it also maps together the Angolan mission with prior moments of entangled African and Caribbean histories. Beto imagines those among the procession:

> a cierta distancia, callados, respetuosos, fieles, patriotas, miles de cubanos en solemne procesión, hombres y mujeres, niños y ancianos, pecadores y arrepentidos, vagabundos, leprosos, minusválidos, mongólicos, cojos, ciegos, mudos, tontos, diabéticos, desesperados, tullidos, tuertos, tuberculosos, sordos, lelos, paralíticos, mancos, tartamudos, cardíacos, desahuciados, asmáticos, sidosos, paranoicos, solitarios, melancólicos, neuróticos, locos, locos, locos, cientos y cientos de pobres locos, algunos incurables como él, Beto Milanés. (237)

> (at a certain distance, quiet, respectful, loyal, patriotic, thousands of Cubans in solemn procession, men and women, young and old, sinners and penitents, vagabonds, lepers, the maimed, the Mongoloid, the lame, the blind, the mute, the half-witted, the diabetic, the desperate, the disabled, the one-eyed, the tubercular, the deaf, the moronic, the paralytic, the handless, the tongue-tied, the weak-hearted, the hopeless, the asthmatic, the AIDS-infected, the paranoid, the solitary, the melancholic, the neurotic, the mad, mad, mad, hundreds and hundreds of poor madmen, some incurable, like him, Beto Milanés. [185])

In its repetitive rhythms and syntax, the passage performs the processions in which devotees to Babalu Ayé participate each December, some of them crawling with stones tied to their ankles or otherwise simulating disease or disfigurement, in order to honor the orisha and ask for healing. Alberto's lists here figures in the preterit, those passed over by history, and thus it serves as a counterpoint to Guerra's configuration of the hyper-real as the revolution's future made manifest through media representation. However, in *Caracol Beach*, the site of their healing and recuperation is imagined not as a reach back in time—as the larger exiled Cuban community's is—but through crossing the geographic divide that separates Cuba from the sites of its diaspora.

In the images with which this chapter began of the infinitely replicating soldier-revolutionaries, the procession is a military march; the figures are idealized military men identical in their physical form and in their multiplicity, symbolizing the revolution itself. Alberto's sick, disfigured, disabled, and "mad" processioners are the inverse of the virile, idealized socialist New Man, while their procession toward the shrine to Babalú Ayé/San Lázaro displaces their devotion from the political center to a religious one—one which itself has a vexed relationship to Cuban officialdom both before and after the revolution.[11] Alberto uses the novel, therefore, as a space to ritually acknowledge those figures who inhabit disappointment, and thus whose representations fall outside of the hyper-reality of the revolution. The novel also serves as a call for bridging the divides that separate the Cuban community from itself: a primary function of the layering together of film and other media with the form of the novel.

To conclude, I would like to return to Alberto's metaphor of the "parapets of words" to argue that the novel explicitly privileges the space of the literary for interrogating the meaning of the contemporary moment's disappointed relationship to its past. One incarnation of Alberto's metaphor of the protective barrier which shields those behind it from enemy fire, sees the accumulation of vacuous rhetoric spilled by writers and politicians as "piles" of words that are disposable, indistinguishable, and meaningless. However, another can read it as an answer to the early revolutionary demand that literary words be used as weapons, another metaphor that permeates early revolutionary texts in Cuba and Angola during the 1960s–1970s. In this second sense, the "parapets" can also be read as offering a potential refuge, a defensive structure which offers a moment of respite. *Caracol Beach*, on the other hand, may only be capable of positing the literary word as offering a momentary reprieve in which to take stock of the historical violence enacted upon those communities through empty political rhetoric, as a way of acknowledging, if not necessarily overcoming, disappointment in the post–Cold War era.

4

Revolution from the South in J. E. Agualusa's *O Ano que Zumbi Tomou o Rio*

An elaborate mythology surrounds Palmares, a historical maroon community located in the Brazilian hinterland, which was destroyed by Portuguese colonial forces in the early eighteenth century. Stories of Palmares imagine it as lying between the colonial New World and Africa, between the past and the present. Historical and popular sources have alternately cast the collection of villages as a cruel kingdom whose inhabitants returned to the barbarous practices of African savages, a utopian collective that served as a refuge for fugitive slaves, and a savvy political challenge to colonial vigilance and organization.[1] They also offer a range of contradictory accounts of the death of Zumbi, the legendary warrior who led the final campaign against Portuguese troops in the late seventeenth century. He is rumored to have died in battle, been imprisoned and beheaded, and to have committed suicide by jumping from a precipice.[2] However, rather than remain buried in a bygone time and a faraway place, stories of Zumbi's messianic return to vindicate Palmares have become enmeshed with Brazilian twentieth- and twenty-first-century politics of social emancipation, movements for racial and political equality, and ideologies of rebellion and revolution.

These historical and geographical translations come together in Angolan author José Eduardo Agualusa's novel *O ano em que Zumbi Tomou o Rio* (2002) (*The Year that Zumbi Took Rio*), a partial restaging of the Zumbi legend in present day Rio de Janeiro. Palmares existed on the liminal edge of the colonial state. Its inhabitants—runaway slaves as well as free people of color—also challenged colonial control by imagining more expansive social roles for people of color than those available in Brazil's colonial period.

Palmares and Zumbi have been retroactively incorporated into imaginaries of Brazil as a nation; however, their histories continue to signal how black history and bodies still straddle the border between inclusion and exclusion. Agualusa's telling of the myth makes fresh use of the colonial indeterminacy that posits Zumbi and Palmares as both part of and outside of Brazil. In so doing, it reactivates a particular model of the twentieth-century messianic revolutionary figure, and emphasizes Angola's distant and contemporary histories as part of broader circuits in the Global South.

The protagonists of *O Ano em que Zumbi Tomou o Rio* are both Angolan exiles in Brazil and socially marginalized Brazilian favela-dwellers who together mount a violent uprising to protest state racism and demand opportunities for greater political participation. The political context that drives the plot thus focuses on contemporary Brazilian racial politics as well as postcolonial Angolan history. The figure of Zumbi is split between Brazilian drug gang leader Jararaca (whose childhood nickname is Cazumbi) and Francisco Palmares, an Angolan arms dealer now exiled in Rio.[3] In addition to the geographical association in his surname "Palmares," "Francisco" was also the name with which a Portuguese priest baptized the historical Zumbi. Jararaca and Francisco articulate diverse motives for revolt: the growing social protest against a long history of institutional racism in Brazil that accelerates in the decades following the *abertura*, the nation's "opening" at the end of the twentieth-century military dictatorship (1964–1985), and the contemporary disillusionment of Angolan exiles who flee the violence and oppressive political environment of Angola's years of colonial and civil war, especially following the 1977 failed coup headed by Nito Alves.

As a consequence of this larger framing, the revolution imagined in *O Ano em que Zumbi Tomou o Rio* cannot be exclusively located in either Brazil or Angola, but neither is it clearly positioned in the possible third space of the diasporic community of transatlantic black solidarity. Rather, I argue that the revolution of Agualusa's novel vacillates between Brazil and Angola and is constructed via a dialogic cooperation among Lusophone subjects that recognizes certain historical similarities as well as contemporary cultural differences among the various Brazilian and Angolan protagonists, as an incarnation of the Cuba-Angola axis that pushes these Global South circuits further into the Southern Hemisphere. In this chapter, I call upon Boaventura de Sousa Santos's discussion of "epistemologies of the South"—the creative potential that can arise out of the contact among different knowledges and systems of knowing—to analyze Agualusa's explicit parallels between the two contexts of Brazil and Angola. In focusing on the characters' geographical and chronological movement in the novel, I show that Agualusa's work ultimately suggests that a transnational reading of Lusophone histories and of revolution might model new modes of understanding in the Global South.

O Ano em que Zumbi Tomou o Rio is primarily set in present-day Rio de Janeiro, Brazil, and is organized around the perspectives of the three primary protagonists: Jararaca, Francisco Palmares, and Euclides Matoso da Câmara, an Angolan journalist who reports on the uprising for the international press. Francisco supplies weapons to Jararaca, a drug trafficker and gang leader turned revolutionary who frames drug violence in the favelas as a response to systematic government neglect and police violence against Rio's marginalized poor and communities of color. Jararaca's demands from the Brazilian government—amnesty for prisoners convicted of drug charges; racial quotas for government representation; an apology from the national government—enrage officials such as the racist army general Weissman, who advocates annihilating the city's poor communities to put an end to the conflict. Nonetheless, as the rebellion escalates and divides the city, Jararaca's increasing visibility and his public denunciation of institutionalized racism eventually recruit sympathizers to his cause, including a reluctant Francisco and Rio's chief of police Jorge Velho, ironically named for the seventeenth-century Portuguese mercenary who oversaw the destruction of Palmares. The novel's third protagonist, Euclides Matoso da Câmara, was once a subject of government-sanctioned torture for his opposing political views and now resides in exile.[4] As the revolt's importance in local, national, and international spheres expands, it eventually leads to some political concessions on the part of the Brazilian government. At the same time, in a clear mirroring of the historical Zumbi dos Palmares's death, both Francisco and Jararaca are presumed killed in the conflict. Yet, the narration of the scene depicting Francisco's death is divided between the first and last chapters of the novel, suggesting that either the Angolan or Brazilian Zumbis—or both—might, like the legendary Zumbi, circle back to initiate a new cycle of revolution.

Revolution has a variety of meanings, each of which serves to bring Brazilian and Angolan characters and histories into contact. Most overtly, Agualusa's use of the term serves to make an explicit connection between the Angolan anticolonial revolution of 1961–1975 and the novel's Brazilian characters' demands to end practices of internal colonization in Rio's periphery: the changes that Jararaca advocates represent a potential transformation of Brazil, both in terms of the marginal characters' concrete rights and the broader public's notions of social inclusion. Further, different interpretations of the term express users' differing perspectives on and position in relation to the contemporary government. The sympathetic characters in the novel cast the uprising as "revolution," defined here as not only the collective violent action implied in "revolt" or "uprising," but as adhering to a particular political project of emancipation and transformation. This characterization contrasts with Brazil's official state perspective in Agualusa's work, which sees it as nothing more than the disordered violence of criminals and miscreants—very much a reflection of the Portuguese colonial state's view of the incipient pro-independence fighters in the African colonies in the 1960s. Interpreting the violent actions of Jararaca and his allies as revolution serves to emphasize the novel's position that the movement's protagonists operate from peripheral spaces only partially incorporated into the Brazilian state, and whose inhabitants have only partial access to Brazilian citizenship.

However, *O Ano em que Zumbi Tomou o Rio* also exploits other possible meanings of the word: revolution in the sense of circular movement, with the associated concepts of revision and repetition. Francisco's melancholy at revisiting his past, for example, provides a counterpoint to the independence-era utopian promise of political change. The novel stages the repetition of the enslavement of African and black subjects as constitutive of historical continuity between the seventeenth-century history of Zumbi, the Angolan struggle for independence, and contemporary Brazil's social apartheid. In building this parallel, Agualusa also suggests that contemporaneous histories of struggle against these legacies in twentieth-century Angola and Brazil are part of parallel revolutionary cycles. At this broader level, revolution serves as a sort of imagined utopian catharsis that opens the possibility for meaningful political and social transformation for its participants and provides a stage for the operations of intercultural translation—the term Sousa Santos uses for transcultural knowledge exchange—in bringing together experiences from across the Southern Atlantic.

The text nonetheless leaves unresolved the question of who comprises the political community that would enact this change and on which such transformation would take effect. As critics have noted, Agualusa appeals for a transnational or diasporic Lusophone community in this novel and elsewhere.[5] I build on this past critical work by calling upon Sousa Santos in order to examine how these exchanges are constructed in the novel and what new knowledge circuits result from them. The chapter proceeds in four parts: the first brings together a discussion of the novel's structure and a more detailed examination of Sousa Santos's theoretical proposal to establish how Agualusa's text offers itself to an interpretation through the lens of intercultural translation. The next three sections analyze different but interrelated areas of overlapping experience that the characters bring to bear on the revolution imagined in the novel: colonial transitions, historical revisions, and new social knowledges that arise via the confrontations and collaborations of the characters and histories. I conclude that the figures of both geographical and temporal displacement in Agualusa's novel offer a model for the ways in which these "epistemologies of the South" might present a productive mode of south-south exchange.

Intercultural Translation and Contamination across the Atlantic

Agualusa, an author and journalist born in Huambo, Angola, left Angola in his late teens and has spent his adult life among various Portuguese-speaking geographies. As one interviewer puts it, "Dividindo-se entre Angola, Portugal e Brasil, Agualusa deixa-se contaminar pelas influências culturais dos caminhos traçados" (Agualusa, "J. E. Agualusa no ritmo da escrita" n/p) (Dividing himself among Angola, Portugal and Brazil, Agualusa allows himself to be contaminated by the cultural influences of the roads he traces).[6] This aspect of the author's biography reflects the preoccupation across his work with the networks that connect various Lusophone communities in the Americas, Africa, Asia, and Europe. Critical reception of Agualusa's literature has emphasized its transnational focus and readership and focused precisely on the trope of travel in space and in history. A sense of "contamination" is central to his Zumbi novel, in which the networks that characters traverse subvert reified notions of national unity or simple linear recycling of history. *O Ano em que Zumbi Tomou o Rio* follows critically admired novels such as 1989's *A Conjura* (*The Conspiracy*) and 1998's *Nação Crioula* (*Creole*) which celebrate ideas of *mestiçagem* (racial mixing) and *crioulidade* (creolity).[7] *O Ano que Zumbi Tomou o Rio* continues these novels' patterns of playing with characters' conflicting national, racial, and geographic notions of identity. These conflicts thus also serve to dramatize the work's harsh and overt criticism of contemporary racial politics in Brazil and violent abuses of power in Angola. But where previous texts by the author traced the colonial triangulation between Portugal, Angola, and Brazil, *O Ano em que Zumbi Tomou o Rio* focuses primarily on south-south exchange and new iterations of the colonial specter that do not pass explicitly through the former colonial metropolis.

The novel comprises eight chapters that circumscribe loops in time and space. The first and last chapters narrate two halves of the same apocalyptic scene in which Francisco and the police chief Jorge Velho contemplate their certain deaths as government helicopters close around them. Each of the shorter sections of the remaining chapters is titled with the name of a city, a locale within the city, and a day and/or time, identifying the starting point for the episode narrated. These markers initially give the impression of a straightforward linear chronology, but the novel quickly undermines this sense of time and place through a variety of techniques that reproduce the circular structure of the chapters and the historical remapping of a familiar legend. *O Ano em que Zumbi Tomou o Rio* repeats locales as points of encounter for different combinations of characters; constantly vacillates between the characters' memories of the past and the narration of the present, often without temporal markers; renames and reuses names for multiple characters; and shifts its narrative perspective as the characters' perambulations lead them to discover secrets known to another. The clashes and encounters traced by the novel's circular structure and citational techniques—framed through the broad idea of revolution—allow for different kinds of knowledge to be gained and sometimes lost.

Sousa Santos proposes the term "epistemology of the South" in a Spanish-language volume of that title, *Una epistemología del sur*, which brings together a number of essays laying out both his critique of colonial-capitalist systems and his proposal for an emancipation project grounded in the counter-hegemonic deployment of difference and multiplicity.[8] He identifies the "South" of his titular concept as a metaphor for the suffering and oppression that world colonial-capitalist systems continue to wreak ("Prefacio" 12). Some of the key terms he proposes lend themselves to an analysis of the nodes of contact that guide Agualusa's novel. In Sousa Santos's essay "Hacia una sociología de las ausencias y de las emergencias" ("Toward a Sociology of Absences and Emergencies") as well as elsewhere, he employs the metaphor of an ecological system which creates the possibility for "multiplicidad y . . . relaciones no destructivas entre los agentes que la componen" (125) (multiplicity and . . . non-destructive relationships between the agents which compose it). This multiplicity might be achieved through cultivating a series of conceptual "ecologies," listed as:

> ecología de saberes, ecología de temporalidades, ecología de reconocimientos, ecología de escalas y pensamiento y acción y, finalmente ecología de productividades (producciones y distribuciones sociales) . . . se trata de una versión amplia del realismo, que incluye las realidades ausentes por la vía del silenciamiento, de la supresión y de la marginalización. (125)

> (ecology of knowledges, ecology of temporalities, ecology of recognitions, ecology of scales and thinking and action, and, finally ecology of productivities [social production and distribution] . . . dealing with a broad version of realism, which includes those realities made absent through means of silencing, suppression and marginalization.)

Sousa Santos's use of "ecologies" exploits the biological metaphor to celebrate both multiplicity and the coexistence of realities and ways of knowing, as well as to argue that the continued existence of disparate ideas, histories, and cultures lies precisely in the survival of other alternatives against which they are defined, which can only continue to exist through interdependence and exchange.

A theory of an "epistemology of the South" thus critiques both the hierarchy inherent in colonial knowledge production, which Sousa Santos calls an "epistemology of the North," and a position of absolute cultural relativism, in which a cultural community or history is considered complete unto itself.[9] He proposes instead a process of what he calls elsewhere *intercultural translation*—"el procedimiento que permite crear inteligibilidad recíproca entre las experiencias del mundo, tanto los disponibles como las posibles (*Refundación del Estado* 52) (the method that permits the creation of reciprocal intelligibility among the experiences of the world, equally those that are available and those that are possible). The methodology of intercultural translation takes as a foundational premise the assumption that all cultures are incomplete and can be enriched through both "dialogue" and "confrontation" with other cultures (55). It is this methodology of intercultural translation that is most relevant to a transnational reading of the revolution in *O Ano em que Zumbi Tomou o Rio*.

The assumptions of an epistemology of the South seek to counteract the colonial and neocolonial suppression of local practices and knowledge. A shared colonial history, the centrality of slavery and its legacies, and the after-effects of empire serve as fundamental links between Brazil and Angola in the novel, as well as between Agualusa's condemnation of contemporary political abuses in both nations. However, just as important to the trans-national networks developed in the novel are those that sidestep the colonial center. That is, the novel explores those networks that do not forge their relationship *solely* on the basis of a figurative passage through the colonial center or solely on resistance to colonial and neocolonial incursion. It is this second aspect of intercultural translation as Sousa Santos imagines it that allows the novel to postulate the productivity of a south-south exchange.

Displacing Colonial Centers: Revolution as Protest

One of *O Ano em que Zumbi Tomou o Rio*'s central challenges is to exorcise the colonial specter and to reanimate the revolutionary hero, which links the narrative both to the historical Palmares's failed resistance to Portuguese encroachment and to one of the central mandates of Sousa Santos's process of intercultural translation. In the novel, this impulse takes the form of a constant return to the notion of collective protest against oppression, mediated through Francisco's memories of his war experiences and hesitation to join the revolt in Rio. Early in the novel, Francisco finds himself exiled in Rio with the intent to leave his past as soldier behind in Luanda; he has deserted his post as colonel in the Armed Forces and fled Angola after discovering a horrifying and compromising secret about the increasingly authoritarian president. However, he is constantly reminded of the experiences he wishes to bury: "Ele, Francisco Palmares, não se esquece de nada. Às vezes isso é bom. Noutras ocasiões pode ser um tormento" (33) (He, Francisco Palmares, never forgets anything. Sometimes this is good. On other occasions it can be a torment).

A chance encounter with the journalist Euclides Matoso da Câmera in a market in Rio de Janeiro launches a flood of memories for Francisco. However, beyond simply reminding him of the turmoil of his wartime experiences, catching sight of Euclides these many years later reminds Francisco that his own actions are implicated in a continuity of violence between Portuguese colonial control and the fictional Angolan president's post-independence regime. Francisco's past plagues him, as he cannot forget his complicity in Euclides's torture and persecution, ending in the journalist's presumed death and burial:

> Euclides passa sorrindo pela secção de carnes. Felizmente não para. O denso fedor das carcaças faz com que Francisco Palmares se lembre outra vez de Luanda. Pagaria muito para que alguém lhe arrancasse do cérebro aquelas imagens, uma por uma, com uma pinça, como se arrancam espinhos. Algumas pessoas tomam medicamentos para melhorar a memória. Ele de boa vontade tomaria alguma coisa para a prejudicar. (33)

> (Smiling, Euclides passes through the meat section. Fortunately he doesn't stop. The thick stench of the carcasses reminds Francisco Palmares yet again of Luanda. He would pay a lot for someone to wrest those images from his mind with tweezers, one by one, the way thorns are extracted. Some people take medicine to improve their memories. He would very willingly take something to damage his own.)

Francisco's sighting of Euclides reminds him of 1977's bloody crackdown on the "factionists," the suspected participants in the failed populist coup led by Nito Alves against Angola's ruling MPLA party. Euclides's torture and presumed death for alleged participation in the coup and Francisco's resulting disillusionment and melancholy upon discovering Euclides's likely innocence thus serve as the novel's point of entry into the ex-colonel's cycles of revising the failures of Angola's political past. This process of revisiting, however, rather than remaining in the melancholic mode of lost possibility, takes place through the new revolutionary cycle initiated in the Brazilian present. While Francisco has fabricated his own death in order to desert his military post and leave Angola behind, discovering that Euclides's death has been falsified as well draws him back into his revolutionary past. For Francisco, "a revolução era a doença dele" (28) (the revolution was his sickness)—a sickness from which not even death can deliver him.

Francisco's horror at his complicity in past violence in part stems from the ruling party's purge of internal enemies initiated in 1977, the urban battles in the civil phase of the war that lasted from 1992 until 2002 (the year of the novel's publication) as well as from the consolidation of colonial practices of torture and repression that secure the novel's fictional unnamed president's authoritarian hold on Angola. Agualusa, in fact, makes the translation of colonial practice to postcolonial corruption explicit in the figure of Monte, the former double agent working for the Portuguese PIDE (colonial police), who becomes the "Great Inquisitor" in the post-independence regime. It is Monte who orders the torture of Euclides and tracks Francisco to Rio in order to suppress Francisco's knowledge of the president's secrets.[10] Francisco holds documents that prove that the president ordered the murder of his own wife, which the ex-colonel wields as a weapon to protect himself against retaliation. However, his contact with Euclides and Monte in Rio reminds him that he has far more in common with Monte than he would like to remember. As Francisco recalls searching the Angolan state archives for information on Euclides's torture, he finds a metaphor for Monte's abuses in the rats found among the files, "acometendo os relatórios da polícia, devorando ansiosas as confissões dos torturados, prosperando e engordando com os segredos do Estado" (26) (attacking the police reports, anxiously devouring the confessions of those tortured, prospering and getting fat on the secrets of the State). The metaphor, however, could just as well apply to Francisco, who prospers by holding the president's secrets as a threat.

The character of Monte reappears as part of Agualusa's more comprehensive portrayal of the collective suppression of the history of the coup and its aftermath in a more recent novel, *Teoria Geral do Esquecimento* (2012) (*General Theory of Forgetting*). Like *O Ano em que Zumbi Tomou o Rio*, *Teoria Geral do Esquecimento* traces the interlinked stories of characters whose experiences are not recorded in official histories and archives. The protagonists of *Teoria Geral do Esquecimento* maintain their silence because they are victims of the brutal repression of political dissent, because they fear revealing what they know or witnessed, or because they are perpetrators of the violence who try to forget their pasts, like Monte who "Evita, inclusive, recordar os anos setenta quando, para preservar a revolução socialista, se permitiram, utilizando um eufemismo grato aos agentes da polícia política, certos excessos" (*Teoria Geral* 65) (Even avoids remembering the seventies, when, to preserve the socialist revolution, they permitted themselves, using a euphemism they owed to the agents of the political police, certain excesses). Agualusa thus establishes an extended critique between the two novels of the erasure of Angola's past in inexistent archives and suppressed memories, as well as the conversion of revolutionary enthusiasm into mourning and decay. This transformation is aptly figured in the graffito one of Monte's victims observes after being shot by a firing squad: the MPLA's rallying cry of "A luta continua, vitória é certa" (The fight continues, victory is certain) has been transformed in the graffito on a nearby wall into "O luto continua" (*Teoria Geral* 34) (Mourning continues).

O Ano em que Zumbi Tomou o Rio extends its portrayal of the specter of the colonizer beyond the figure of Monte through the other characters' frequently confused and mistaken familial and national identifications. This phenomenon arises from what critic Phillip Rothwell calls the loss of the "lusotropical father" in the postcolonial era (*A Canon* 22). In his analysis of absent paternity in Portuguese literature, Rothwell takes up the links forged between the colonizer and the colonized via Brazilian sociologist Gilberto Freyre's concept of *lusotropicalismo* (lusotropicalism) developed in Freyre's landmark 1933 study of the formation of the patriarchal national family, *Casa-grande e senzala* (*The Masters and the Slaves*).[11] In Freyre's work, lusotropicalism, the social ideology that argues for the special proclivity of Portuguese colonizers to adapt to the "tropics" and mix with indigenous populations, is enacted through the colonial father. Rothwell observes that while the colonial enterprise is seen as biologically and culturally productive for the colonies, it leaves in its wake a patriarchal absence in the metropolitan center (*A Canon* 24). In *O Ano em que Zumbi Tomou o Rio*, this phenomenon shifts south: the Brazilian and Angolan characters come together in part as a result of patriarchal abandonment. Francisco's bourgeois father exiled in Portugal disowns him when he runs away to join the Angolan MPLA's armed forces. Not only does Francisco trade the colonial "fatherland" for the *pátria* of his birth, he trades Angola for a Brazilian stepfather when he settles in Rio, while the death of the national patriarch, the Angolan president, saves him from assassination.

The trope of the lost and replaced fatherland also bears meaning for Euclides. An orphan, Euclides is raised in Angola by the Brazilian priest Padre Eusébio de Queirós Coutinho Matoso da Câmara, who tells Euclides that "hoje não sei bem dizer a que chão pertenço" (66) (today I don't know exactly what land to say I belong to). This national indeterminacy prefigures Euclides's position as the journalistic translator of the revolutionary experience to the larger international public. Similarly, Jararaca's father abandons the family when his son is young, and as Jararaca rises in power and visibility, his father is conscripted by Brazilian government officials to assassinate his son but is himself killed on his mission. The literal and symbolic patricides in the novel dismantle old patriarchal familial tropes of national and racial belonging. Instead, the characters construct new fatherlands imagined as founded on the precipice of Francisco's and Zumbi's deaths—a transitional space between Brazil and Angola, with the African-Brazilian Zumbi as its head.

Francisco witnesses the police murder of another father figure, a priest, together with a group of young children, while visiting Jararaca in his neighborhood of *Morro da Barriga* (Belly Hill/Mountain) to finalize an arms deal.[12] This last patricide finally forces Francisco to move from the position of indirect facilitator to direct participant in the revolution in Brazil. As a procession of children dressed as angels in celebration of Saint Sebastian passes through the plaza, they are caught in the crossfire of a sudden battle between the police and the drug traffickers. The episode is a clear reference to the 1993 murder of eight children sleeping in front of the Nossa Senhora de Candelária church in Rio de Janeiro; the perpetrators were off-duty police, and the news made international headlines. Observers and activists protested the unrestrained extrajudicial violence, and Agualusa levies a similar critique against the Brazilian state through Francisco's shock at the murder of one of the children. When Francisco sees one of the children passing through the plaza shot in front of a wall adorned with the graffito "o povo das favelas quer cidadania" (121) (the people of the favelas want citizenship), he finally comprehends the message that the inhabitants of the peripheral favela communities live beyond the protections of the law and are excluded from the national community. He gives up his protestations that "esta guerra não é minha" (120) (this war isn't mine) while Jararaca pushes a gun into his hands. By firing back, Francisco gives himself over to the possibility of either a further disillusionment or a redemptive cure to his "revolutionary sickness" in the present.

Francisco's hesitation to join the revolt makes visible the claim repeatedly reiterated in the novel that Rio's "social apartheid" (to borrow a phrase from Sousa Santos) is inherited from slavery and colonial rule. Francisco's past experience in what he calls war in the "classic sense" (55)—conceived through an intelligible distinction between war and peace, ally and enemy—fits into a colonial world order in which political and social control are vertically integrated via the metropole-colony axis. However, Jararaca's revolution operates from what Sousa Santos calls an urban cartography formed by internal zones of "civilization" and "savagery" in his city, which in the postcolonial era have replaced the geographic divide between Europe and its colonies (*Una epistemología* 174). Operating from this peripheral space, Jararaca becomes a "soldier" not by profession or training but out of the impulse to fight back against the excess of state violence exercised without legal impediment in urban zones of "savagery." In this sense, he shares a point of departure with the early anti-colonial fighters in Portugal's African colonies, dismissed by the Portuguese dictatorship as "terrorists" against the colonial state. Jararaca defends his illegal drug business as undermining the capitalist system and co-opts the vocabulary of war to protest the narrative of Brazil's successful transition to a post-dictatorial democracy. Jararaca's perspective reveals a situation of internal colonization and exclusion, enforced using the language of legality—police violence is justified because the revolutionaries are criminals—and of democracy, in that their actions threaten the stability of the state. Indeed, the novel ultimately proposes that the parallel between Jararaca's perspective from Rio's margins and Francisco's observations of postcolonial Angola provides terms for translating postcolonial situations across the Atlantic.

Historical Revisions

The alliances among Jararaca, Francisco, and Jorge Velho bring to the forefront the process of historical translation that structures *O Ano em que Zumbi Tomou o Rio*. The novel describes two valences of circulating movement: first, the synchronic development of parallel moments of postcolonial protest shared in the transatlantic circulation of characters and literary texts between Angola and Brazil and, second, a diachronic resurgence of past moments of rebellion against slavery and racial oppression, pointing to another period of Angolan and Brazilian exchange in the era of the trans-Atlantic slave trade. Francisco's and Euclides's "rebirth" in Rio are central to this convergence, as they parallel the messianic myth of the historical Zumbi's eventual return. Jararaca also brings this history forward in his re-embodiment of the seventeenth-century warrior figure in the racially divided physical and cultural landscape of contemporary urban Brazil, placing Zumbi into contact with Francisco's reinvigoration of the twentieth-century revolutionary hero. Suggesting that maps of time and space intersect in this network, the novel not only insists on a dialogue between Brazil and Angola, but also introduces a kind of revolutionary time into the characters' revisiting their individual and collective pasts. In *O Ano em que Zumbi Tomou o Rio*, revolution is configured as process of historical revision, and its cyclical resurgence has both destructive and constructive potential.

The proximity between Angola and Brazil is framed in terms that go beyond their linguistic and historical similarities as Lusophone countries formerly colonized by Portugal. The foundational history that links Angola to both Palmares and contemporary favelas is the history of slavery, the trans-Atlantic slave trade, and the legacies of how the enslaved fought back against the colonizers. Matthias Röhrig Assunção estimates that 3.8 million of the enslaved Africans who were shipped to Brazil embarked from the ports of West Central Africa between the sixteenth and nineteenth centuries, and identifies "Angola" as a dynamic signifier of a range of cultural and religious practices that have become embedded in colonial and post-independence Afro-Brazilian life.[13] The historical imaginaries of Palmares are symptomatic of this legacy: the settlement was known among its inhabitants as "Angola Janga," a name (mis)translated by the Portuguese colonizers as "Little Angola." John K. Thornton suggests the name of "Angola Janga" is indicative of the centrality of Angolan social structures in constructing the unity, complexity, and resilience of the city (784–88). As Ineke Phaf-Rheinberger notes, Agualusa's novel serves as part of a contemporary literary tradition in which "Criticism, subversion, and armed resistance against (the consequences of) slavery on all levels of daily life are . . . the main motifs" (122). *O Ano em que Zumbi Tomou o Rio* thus calls upon a collective memory of Palmares as part Africa and part New World, and therefore points to a longer record of relations between the two largest Portuguese colonies that centers a shared history of struggle against colonial occupation and violence.

In addition to recycling Jorge Velho's and the two Zumbi characters' names, the novel cites in Jararaca's home community of the Morro da Barriga yet another reference to the historical Palmares's location on the *Serra da Barriga* (Barriga Mountains). Thus, when Francisco sets foot in the Morro da Barriga, he steps into both a time more remote than his own past and an almost predetermined future: like Zumbi, he will join the fight. Jararaca's choice of the flag of the *Clube Militar Angolano* (Angolan Military Club) as the emblem for his army, the *Comando Negro* (Black Command), also obliquely points to another parallel between the novel's description of "conscripts" in the war against social apartheid and Angola's postindependence history.[14] The protracted years of war in Angola and its extension from rural to urban areas meant that few Angolans had been able to escape the direct consequences of its violence. Just as Jararaca posits involvement in the movement as an ideological choice, novels such as Pepetela's *Parábola do Cágado Velho* (*Parable of the Old Tortoise*) (1996) and Sousa Jamba's *Patriots* (1990) illustrate how in wartime Angola, regional, ethnic, or familial connections were politicized, resulting in literal or ideological "conscription" to one faction or another.

The "Comando Negro" referenced in Jararaca's revolutionary organization also invokes a fictional, militarized iteration of Brazil's *Movimento Negro Unificado* (United Black Movement), founded in São Paulo in 1978 with the help of famed black rights activist and experimental playwright Abdias do Nascimento. The first major black rights organization after the dissolution of the 1920s–1930s political party the *Frente Negra Brasileira* (Black Brazilian Front), the MNU was instrumental in placing political and social equality for Afro-Brazilians back into national debates that for decades had been dominated by ideologies of "racial democracy." This term is most commonly associated with sociologist Gilberto Freyre's defense of the value of racial miscegenation in Brazil's social and cultural history. Freyre justifies ideas of the exceptional nature of Brazil's race relations and the absence of racial prejudice in its society, and the notion of "racial democracy" was supported in the 1950s by black cultural activists like Nascimento as an ideal to which Brazil could aspire, if not a description of its realities (P. Alberto 12).[15]

As racial democracy became increasingly linked to the denial of structural racism in Brazil during the latter half of the twentieth century, Nascimento and other black leaders denounced the ideology; they looked to the civil rights protests in the United States as a more fruitful model for demanding social equality (Guimarães 130). However, Guimarães additionally notes that the accelerated movement away from "racial democracy" during the *abertura* of the 1970s–1980s was also founded in part in African decolonial thought (132–33). Seeking to concretize the shift from an ideology of patriarchal benevolence to one of active resistance, black activists promoted replacing the celebration of the centenary of abolition in 1988 with a national holiday devoted to the anniversary of Zumbi's death. Cultural projects that evidence this shift include *Cadernos Negros* (1978), literary anthologies which highlight Afro-Brazilian writers and *Quilomboje* (1982), a literary circle and journal whose name is a portmanteau of the two words *quilombo*—a maroon community—and *hoje*, "today." As Emanuelle Oliveira points out, these projects sought to create a political and cultural space for the formation of black community, inspired jointly in the African wars of liberation and the anti-colonial and anti-slavery past:

> Since they have been denied an appropriate place in society, Afro-Brazilian intellectuals have sought to reconstruct a political imagery that would enable blacks to envision themselves within a historical, cultural, and political framework. They place themselves within a macro experience (liberation wars in Africa) and a micro scenario (the re-emergence of social movements in Brazil), thus allowing themselves to actively participate in the construction of their identities. (55)

The shift away from racial democracy to recognizing black historical protagonism set the stage for the resurgence of Zumbi as both a national and trans-national figure through the turn of the twenty-first century, reflected in Agualusa's choice of source material.

O Ano em que Zumbi Tomou o Rio extends this trend in casting the work of Brazilian movements for racial equality of the twentieth century as parallel to the African decolonization movements of the 1950s-1970s. During approximately the same period as Angola's anti-colonial war of 1961-1975 and civil conflict of 1975-2002, the leftist opposition to the Brazilian military dictatorship of 1964-1985 included protests against racial inequality, which grew into well-developed black Brazilian activist movements that continue to protest institutionalized racism into the twenty-first century. The ways in which these contemporary historical moments intersect are the foci of David Brookshaw's article on Agualusa and Brazilian writer Francisco Maciel, as well as Jerry Dávila's study of Brazil's relationship to African decolonization. Agualusa's adoption of this contemporary narrative of resistance signals two important ways in which *O Ano em que Zumbi Tomou o Rio* models epistemologies of the South. The joint resistance of the intellectual Francisco against authoritarian rule in Angola and Jararaca against marginalization in Brazil suggests a translatability between the objects of their opposition located outside the old colonial triangulation, as well as a translatability in the form of their resistance: revolution. The fundamental conflicts that the two Zumbis face are thus posited as parallel as well: in Francisco's case, political heterodoxy and exile, and in Jararaca's, racism and racial exclusion.

Just as the novel stages the struggle to find a mode of productive epistemological resistance against the confines of national narratives and the weight of colonial history, Euclides da Câmara struggles for an adequate grammar to translate the conflict to his international readership. As the journalist sits observing the water that serves as the liquid bridge between Rio and Angola he sees an allegory for Brazil's racial divides among the sea birds perched on a boat:

> Uma dezena de grandes aves pretas, biguás, permanecem em pé e imóveis, no seu interior, muito bem alinhadas, o bico voltado na direção do vento. À proa resplandece uma garça. Euclides descobre naquilo uma alegoria do Brasil: um país de negros escravizados, remando, remando sempre—e sempre, sempre, um colono branco à proa. Afugenta as duas garças, que gritam e se vão. (45)

> (A dozen large black birds, cormorants, are standing motionless, lined up inside the boat, with their beaks pointing with the wind. At the prow shines a heron. Euclides discovers in that image an allegory of Brazil: a country of black slaves, rowing, always rowing,

and always, always a white colonist at the prow. He scares away the two herons, which screech and fly off.)

The novel, however, undermines the simplified metaphor in which the black masses, here the cormorants, can be liberated simply through a process of eliminating white leadership. In so doing, it undermines some of the most simplified of the Palmares mythologies—that of a utopian black commune that achieves harmony solely through its distance from the corrupt European colonial apparatus.[16]

In a clear reference to the boat scene, in the chapters that describe the end of the uprising, Francisco watches a fleet of military helicopters close in over the rebels. In the blades of the helicopters, he sees that "bandos de biguás, garças, patos, lançam-se enlouquecidos contra as hélices, e o sangue brota e alastra, soprado pelo vento forte, até se derramar numa chuva de fim de mundo sobre o asfalto quente" (11) (flocks of deranged cormorants, herons, ducks throw themselves against the propellers, and their blood splatters and spreads, carried by the fierce winds, until it splashes in an apocalyptic rain onto the hot asphalt). The violent "revolving" of the helicopter blades, symbolizing the revolutionary machine, destroys the birds; it thus literalizes the material consequences of "revolution." While Euclides observes the historical residue of the slaving system, it is uncertain in the present day whether the "bloody apocalypse" can erase it, and the annihilation of the birds in the blades of the helicopter points to the same devastating end for both the metaphorical masters and the enslaved. Their fate, therefore, also recalls the torture and killing of the political dissidents that Euclides himself escaped. *O Ano em que Zumbi Tomou o Rio* asks whether, after the return of Zumbi in the "apocalyptic" violence of armed uprising, the demands for social equality issued by the revolutionaries can be translated to the new time and space that revolutionary time imposes.

The apocalypse that Francisco witnesses opens a possibility for interpreting Euclides's metaphor of the birds beyond solely promoting a series of organized uprisings against the Brazilian state. The question is whether the annihilation of the birds signals the futility of revolutionary action. Francisco José Sampaio Melo reads the results of the rebellion as a failure: Francisco and Jorge Velho face capture or death as they pause on the precipice of the Morro da Barriga, referencing one version of the historical Zumbi's alleged suicide by jumping from a precipice (160). In the aftermath of the rebellion, Jararaca's body is identified, but reports of his reappearance circulate, nonetheless, reproducing another version of Zumbi's disappearance. While some of Jararaca's demands are met by the government, others are rejected. Regardless, Francisco insists that the localized practices of resistance might still yield some measure of emancipation.

For Francisco, however, the potential for emancipation seems to only exist in a place where he can shake off the weight of past revolutionary disillusionment—in Brazil rather than Angola. Hearing of the Angolan president's death, Francisco counters Euclides's optimistic forecast that a new president heralds new political possibilities in Angola: "Em Angola talvez seja possível derrubar o regime, mas não vai mudar nada. Aqui, ao contrário, podemos até perder esta batalha. Mas depois da nossa derrota, acredita, nada será como antes. Mesmo derrotados, teremos vencido" (248) (In Angola perhaps it is possible to topple the regime, but it won't change anything. Here, on the contrary, we could even lose this battle. But after our defeat, believe me, nothing will be like before. Even if we are defeated, we will have won). Seen on solely national terms, Francisco is expressing a pessimistic fatalism about the future of Angola, while he sees more possibility for social and political change in Brazil. But the novel systematically undermines the stability of the poles of "here" and there." Francisco's insistence on the utility of repeating Zumbi's resistance in a new time and of restaging revolution on a new Atlantic shore point not just to Brazil as offering the possibility for social change that no longer exists in Angola. Rather, his use of the collective first person suggests that the success of the revolt in Brazil depends in significant ways on the mutual participation of those from both shores of the Atlantic. The figurative location of the revolutionary victory as between the spaces of "here" and "there" suggests that its full meaning is accessible only via networks of knowledge that include multiple times and locations.

The Way to New Knowledge

The process of historical revision and translation of national histories models the encounters among Agualusa's characters that lead to new types of knowledge. However, these encounters suggest that "knowing from the south" is as likely to be a difficult and thorny process without resolution as a straightforward aggregation of facts, memories, and experiences. From his first interactions with Jararaca, Francisco discovers that each of them must revise what and how they know and experience the world. The relationship between the two is initially built through Francisco's illegal weapons sales to Jararaca; Francisco sees his own wartime experience fighting for independence from Portugal and defending the postindependence leadership as another figurative weapon he possesses and which Jararaca lacks. However, he discovers that his understanding of war clashes with the knowledge that Jararaca and his dealers have obtained by learning to survive in Brazil's racialized system of social exclusion and violence. When Francisco expresses his hesitation to release the arms to

Jararaca's men without "proper training," he warns Jararaca that "estes tipos não sabem o que é uma guerra. A bem dizer nunca tiveram nenhuma" (54) (these guys don't know what a war is. The truth is that they've never had one). Jararaca quickly corrects him:

> O que está acontecendo nesta cidade é uma guerra. Uma guerra, sim, tá ligado?! Faz ideia de quantas pessoas morrem por ano nas favelas cariocas? . . . Oito mil pessoas, mais de vinte e duas a cada dia, tá ligado?! . . . Sou traficante . . . porque meu povo está escravizado pelo sistema . . . Ou você entra no movimento, e morre jovem, mas como um homem livre, ou você envelhece sem deixar jamais de ser escravo. (55)

> (What's happening in this city is a war. A war, got it? Do you have any idea how many people die each year in Rio's favelas? . . . Eight thousand, more than twenty-two every day, got it? I'm a drug dealer . . . because my people are enslaved by the system . . . Either you join the movement, and you die young as a free man, or you get old without ever escaping slavery.)

The exchange between the two characters models an intercultural translation project, where the idea of war acquires new meanings for Francisco in a new context. Francisco is at first unable to assimilate the Brazilian favela-dwellers' armed resistance against their rivals and the representatives of the state—the police—into his idea of armies facing armies in formal conflict. He eventually revises his opinion and accepts the interpretation that Jararaca and his men are staging a series of violent political interventions against the contemporary legacies of slavery—that is, a war. His declaration that "they've never had one" can be read as a reference to Brazil's lack of a singular event of what Howard Winant calls "apocalyptic national conflict" over racial inequalities ("Rethinking Race" 191). In fact, the weight of such a conflict in Angola partially drives Francisco's melancholy, and this in turn leads David Brookshaw to argue that the novel is "deeply and fundamentally about Agualusa's homeland" ("Race Relations" 164). I do not dispute this characterization, but also argue that Jararaca's perspective nonetheless politicizes the deaths of Rio's marginalized, and his reframing serves both to force Francisco to revise his understanding of "war" as well as to relate Angola's colonial and postcolonial wars to the broader context of Brazil's racial history.

The familial genealogies critiqued in the novel extend to racial imaginaries as well. *O Ano em que Zumbi Tomou o Rio* repeatedly presents both tired stereotypes and conflicting racial knowledges in the voices of many of the characters, and then interrogates or undermines their utility to the social transformation that the revolutionaries seek. At various moments in the novel, Francisco and Euclides are mistakenly identified as Portuguese because of their accents; the organizer of a Conference of Black Writers in Portuguese is dismayed to discover that the African poets he has invited are indeed white; and the Brazilian characters alternatively declare themselves "black" or "brown" depending on whether the situation calls for declaring black solidarity in the Morro da Barriga or integrating into the hegemonic national imaginary of Brazil. This epistemological confusion signals the search in the novel for a kind of vocabulary that slips outside the tendency to subsume racial discourse under notions of national unity or through the specter of the colonial metropolis.

The figures of Jararaca and of Jacaré, the rapper who becomes the voice of the rebellion, demonstrate these conflicting racial knowledges in their encounters with the Angolan protagonists. In an interview with Euclides, Jararaca articulates what the novel clearly presents as the ironic nature of the vocabulary the characters use to discuss race: while, on the one hand, Jararaca agrees with Euclides's observation that the racialized social fracturing divides the city into Sousa Santos's zones of "civilization" and "savagery," on the other, he answers Euclides's follow-up question about his own racial identity by negating the suggestion that he is black: "Eu? Sou pardo, não é?! Moreno escuro" (84) (Me? I'm brown, right? Dark brown). Jararaca here reveals the complexity of racial formation in the Brazilian context. He appeals to black solidarity expressed in the name of his army—Black Command—and repeats his commitment to racial solidarity throughout his interviews and public statements about the reasons for the uprising, at one point demanding that his interviewer be black. Jararaca's position thus exemplifies what Howard Winant and others have analyzed as the accelerating pace of black political organization in the late twentieth and early twenty-first centuries, and the increasing efforts of figures like Nascimento to unite organizations working for racial equality. Yet, Jararaca's self-identification as "dark brown" also references the complicated vocabulary of color gradation in Brazilian Portuguese. As Brazil has historically assured greater social mobility for lighter skin tones, a proliferation of racial vocabulary captures the degree to which socially meaningful differentiation results in increasingly complex racial taxonomies. Jararaca's subtle expression of a desire for integration is repeated in the verses of the rapper Jacaré's anthem for the revolution entitled "Preto de Nascença" (Black by birth), which catalogs examples of racial discrimination, calls for black solidarity, and ends with a nationalistic appeal using verses taken from Brazil's national anthem.

The Angolan characters, however, complicate the intelligibility of racialized social castes as established by the organizing concept of the Brazilian nation. Repeatedly, the narrator either describes Francisco's elegant appearance and princely demeanor as out of place among the dwellers of the Morro da Barriga or his and Euclides's dark skin as standing out among the customers of the expensive hotels, clubs, and restaurants they frequent. When a taxi driver complains about the "blacks" causing trouble for the city, Francisco points out his own racial solidarity with the perpetrators, but the taxi driver is unable to assimilate Francisco as one among them, protesting, "o senhor é um homem de bem!" (116) (you're a respectable man!). And yet Francisco warns elsewhere that someone who elides blackness by choosing the vocabulary of lighter skin gradations "kills" a black person (37). The novel thus positions the vocabulary of racial solidarity as a strategic intervention that Francisco's foreign voice offers in the Brazilian context, where open discussions of racial identity and racial prejudice have a long history of suppression.

The novel's exposure of the contradictions in racial identifiers, however, is not bounded by Brazilian national territory. Again, it is through the confrontation of different national and racial signifiers that the novel posits new racial understandings. Jararaca and other characters repeatedly refer to Euclides and Francisco as "Portuguese" or the sometimes-derogatory slang term "portuga." In the same scene where Jararaca declares himself "dark brown," Euclides corrects him: "Não sou português, senhor Jararaca, sou angolano" (84) (I'm not Portuguese, Mr. Jararaca, I'm Angolan). Jararaca's response reveals the slippage between racial and national identifiers: "Português, japonês, angolano, é tudo a mesma raça" (Portuguese, Japanese, Angolan, it's all the same race). In positioning himself on one end of a dichotomy between his perceived group of "us" (Brazilian) and everyone else, Jararaca seems unable to break out of racial identifiers vertically aligned with national belonging: the exclusion against which he protests is posited here in solely national terms. Coming closer to Francisco's position, however, the police chief Jorge Velho positions black racial identifiers and solidarity as the strategic answer to systemized exclusion that emanates from a place of privilege, observing, "alguns de entre nós se descobriram negros porque não os deixam ser brasileiros" (252) (Some among us discovered they were black because they were not allowed to be Brazilian).

With this statement, the novel seems to offer a criticism of discourses of black solidarity as rooted in colonial ideologies of race and linked to the consolidation of otherness: as Jararaca points out elsewhere, a black Brazilian with a white great-grandparent would not call him or herself white. David Theo Goldberg's concept of "racial knowledge" defined as naturalized knowledge produced about a racial Other helps elucidate how Jararaca reproduces the language of state-sponsored racism. For Goldberg, racial knowledge is fundamentally relational: Jararaca's mapping together of blackness and Brazilianness exposes how this sort of racial knowledge "establishes a library or archive of information . . . socially managed, regulated by the general concerns of a social authority, and self-imposed by the specific concerns of the disciplinary specialist" (150–51). While black solidarity is the ostensible driver of the rebellion, both Jararaca and Jacaré insist that the Angolan characters are "different," and their nationality appears in media accounts of the violence as a mark of "foreign mercenaries" fanning the racial flames and further threatening the state's vigilance and discipline of Rio's racialized zones.

Nevertheless, the white Jorge Velho and Francisco's show of solidarity with the favela uprising also points to a project of national and transnational integration that more closely approximates the "roads of contamination" celebrated elsewhere in Agualusa's oeuvre. Euclides, in this scene and elsewhere, continues to question what Jararaca knows and does, and through his filter the friction between the colonial epistemologies and alternative notions of racial knowledge, including nonnational solidarities, models Southern epistemologies. These misidentifications and corrections underline, for critic Malcolm McNee, two important ideological aspects that guide Agualusa's work: first, the celebration of mixing or contamination, and second, his promotion of *lusofonia*, the theoretical configuration that seeks to link the Lusophone areas of the world without the necessity of passing through the figurative organization of the colonial metropole. McNee analyzes the transition from the "lusotropical" metanarrative founded in Freyre's proposal of the particular "openness" of Portuguese colonizers to idealized racial synthesis toward the more recent theoretical conversation around "lusofonia" to which Agualusa and Sousa Santos have both contributed. There is, as McNee makes clear, an important distinction between the lusotropicalist ideal of *mestiçagem* (racial mixing) and the overlapping encounters that Agualusa's work models. According to McNee, Agualusa "at times seems to veer away from *mestiçagem*, that is, away from the latter term's emphasis on cultural and sexual mixing and toward a sense of displacement, dislocation, and the aggregation of difference, rather than its transcendence" (18). This aggregation of difference operates in *O Ano em que Zumbi Tomou o Rio* via the confrontations and corrections that come out of the characters' differing ideas of race and belonging, and are also developed in the form of the novel itself.

The final aspect of intercultural translation that I examine is the form of *O Ano em que Zumbi Tomou o Rio*, which inscribes the unstable, whirling, circular movement of the metaphor of the helicopter blades. As noted above, the parallel chapters narrating Francisco's and Jorge Velho's demise as the first and the last chapters of the novel structure the events as part of historical cycles with the possibility of reencounters in time and in space. In the same way that the novel recycles the mythology of Zumbi, it incorporates literary citations, musical lyrics, and film references from across the Lusophone world, as well as from other languages. Francisco's chauffeur speaks only in the verses of Angolan poet Ernesto Lara Filho, and Francisco and Euclides's thoughts frequently reference other works of literature. Euclides's name, in fact, is likely a reference to Brazilian journalist Euclides da Cunha, whose 1902 work *Os sertões* (*Rebellion in the Backlands*) was based on da Cunha's journalistic reporting on the Canudos War of 1896–97.[17] Through his observations, da Cunha came to sympathize with the rural revolutionaries. Luiz Valente's characterization of da Cunha's resultant political positioning could apply just as easily to Euclides's readings of the Brazilian favelas as well as to his own persecution and exile: "da Cunha pinpoints a fundamental characteristic of Brazilian republican history, which, to borrow one of the author's most felicitous formulations, could be called a 'crime against our nationality': the construction of the Brazilian republic is being carried out by excluding the majority of Brazilians" (15). As Agualusa's portrayal brings forward, this process of racial exclusion is a continuous phenomenon from the nineteenth to the twenty-first centuries. A more recent reference incorporated into the novel, as Brookshaw has noted, is found in the way in which Jararaca's character recalls the story of the passengers of a Rio bus taken hostage in June 2000 by Sandro do Nascimento, a survivor of the massacre of children at the Candelaria church; the episode was retold in the documentary film *Bus 174* (with whose protagonist Jararaca shares a legal name) ("Race Relations" 166). In its jumbling of current politics, history, and literature, Agualusa's novel can be read as playing with popular Brazilian literary genres like the romance-reportagem (novel-reportage, or a non-fiction novel), which for Randal Johnson secures its audience's sympathy through the manipulation of documentary and journalistic discourses that encode contemporary social realities that the audience shares and recognizes (46).

However, Agualusa's work also undermines the perspective of the "outsider's gaze in" by privileging the narrative perspective of multiple characters who are simultaneously foreigners—Angolans—and at other times homogenized with the favela-dwellers in black solidarity. The novel thus toys with a readership hungry for the kind of "exposé" of the "truth" about poverty, violence, and racial inequality that the national and international reception of these works has represented. *O Ano em que Zumbi Tomou o Rio* thus risks falling close to another stereotype that casts favela communities as reliant on the patronage of outsiders to rescue them from their degradation.[18] However, the realities that the characters in Agualusa's novel live evade easy packaging. Their experiences are narrated not only in their own voices, thoughts, and memories, but through multiple textual incarnations. Euclides's journalistic work organizes and communicates the rebellion for an international audience but remains outside the text of the novel. Francisco's interactions with his surroundings and with his own past, conversely, are continually presented through poems and other literary texts and song lyrics. Rather than a depoliticized pastiche, this textual palimpsest exemplifies Agualusa's model of the networked exchange of literary knowledge. In one example early in the novel, Francisco recalls another near death and rebirth in a car accident that almost killed him. As he waits for death, he recalls verses of the poems "O Cão do Nilo" (The Dog of the Nile) and "Posposição" (Postponement) from the collection *O Escriba Acocorado* (The Squatting Scribe) by twentieth-century Mozambican poet Rui Knopfli.[19,20] The poems contemplate death and forgetting; "Posposição" posits literature as a resistance against annihilation:

> Escrevo sentado sob a fraca luz que do alto desce.
> Escrevo contra o silêncio. Não tenho já nome aqui.
> Por certo os outros têm a História a seu favor.
> Ausculto a ténue respiração da noite e da quietude.
> Sob o débil crepitar do metal percorrendo o papel
> soa perturbada a harmonia distante do universo. (Agualusa 33)[21]

> (I write seated beneath the weak light that descends from on high
> I write against silence. I no longer have a name here.
> Certainly others have History in their favor.
> I auscultate the tenuous respiration of the night and tranquility.
> Under the weak scratching of metal traversing the page
> uneasy, the distant harmony of the universe sounds.)

The poem's meditation on literature's immortality, incompletely rendered in Francisco's mental recitation, echoes the novel's structural proposition of reframing and translating histories that have occurred in other times and other places to construct new possibilities in the present. In fact, in the final note that accompanies Knopfli's poems, the poet makes precisely this point: quoting an essay from Borges, he contends that in choosing literary models, writers remake their precursors at the same time that their past models shape their own texts in unanticipated ways (43). Knopfli follows this final note with a list of allusions to other poetic texts from which he has drawn verses and figures throughout the poems. This is a technique that Agualusa adopts as well in a note to the reader at the end of *O Ano em que Zumbi Tomou o Rio*, though, like Knopfli, he lists only a small portion of the texts and works he has referenced throughout the novel. In a deliberate way, Agualusa, via

Knopfli, thus performs in the formal composition of the novel the historical revision and trans-historical translation that serve as the underlying project that animates Jararaca's revolution in the favela.

Francisco's onetime associate Monte, who in addition to being a torturer and spy is a poet turned speechwriter for the dictatorial Angolan president, reflects the palimpsestic technique of Agualusa's novel itself. Monte plays a game with his friends and acquaintances, who challenge him to incorporate random or incongruous literary quotes seamlessly into the president's speeches. In this way, the literary text is exploited for its very plasticity, and the act of citation signals the lack of stability of the rearranged literary text when fragmented and transported to new contexts. The problematic that the novel thus leaves us with is the role of the literary text in communicating both past histories and future possibilities: Is the victorious result of the revolution a specious one, or has meaningful change taken place for the marginalized characters whose lives the novel presents? Is Agualusa's incorporation of diverse cultural figures, tropes, and references simply a literary game? Or might it be calling upon a community of intellectuals and activists to contribute to the revolutionary project of reinforcing a new literary knowledge as a means of mediation among political subjects?

In his article "The Other Side of the Process," Winant notes that postures of collective rebellion as a contestatory political stance only come about in Brazil from the 1960s on, through an imaginary that links to circulating notions of black identity and culture that supersede the national configuration through which integration and racial democracy had operated. It is no accident, therefore, that the same era marks the development of political and cultural allegiances that foment Angola's independence movements around ideas of internationalist solidarity, or that in the subsequent decades, the rhetorics of these solidarities become inextricably linked to Angolan authors' examinations of these periods. As an example, in the context of *O Ano em que Zumbi Tomou o Rio* that the rebellion is only imaginable—articulable—through the language and vocabulary of a transnational community: Zumbi is divided between characters that represent Africa and Brazil, indicating a "marking" process of the marginalized favela as neither fully Brazilian nor fully outside. Thus the bodies on which antirevolutionary crackdowns operate are not fully subject to the nationalized state power on either side of the Atlantic: Francisco, Euclides, and Jararaca are killed and reborn in new national spaces. The failures of the Angolan revolution, linked to ongoing violence and the consolidation of authoritarian power in Agualusa's work, can be reimagined in Brazil via the shifts that allow the racial conflict to be interpreted through these super-national imaginaries. The figure of the revolutionary that Agualusa activates indicates these geographical and temporal crossings as well.

The novel relies on a particular model of active revolutionary resistance that circulated in the mid-twentieth century as part of the ideology of the socialist New Man. In analyzing this trope in the Cuban context, Hernández Salván focuses on the central mechanism of apocalyptic violence and masculine heroic sacrifice to bring the revolution about, rooted in Guevara and Fanon's theorization of violence as the means through which colonized peoples will bring about national liberation (44–50). This is very much the model posited in Francisco's and Jararaca's understanding of social transformation. In this sense, the Angolan revolution serves as a surrogate foundational violent event for twentieth-century Brazil, while Zumbi's historic resistance is retroactively mapped as a foundation of Angola's anti-colonial war. Agualusa's 2014 novel *A Rainha Ginga e de Como os Africanos Inventaram o Mundo* (*Queen Nzinga and how Africans Invented the World*) is exemplary in this respect. The novel deals with the history of Nzinga Mbande/Ana de Sousa (1582–1663), ruler of the Ndongo and Matamba kingdoms in what is now northern Angola, and a fierce resister against Portuguese incursions into her territory. Not only is the novel another example of the reactivation of a historical figure of resistance to colonial occupation but, as the subtitle indicates, it recenters world Atlantic history on the active role of black and African protagonists. In this sense, *A Rainha Ginga*, like *O Ano em que Zumbi Tomou o Rio*, perpetuates revolutionary ideology where revolutionary action opens new windows onto a history of resistance suppressed by colonial occupation. The historical reach back additionally hearkens to the ideological underpinnings of revolution as enabling the composition of a new historical and literary genealogy that traces this violent revolutionary resistance in a direct line from the colonial past to the postcolonial present. Francisco's exhaustion and disappointment with revolution do not prevent the instantiation of another revolutionary movement on the other side of the Atlantic.

For critic Pires Laranjeira, Agualusa's novel fails as a valid literary work because of its "irresponsible" postmodern incorporation of truth and fiction ("Vale tudo?"). Certainly, *O Ano em que Zumbi Tomou o Rio*'s complex engagement with the interactions of texts and histories resists some of the theoretical models we commonly use to read literature in the Global South. The novel might even resist some aspects of the rubric I have applied here: Sousa Santos's epistemologies of the south has an optimistic thrust that is sometimes obscured in the novel. However, this very tension is precisely what Agualusa's work has to offer. In drawing from transnational connections forged through a long history of resistance to slavery and colonization as well as a recent contemporary revolutionary alliance, this novel suggests that post-revolutionary disappointment can also serve as a point of departure for a new revolutionary cycle, one that incorporates the new configurations of knowledge gained from elsewhere and other times. In the context of the disappointment outlined by this novel, the "lack" or loss that such a term implies might be the very component that serves as the grounds, and not just as a symptom, for an alternative community that escapes from the limits of the revolutionary past.

Part III

Genre, Style, and Empire

5

Deferred Time and Belated Histories in Leonardo Padura's *El hombre que amaba a los perros*

In 2007, Cuban essayist and intellectual Ambrosio Fornet gave a speech entitled "El quinquenio gris: revisitando el término" (The Gray Five Years: Revisiting the Term), a surprisingly frank reevaluation of the difficult first half of the 1970s. Fornet had termed the period "gray" for its turn to imposed socialist-realist literary models and suppression of political and literary creativity in favor of "el burocratismo y la rutina" (380) (bureaucratism and routine).[1] The period of 1971–1976 came on the heels of Cuba's turn away from European allegiances and toward rhetorics of decolonization and solidarity with the then-called Third World, saw the beginnings of Cuba's mission in Angola, and occurred in parallel to the island's rapprochement with the Soviet Union in the political, economic, and artistic spheres. This chapter considers a novel that engages with the larger Cold War framing in which the internationalist missions in Africa were inevitably inscribed: though Cuba's relationship with the Soviet Union was officially one of "amistad entre los pueblos" (friendship among peoples), the legacies of this friendship are contested, often producing both nostalgia and "pain and consternation," as Jacqueline Loss has explored (21). The inheritances of this period for the first Cuban generations who grew up with the revolution is the primary subject of Cuban novelist Leonardo Padura Fuentes's novel *El hombre que amaba a los perros* (2009) (*The Man Who Loved Dogs* [2014]). The novel traces the three interlinked stories of Leon Trotsky, his Catalonian assassin Ramón Mercader, and the fictional Cuban novelist Iván Cárdenas. The novel, however, also stages the reconsideration of Cuba's relationship with other revolutionary movements and powers from the geographic and ideological margins. This chapter considers Padura's novel as part of a recent movement among Cuban intellectuals to reconsider what Fornet calls "los deletéreos efectos" (the deleterious effects) of the forced orthodoxy of the *quinquenio gris* as a result of the imposition of Soviet-style bureaucracy and associated oppressive ideological rigidity (400). Padura's portrayal of this era in Cuba, controversially, places the *quinquenio gris* into the context of the global effects of Soviet imperial politics. In *El hombre que amaba a los perros*, the teleological temporalities of the revolution are broken in multiple ways: the novel thematizes waiting and deferral rather than the action and progression associated with works of enthusiasm, its narrative time advances asynchronously among the three protagonists, and its organization follows the logics of both detective and historical fiction.[2]

Padura's novel is a nearly 800-page work of primarily historical fiction. The three main characters, Leon Trotsky, Ramón Mercader, and the Cuban writer Iván, each enters the text at a moment of frustrated estrangement from collapsing political projects. The novel begins with Trotsky's story upon his banishment to Kazakhstan in 1928, and follows him through Turkey, Norway, and finally to Mexico where his fateful encounter with Ramón Mercader takes place. Mercader is plucked from the battlefield of the Republican cause in civil war Spain, trained in the Soviet Union as an assassin, imprisoned in Mexico for twenty years after assassinating Trotsky, and then passed between the USSR and Cuba before his death from cancer in 1978. His character links the three protagonists and the spaces they move through together. He meets Iván in Havana in the late 1970s, where Mercader is living under the assumed name of Jaime López, and indirectly confesses to Iván the story of his recruitment, training, and assassination of Trotsky as a Soviet agent. Iván, alienated from writing after a short story he composes as an enthusiastic youth is rejected as counterrevolutionary, begins to write López's story decades later, leaving it to be found by his best friend when Iván is crushed to death by the collapsed ceiling of his decaying Havana apartment building. The deferred act of writing—Iván's slow accumulation of the details of López's story and identity over several decades, terminating in a partially composed account of the history—is central to the novel. This chapter considers how waiting and the deferred act of writing revise the advance of messianic and teleological time through which revolutionary action has been read.

Leonardo Padura Fuentes (b. 1955) made his initial mark on post-Soviet Cuban literature in the 1990s through his Mario Conde detective series, and more recently through a series of historical novels that reconsider distinct moments in Cuba's past and its entanglement in major world events: the political leanings of Cuba's nineteenth-century national poet José María Heredia in *La novela de mi vida* (2002) (*The Novel of My Life*); Hemingway's final days in Cuba in *Adiós, Hemingway* (2005); or art that disappeared after Havana's 1939 denial of entry to the SS St. Louis, resulting in the deaths of hundreds of its Jewish passengers in *Herejes* (2013) (*Heretics*). Angola has left its mark on Padura's fiction as well, and the Angolan experience is one of the central indicators of the post–Cold War disappointment that pervades the Mario Conde series, via Conde's best friend Carlos who is paralyzed due to injuries suffered in the war. Padura himself served as a journalist in Angola for a year between 1985 and 1986, and has spoken about the effect the experience had on his literature: "Vi las actitudes más mezquinas de los cubanos allí en Angola y . . . las más hermosas y más altruistas. Eso me enseñó a entender algo de la condición humana que después he tratado de reflejar en mis libros" (Pérez n/p) (I saw the most mean-spirited attitudes of the Cubans over there in Angola and the most beautiful and altruistic ones. That taught me to understand something of the human condition that since then I've tried to reflect in my books). In addition to the veteran character in the Mario Conde series, the author has written several short stories whose protagonists are veterans of Angola including "La Puerta de Alcalá" and "Según pasan los años" (As the Years Pass) both included in the collection *La Puerta de Alcalá y otras cacerías* (1998) (*The Puerta de Alcalá and Other Searches*). These stories focus on the intimate, personal loss of the post-Cold War transition—the protagonists' loss of friends to the war and to exile or lovers to loneliness. However, I have chosen to focus this chapter on *El hombre que amaba a los perros* rather than these stories about Angola precisely for the way that the novel captures the larger debates about the complex inheritances of Cold War divisions not just between the superpowers, but between the Soviet Union and the socialist world in the Global South. Padura's portrayal of the Soviet influence in Cuba reinforces Rojas's thesis about Cuba's underdevelopment, though reconfiguring it as temporal belatedness that results from the period of Sovietization in the 1970s. In this way, the novel implicitly reinforces some of the rhetorical grounds justifying Cuba's Angolan mission and identification with the Third World more broadly, casting Cuba as the unfortunate target of destructive manipulation by the Communist superpower, as opposed to the island's horizontal solidarity across the Global South.[3]

Anke Birkenmaier places Padura's fiction as an inheritor of both the explosion of the "novela negra," the hardboiled detective novel in Spanish, as well as two distinct traditions that define twentieth-century Cuban fiction: first as part of the generation of disenchanted writers who document the economic and social crises introduced by the fall of the Soviet Union and Cuba's euphemistically named "Período Especial en Tiempos de Paz" (Special Period in Times of Peace) during the 1990s, and second as the long line of authors of historical novels that re-center the construction of world history on the so-called peripheral spaces of Latin America (13–17). To these traditions I add the pivotal moment of the 1970s and the *quinquenio gris* as the era that introduced the detective novel into the Cuban tradition, a genre associated with the socialist realism embraced by the state. This is also, of course, the era in *El hombre que amaba a los perros* during which Iván, a metonymic representative of what Padura and his contemporaries refer to as the "lost generation" of writers, is judged politically suspect and thus refused the state patronage that would allow him to continue to write.

Iván's story, intercalated among alternating chapters that narrate both Trotsky's and Mercader's lead-up to their encounter in Mexico City, turns out to be both the narration of a history unknown to his generation until the post-1989 realignment of world geopolitics, and the deferral of that narration to beyond the final pages of the novel. Iván first meets Mercader on a Cuban beach in 1978, as Mercader is dying of likely radiation poisoning. Over the course of several months, he tells Iván the story of his recruitment by the NKVD, his training and preparation, and his eventual assassination of Trotsky, about which the historical Mercader was famously silent from his conviction in Mexico in 1940 until his death in 1978.[4] However, he disappears before finishing the tale, and Iván only gets access to the final pieces in installments over the following decades. The first comes in 1983, in a letter that recounts Mercader's utter disillusionment with the Soviet machine that had recruited, trained, and ultimately isolated and possibly murdered him, delivered years later by Mercader's terrified nurse; the second in the anonymous package containing the 1990 biography of Mercader written by his brother Luis; and a third, in 1996, when Mercader's driver and minder visits Iván and fills in the details of Mercader's final weeks and death.

Birkenmaier reads in Padura's work a blurring of the genre categories that would ostensibly separate detective and historical works. This differentiates his fiction from other canonical twentieth-century authors of historical novels such as Alejo Carpentier:

> if one follows Padura's path from the detective novel to the historical novel, it is quite clear that his fiction is not so much preoccupied with cyclical, mythic history or with origins, than with what Roger Caillois has called the inversion of time, typical of the mystery novel: the substitution of the order of occurrence by the order of discovery. Padura's historical novels often feature, just like his detective novels, an enigma . . . that is subsequently uncovered by the lead character, a scholar or a witness who employs just the same means of logic and investigation that a detective would employ. (17)

This method of organization following the "time of discovery" rather than the order of occurrence is intimately linked to the ideology of time that the novel unravels as part of its critical examination of the Soviet Union's place in Cuba's post-revolutionary history. In *Dreamworld and Catastrophe*, an examination of the impact of the Soviet Union on the political philosophies of the twentieth century, Susan Buck-Morss argues that while the logic of nation-states is fundamentally one governed by a concept of geographic space, socialism is governed by time: "Class revolution is a historical event understood as an advance in time. What constitutes a victory is described in terms of historical progress rather than territorial gains" (23). Historicizing the temporal gains as constitutive of progress through writing and other arts becomes the hallmark of the Soviet model, and allows the revolutionary event, the breach in the course of history, to not only take meaning but to be recast as the causal force that produces the lived present (62). While Buck-Morss's notion of a forward-moving temporality predicated on a Hegelian configuration of history describes the underlying ideology that drove the expansion of socialisms across the globe, *El hombre que amaba a los perros* reinscribes that movement in the specific geographies that trace its uneven expansion and divergent development. We might see this geographical reinscription as a kind of inversion of Trotsky's thesis of uneven and combined development, tracing the path of the collapse of leftist political projects, rather than their advancement. The novel picks up the stories of the three protagonists not at the moment of revolutionary enthusiasm and possibility, but at the places and times of their marginalization: Trotsky in 1928, upon his first exile to the margins of the Soviet empire in Kazakhstan, Mercader in 1937 at the time of his recruitment to the NKVD and subsequent abandonment of the Spanish Republican cause, and Iván as he buries his wife after her death in 2004 and then recalls his estrangement from Cuban revolutionary orthodoxy in the 1970s. The protagonists thus trace the movement of a feeling of revolutionary possibility among the international Left as the sites of its new, possible utopias moved South: both Mercader and Trotsky end up in Mexico, and Mercader eventually in Cuba, where he meets Iván. Thus, their paths also follow the inevitable futurity of disappointment—or in Wendy Brown, Marta Hernández Salván, and Enzo Traverso's slightly different configurations, leftist melancholy as one of the consequences of disappointment—signified in the deadly collapsing roof of Iván's Havana apartment building.

Central to *El hombre que amaba a los perros* is the specific act of waiting, as a measure of time deferred and a counterpoint to the rushed sense of history on its way to the future associated with revolutionary events. Trotsky's entire exile is marked by waiting for both information—news of where he would go next, as the novel traces his exile from Kazakhstan to Turkey, Norway and finally Mexico—and for the inevitable attempts on his life that he expects from Stalinist agents. Even his death is deferred: Mercader's imperfect assault with the infamous icepick leaves Trotsky alive for a day after the attack. Similarly, Padura's depiction of Mercader focuses on the slowing of time as he waits for orders, for the proper moment to carry out his attack, and then on the decades that pass before he finally reveals his story to Iván. Iván, like the others, is frozen into inaction by the censorship of his "counterrevolutionary" story, his subsequent marginalization as a result of the *quinquenio gris*, by the crisis of the Special Period, and by attending to his wife as he waits for her inevitable death. Though the novel begins and ends with Iván in 2004, the intervening chapters advance largely chronologically, alternating among the perspectives of each of the protagonists. However, the advancement of time is asynchronous: not only does the cosmological time of each protagonist's story differ, time has a different value for each. The amount of time elapsed, the passage from one place and one event to the next for each protagonist, proceeds out of step with the others. In the case of each of the three protagonists, waiting contributes further to this asynchronous passage of time in the novel that counteracts the notion of an accelerated, synchronized march of world events toward an inevitable fulfillment of imagined utopian futures.

The Drive South

The organization of *El hombre que amaba a los perros* interrupts two associated modes of time: the continuous time of the realist historical novel, as well as the messianic, revolutionary time of imminence associated with the urgency to create new literary form and redress the failures of pre-revolutionary history in the first decade of the Cuban Revolution. This section will advance with the following goals: first, to link this early notion of messianic time in revolution to a global leftist drive that locates the future in the Global South, and, second to examine how the *quinquenio gris* foreclosed this notion of time and its accompanying literary innovations. The juxtaposition of these two temporal modes opens the possibility of a reading of *El hombre que amaba a los perros* as a metaliterary contemplation of the continuous deferral, stagnated time, and waiting that defers the composition and publication of Ivan's novel, that is, precisely *El hombre que amaba a los perros* itself, beyond the final page of Padura's text.

The late 1960s mark an intersection of two geopolitical configurations of time in Cuba. A number of the primary texts that develop the "decolonizing thesis" of the Cuban Revolution promote a configuration of time in which Cuba, looking south, figures as the vanguard of the global leftist future, and thus as the ideological inheritor of the particular revolutionary history traced in Padura's novel. In 1966, the first Tricontinental Congress was held in Havana; world leaders from across Africa, Asia, and the Americas met to discuss a program of mutual support for worldwide anti-imperial and anti-colonial action. The resulting journal, *Tricontinental*, published by the Organización de Solidaridad de los Pueblos de África, Asia y América Latina (Organization of Solidarity of the Peoples of Africa, Asia and Latin America; OSPAAAL) contained reports of revolutionary and leftist-aligned actions across the three continents, and was the primary site of development of the tricontinentalist ideology. Anne Garland Mahler, for example, has looked at how among images in the journal, the abstraction and repetition of particular forms—the stylized outline of guns, folkloric figures turned into soldiers, etc.—indicate a particular translatability of anti-imperialist ideology abstracted from either nationalist particulars or biological notions of race, that could and should be repeated across the three titular geographies of Asia, Africa, and Latin America ("Beyond the Color Curtain"). This iterability of revolution appears repeatedly in written texts about Tricontinentalism as well. As Besenia Rodríguez has argued, the Cuban Revolution comes to represent a benchmark for other anti-colonial and anti-imperialist movements, in essays and theoretical and cultural texts from across the areas represented by the movement; Stephen Henighan has made a similar case in a broader context ("The Cuban Fulcrum"). This abstraction and iterability of revolutionary movements also function on a temporal level, introducing a kind of immanent revolutionary present into the way that tricontinentalism conceives of how movements are linked in different places, but also in different times. This linkage could be figured, certainly not coincidentally, in both Ernesto "Che" Guevara's and Trotsky's notions of continuous revolution. Within this accelerated, circular movement, the Cuban Revolution represents an incarnation of the socialist immanent future, allowing the coexistence of both a time of belatedness across the Third World and a time of fulfillment or surpassing the (neo)colonial and underdeveloped past in the model of the Cuban Revolution. These ideas inflect the language of a number of the speeches from the First Tricontinental Congress, as in the examples from Bissau-Guinean revolutionary leader Amílcar Cabral's and Angolan Mário Pinto de Andrade's addresses discussed in the introduction. They are also articulated clearly in Guevara's famous last political address before his death, "Mensaje al Tricontinental" (Message to the Tricontinental), which was published as a supplement to the journal *Tricontinental* in 1967.

Guevara refers to the "continentes atrasados," the "backwards" or "lagging" continents, in terms not of the necessity that they "catch up" to the imperialist societies of North America and Europe, but rather in terms of their potential to either follow the dead-end, stagnant model of the Global North or choose the liberating path of revolution as modeled in Cuba and elsewhere. His projections reinforce both the idea of accelerated concurrence of revolutionary time across the three continents and their projection into an almost-fulfilled future:

> Nuevos brotes de guerra surgirán en estos y otros países americanos . . . e irán creciendo, con todas las vicisitudes que entraña este peligroso oficio de revolucionario moderno . . . Poco a poco, las armas obsoletas que bastan para la represión de las pequeñas bandas armadas, irán convirtiéndose en armas modernas y los grupos de asesores en combatientes norteamericanos, hasta que, en un momento dado, se vean obligados a enviar cantidades crecientes de tropas regulares para asegurar la relativa estabilidad de un poder cuyo ejército nacional títere se desintegra ante los combates de las guerrillas. Es el camino de Vietnam; es el camino que deben seguir los pueblos; es el camino que seguirá América. (256–57)

> (New outbreaks of war will emerge in these and other American countries . . . and they will continue to grow, with all the vicissitudes that this dangerous occupation of the modern revolutionary entails . . . Little by little, the obsolete weapons that are sufficient to repress small armed bands will turn into modern weapons and the groups of advisers will become North American combatants until, at a certain moment, they will be obligated to send growing numbers of regular troops to assure the relative stability of a power whose puppet national government is falling apart before the guerrilla fighting. This is Vietnam's road; it is the road that all peoples should follow; it is the road that the Americas will follow.)

The grammar of this accelerated futurity is registered in the repetition of the future tense verbs and their implication of inevitable fulfillment; Guevara pays lip service to the local, regional, and national differences across the three continents, and yet articulates a kind of revolutionary formula for development that will translate across the geographies of the Third World. This model of continuous revolution around the Global South is posited explicitly to distinguish third-world revolution from the progress of the Soviet model, and to propose the possibility of fulfilling the messianic revolutionary time that the Cuban Revolution represents elsewhere across the Americas, Asia, and Africa. These are precisely, however, the ideas that Padura's novel dismantles.

The other notion of time that *El hombre que amaba a los perros* challenges posits Cuba as a "latecomer" to Soviet futurity. As we have already seen, the late 1960s initiated Cuba's approximation to the Soviet Union; considering Cuba as site of "underdevelopment," the axis between the Cold War superpower and the island nation would figure the USSR as the socialist future made manifest. In this configuration, "underdevelopment" in its temporal incarnation figures as belatedness. This belatedness was made concrete in the emblematic two-day delay in Fidel's response to the 1968 Soviet invasion of Prague; his lukewarm confirmation of support for the Soviets marked the beginning of the "Soviet turn" that continued into the 1970s, and which many Cubans saw as a betrayal of Guevara's ideals of third-world revolution. Therefore, we may also see the late 1960s and the early 1970s in *El hombre que amaba a los perros* as the beginning of a temporal modality of deferral: it is, after all, during this time that Iván falls away from the revolution. He notes, precisely, the deferral of the future toward which he and his generation have been laboring, results in falling "out of time" with the external world:

> yo era un romántico . . . siempre armado con aquel compacto entusiasmo militante y aquella fe invencible, que nos imbuía a casi todos, en la realización de casi todos los actos de nuestras vidas y, muy especialmente, en la paciente aunque segura espera del luminoso futuro mejor en el que la isla florecería, material y espiritualmente, como un vergel.
>
> Creo que en esos años nosotros debimos de haber sido, en todo el mundo occidental civilizado y estudiantil, los únicos miembros de nuestra generación que . . . vivimos sin saber que estaba naciendo la música salsa o que los Beatles (Rollings y Mamas *too*) eran símbolo de la rebeldía y no de la cultura imperialista, como tantas veces nos dijeron; y, además, como cabía esperar, entre otras manquedades y desinformaciones, habíamos sido, en su momento, los menos enterados de las proporciones de la herida física y filosófica que habían producido en Praga unos tanques algo más que amenazadores, de la matanza de estudiantes en una plaza mexicana llamada Tlatelolco, de la devastación humana e histórica provocada por la Revolución Cultural del amado camarada Mao y del nacimiento, para gentes de nuestra edad, de otro tipo de sueño, alumbrado en las calles de París y en los conciertos de rock en California. (100)

(I was a die-hard romantic . . . always armed, with that compact militant enthusiasm and that invincible faith that imbued almost all of us in carrying out almost all of the acts of our lives and, especially, in the patient although certain wait for the luminous better future in which the island would flourish, physically and spiritually, like a garden.

I think that in those years we must have been the only members of our generation in the whole of Western student civilization who . . . lived without knowing that salsa music was being born or that the Beatles (The Rolling Stones and the Mamas and the Papas *too*) were the symbol of rebellion and not of imperialist culture, as we were told so many times; and besides, as should be expected, amid other shortcomings and disinformation, we had been, at the time, the least informed about the extent of the physical and philosophical wounds produced in Prague by tanks that acted as more than threats, about the massacre of students in a Mexican plaza called Tlatelolco, about the historic and human devastation unleashed by our dear Comrade Mao's Cultural Revolution, and about the birth, for people of our age, of another kind of dream, kindled in the streets of Paris and in rock concerts in California. [67])

Iván's lament figures his generation as trapped between competing temporal paradigms: the paradigm of the "patient although certain wait for the luminous better future," which entails a life "without knowing," versus the cultural impact of the global youth movements whose participants, like revolutionaries before them, sought to arrest the time in which they were living. Padura places the blame squarely on the sovietization of the Cuban bureaucracy; the novel, in its work of historical unmasking, thus promotes the thesis that the failures of the cultural policies of the 1970s were already observable in the administration of the Soviet Union decades before.

This thesis is supported in Buck-Morss's analysis: she argues that by the late 1920s, Soviet art had ceded its position as the avant-garde to functioning as the mechanism of enforcement of a political vanguard, buttressing not just the party's version of history and reality, but its unquestioned right to direct the social future of the people. The collapse of all futures into the political one has the ironic effect in the cultural sphere of foreclosing the potentiality of the aesthetic to "arrest time"; it is therefore a "colonization of time":

Bolshevism's claim to know the course of history in its totality presumed a 'science' of the future that encouraged revolutionary politics to dictate to art. Culture was to be operationalized. Its products would serve 'progress' as the latter's visual representation . . . Artistic revolution came to be distinguished from political revolution, of which it was merely symptomatic. Constrained by the historical goal, revolutionary culture became sedate, conserving a past that appeared to lead meaningfully into the present eschewing new primitivisms that blurred the line of progress, appealing to the masses by means of conventional art forms in order to mobilize them for movement 'forward' in time. . . .

In acquiescing to the vanguard's cosmological conception of revolutionary time, the avant-garde abandoned the *lived* temporality of interruption, estrangement, arrest—that is, they abandoned the *phenomenological experience of avant-garde practice* . . . The avant-garde philosophically understood, as a temporal structure of experience, is a cognitive category: it is 'aesthetics' in the word's original sense of 'perception through feeling.' (49; 62)

Buck-Morss's critique, like Iván's, is not solely of how the Soviet and, later, the Cuban models subjugated artistic production to political orthodoxy. Rather, both signal a mode of thought where the revolutionary is located fundamentally in the aesthetic. This may be one of the critical functions of the ways that Padura's deployment of the historical novel and detective fiction genres, as two of the primary genres associated with socialist realism in Cuba, challenges some of the tenets of socialist realism, including its heroes' tendency toward restoring the social order. *El hombre que amaba a los perros*, like Padura's Mario Conde detective novels of the 1990s, is conditioned by a pervasive corruption of the social sphere, which in José Antonio Michelena's view, revealed areas of conflict previously unmentionable in revolutionary literature (17). Iván, too, evidences this focus on the aesthetic by sandwiching his lament about his generation's belated realization of the political impact of events such as the Prague Spring, the massacre at Tlatelolco, and the Cultural Revolution between examples of the music that register, too late, a heterogeneity of revolutionary expression. By defending an awaited revolutionary future that does not materialize, he is kept from the phenomenology of another revolution underway: the Beatles, Paris, the Rolling Stones, part of what Traverso argues is the first global revolutionary culture (12). The silencing of countercultural music is, for Iván, to have failed to witness its historical rupture, to have lived out-of-time.

The movement of the revolutionary future to the South, as it is traced geographically by the three protagonists of *El hombre que amaba a los perros*, thus also opens up a number of different temporalities. However, this course remains peripheral to the protagonists' paths and actions. Or, perhaps better stated: the protagonists remain on the periphery of the revolutionary action that continues in its historical progress either elsewhere or among other actors. In this sense, the hope for the revolutionary future is simultaneously the path of disappointment: in each case, the deferral of that futurity constitutes the two simultaneous affective modes.

Waiting

The temporal deferral that Iván laments frequently takes the form of waiting in *El hombre que amaba a los perros*. The reader encounters Mercader, Trotsky, and Iván in marginal spaces, where they wait: for the passage of time, for a change in conditions, or for orders to act. These spaces thus also serve as pivot points between the accelerated pace of the revolutions-in-action around them, and the slowing, thickening of time that waiting produces. We first encounter Trotsky in exile in Kazakhstan, waiting to find out his fate; the rest of his perambulations are also characterized by his waiting for the inevitable attempts on his life, as well as the imprisonment, persecution, and death of his family members. Mercader is called away by his mother to be recruited by the Soviet agent Kotov, and subsequently waits for his orders to come down from Stalin while the faltering Republican effort collapses around him. Iván, who has spent decades trying but failing to write Mercader's story, buries his wife after her long, slow decimation due to cancer, and closes himself in his apartment to wait for the arrival of a hurricane. While the act of waiting links the characters, however, their waiting is not all of the same kind. In his reading of Penelope's waiting in *The Odyssey*, Harold Schweizer argues that Penelope introduces two competing notions of waiting: she weaves Laertes's burial shroud during the day to hasten her selection of a suitor to replace Odysseus but at night unravels it to defer the moment of selection. The first type of waiting is figured in the rhythmic, measured daytime weaving as an act of structured time, while in the second type, time's structure falls away:

> nightly [the shroud] is reduced to a tangle of threads, when waiting is no longer directed toward the future, but simply endured. Such waiting is not waiting *for something* but waiting *for something to pass*. No text, no cloth, no weaving is there to assure us of the moral or psychological soundness of the person who must have passed through that unplotted time. This is one of the implications of Penelope's unraveling of the shroud at night. It is a time

unaccounted for, a refusal of conventional patriarchal narrative, a refusal of the beauty Erymakkos wants to see, a refusal of the luxuries that would distract her from the passage of time. (287)

It is clear that each of the three protagonists engages in the first type of waiting, *waiting for something*, waiting to hasten the arrival of an event. While Trotsky's waiting is, in a perverse way, fulfilled by his murder, Mercader, released from prison and living in Moscow, must discharge the object of his waiting: while his younger brother dreams of obtaining permission to leave the USSR and returning to Spain, "Ramón, en cambio, sabía que a él nunca le permitirían abandoner el territorio soviético y que, además, ningún país del mundo, empezando por España, se dignaría recibirlo. . . . dijo en voz alta: —*Jo sóc un fantasma*" (735–36; 742) ("Ramón, in contrast, knew he would never be allowed to leave Soviet territory and that, in addition, no country in the world, starting with Spain, would deign to receive him . . . he said out loud: '*Jo sóc un fantasma*'" [553; 558]). Mercader's waiting, like Iván's after his censure and the beginnings of his disappointment, loses its transitive function. The second kind of waiting—waiting as slowing, rather than hastening time; waiting to endure, rather than to hurry time's fulfillment in the next event—is figured in a scene where Mercader searches in vain for the apartment of his Soviet handler: "Los números que debían identificar bloques, edificios, escaleras, habían sido borrados hacía tiempo por la nieve y la lluvia. Los letreros de las calles se habían esfumado y, sobre cada pedestal reciclado (llegaron a contar cuatro), se levantaba una de las estatuas de un Lenin ceñudo y avizor, fundidas en serie y con trabajo voluntario. Pero ninguno de aquellos Lenin indicaba hacia ningún lado" (722) ("The numbers that ought to identify blocks, buildings, and stairways had been erased long ago by the snow and the rain. The street signs had disappeared and, over each recycled pedestal (they counted four), rose one of the statues of a frowning and watchful Lenin forged in series by voluntary labor. But none of those Lenins were pointing anywhere" [543]).

Waiting wrests the three characters not only out of the *times* of their protagonism in the construction of the three revolutionary movements underway—the Soviet, the Spanish, and the Cuban—but out of the circuits of knowledge and of art that should or could accompany the accelerated march toward the future. In this sense, both Mercader and Trotsky foreshadow Ivan's eventual melancholy at coming of age out of step with others of his generation. Iván's *waiting for* the promised future has the ironic effect of his ignorance of either the facts or the global impact of events that were repressed or carefully framed through limited mass media and select historical texts. In fact, the experience of reading *El hombre que amaba a los perros* is the inverse of the experience of the novel's protagonists: when time slows for the protagonists, Padura simultaneously slows the experience of reading the novel, but not because information is being withheld. Rather, the reader slows due to the considerable accumulation of historical and imaginative detail. In one example, Mercader, as he waits for his orders from his Soviet handler in Barcelona, immediately experiences the sudden arrest of the flows of time as being cut off from the sources of information on which he had previously depended:

> Su estricto sentido de la responsabilidad lo conminó a permanecer a la espera y gastó sus ratos de ocio en compañía del joven Luis, con el que solía jugar al fútbol. . . . En su aislamiento, Ramón no conseguía tener una comprensión clara de los acontecimientos que se sucedían. Los periódicos de las distintas facciones republicanas llegaban a sus manos troceados por una censura elemental, que se contentaba con levantar los textos y dejar en blanco los espacios que habían ocupado los trabajos condenados. Solo los diarios comunistas, libres de la censura que el Partido se encargaba de ejercer sobre los demás periódicos, escapaban a aquella orgía de mutilaciones. (212–13)

> (Due to his strict sense of responsibility he waited, spending his free time in the company of young Luis, with whom he played soccer. . . . In his isolation, Ramón couldn't gain a clear understanding of the events taking place. The newspapers from the different Republican factions that reached his hands were cut in pieces by a crude censorship that contented itself with removing words and leaving blanks in the spaces formerly occupied by the condemned works. Only the communist dailies, free of the censorship that the party exercised over the rest of the newspapers, escaped that orgy of mutilations. [154–55])

Padura immediately fills in the censored events for the reader, however, using extensive detail to explain the context of 1937's explosive *Jornadas de mayo* (May days), in which the violent confrontation among the various competing anarchist, socialist, and communist parties began to derail their allegiance against the Francoist Falange and the Spanish Nationalists. This same effect plays out in the central event of the novel, Trotsky's assassination itself, which takes place over three chapters as Mercader stops, starts, paces, reconsiders, doubts himself, and finally commits the murder. The novel thus subjects the readers to a similar experience of thickened, slowed time as its protagonists, where both characters and readers experience historical and narrative events as belated. Simultaneously, it restores the transitive function to its readers' experience of waiting: the readers are *waiting for* the details of a history/story whose ending they have already seen, and whose effects they are already living.[5]

Writing and Time

The different relationships that the three protagonists of *El hombre que amaba a los perros* have with writing concretizes the novel's relationship between revolutionary aesthetics and waiting. Trotsky's pace of written production accelerates during the period of his exile; in contrast to Mercader and Iván, he has networks that bring him news of his faraway friends, compatriots, and family, including the deaths of each of his children. Padura's imaginative access to Trotsky as a character is, fundamentally, through Trotsky's extensive bibliography composed in exile: *El hombre que amaba a los perros* traces, among other texts, Trotsky's composition of his autobiography, his history of the October Revolution, his biography of Stalin, and his manifesto co-authored with Breton. Trotsky therefore serves as the figure at the center of the novel's alternative narration of Stalin's consolidation of power. The plot moves forward by Trotsky's frenetic pace of authorship, and by letters, messages, and texts that he receives from others, including the information that an assassin, arriving from Paris, was planning his murder (475). The chapters focused on his character, in fact, frequently begin with an action— a movement, the arrival of a letter, etc.—and then lapse into long, detailed historical discourse that serves to interpret the historical events underway at the time: "Como permanecía casi todo el día encerrado en su habitación de la Casa Azul, Liev Davídovich había aprovechado su tiempo y había escrito un análisis sobre el fin previsible de la guerra civil española y la derrota de un movimiento revolucionario que, quizás, hubiera podido retrasar y hasta evitar la conflagración europea . . ." (509) ("Since he spent almost the whole day holed up in his room at the Casa Azul, he made the most of his time by writing an analysis of the foreseeable end of the Spanish Civil War. Spain's revolutionary movement, if successful, could perhaps have delayed and even prevented the European War . . ." [380]).[6]

The style of ordering events and interpretations, or correcting the scant historical record from which Trotsky remained largely absent in Cuba, leads Padura's contemporary Antonio José Ponte to argue that the novel suffers from a kind of genre confusion, (unsuccessfully, in Ponte's view) straddling historiography and fiction. Ponte maintains that Padura's portrayal does not adequately address the central question of the Cuban regime's implication in the most repressive and abusive measures inherited from the Stalinist apparatus ("El asesino" n/p).[7] Odette Casamayor-Cisneros, alternatively, argues that "El líder asesinado por Mercader aparece en el libro como el último creyente puro en el comunismo, postrera imagen de la integridad ética, y contrasta con el 'demonio' Stalin y el resto de los comunistas que—a favor o en contra sea de Trotski o de Stalin—fueron perdiendo la fe en el sueño original" (125) (The leader assassinated by Mercader appears in the book as the last pure believer in communism, the ultimate image of ethical integrity, and contrasts with Stalin the demon and the rest of the communists who—whether for or against Trotsky or Stalin—were losing faith in the original dream). Casamayor-Cisneros's characterization meshes with Jacqueline Loss's observations that Trotsky occupies a particular place in some recent reconsiderations of Soviet inheritance in Cuba as the idealized opposite of Stalin (13; 29). Loss cites Celia Hart Santamaría's 2013 essay that recuperates Trotsky as the harbinger of the "pure revolution" that is Cuba's way forward after the fall of the Soviet Union (47). Casamayor-Cisneros's, Loss's, and Hart Santamaría's readings, therefore, signals one of the central imaginative functions of Padura's idealized portrayal of Trotsky. Schweizer sees an allegory of writing in Penelope's waiting, both by weaving and unweaving (280; 291–92). In his writing, Trotsky enacts Penelope's daytime weaving as the patterned, rhythmic, ordering of events that in some instances counteract the version of events that Mercader perceives, and in others, fills in the details of a history that lies beyond Iván and his generation's cognizance. If Trotsky is the last "pure communist," in the novel, his characterization represents a fundamental *as-if* proposition: how would Iván's world have been different if Trotsky's texts had been available to Iván and his contemporaries?

Both Mercader and Iván display much more tortured relationships with writing, and this feature is emblematic of one of the novel's central theses that links the foreclosure of imaginative political and artistic horizons with bureaucratic statism inherited from Stalin's oppressive regime. For Iván, the act of closing and circumscription of the 1970s have the effect of slowing, even halting measures of time far beyond the temporal boundaries of the precise dates of the *quinquenio gris* between 1971 and 1976. Fornet sees this transition as cutting off the close allegiance between the political and the artistic vanguard of the 1960s. As he puts it, through this process, "Los nexos de continuidad (política y artística) habían sido cuidadosamente rotos o reducidos al mínimo" ("El quinquenio" 394) (The links of [political and artistic] continuity had been broken or reduced to a minimum). The two adjectives that Fornet uses, "rotos," "reducidos," could also describe the very process of circumscription, periodization, or definition in the precision of the "quinquenio" that Fornet had coined in the 1980s to describe this period. In both Fornet's speech revisiting the *quinquenio gris* and in Padura's novel, the prescribed aesthetic and concomitant program of censorship of non-conforming cultural expression during the 1970s not only produced a generation of "formulaic, normative" literature, but also caused deep scarring in Cuba's collective intellectual psyche. Loss suggests that the evidence of this scarring continues to register in twenty-first-century discussion of Soviet influence in Cuba: "The 2007 appearance of Luis Pavón Tamayo, president of the Consejo Nacional de Cultura (National Council on Culture) between 1971 and 1976 . . . on the television show *Impronta*, which was dedicated to those Cubans who left important marks within the cultural realm, sparked contentious debates on the Sovietized past and Cuban present on the island and abroad" (13). For Fornet, this effect of scarring was all the more pronounced precisely because the early years of the Revolution had turned being a writer into a profession—a possibility he points to as impossible during the years prior to 1959.

The path of a writer is the one that a young, idealistic Iván imagines for himself after his first book of short stories wins honorable mention and publication in a contest. From his post-1989 vantage point, however, Iván calls his younger self a "diligent simian" in his reproduction of the literary ideology that dominated during the 1970s:

> relatos sobre esforzados cortadores de caña, valientes milicianos defensores de la patria, abnegados obreros cuyos conflictos estaban relacionados con las rémoras del pasado burgués que todavía afectaban a sus conciencias . . . herencias que, esforzados, valientes y abnegados como eran, sin duda se hallaban en trance de superar en su ascenso hacia la condición moral de Hombres Nuevos . . . (98)

> (stories about hard-working sugarcane cutters, brave soldiers defending the homeland, self-denying workers whose conflicts were related to the hindrances of the bourgeois past still affecting their consciousness . . . legacies that, hardworking, brave, and self-denying as they were, they without a doubt found themselves in the midst of overcoming on their ascent toward the moral condition of New Men . . . [66–67])

We see a clear parallelism between Iván's naïve aspirations and the socialist realist model that Fornet critiques as "la literatura como pedagogía y hagiografía, orientada metodológicamente hacia la creación de 'héroes positivos' y la estratégica ausencia de conflictos antagónicos en el 'seno del pueblo'" (384) (literature as pedagogy and hagiography, methodologically oriented toward the creation of "positive heroes" and the strategic absence of antagonistic conflicts in the "nation's core"). After he writes a second work about a young revolutionary's self-doubt and questioning of his duties, Iván is reprimanded, sent to complete his social service in a far-away province as a presumed re-education measure. He eventually gives up both writing literature and his profession of journalism to edit an obscure veterinary journal, refusing to consider writing again until decades later when he begins to assemble the pieces of the story of Ramón Mercader.

Padura's portrayal of Mercader also contributes to this metaliterary construction. Mercader frequently contemplates himself as an unwritten fictional creation, positing the possibilities of other Mercaders who *could have existed* outside of his single historical epithet as the Soviet agent who assassinated Trotsky:

> muchas veces Ramón se empeñaría en el desafío de imaginar qué habría ocurrido con su vida si hubiera dicho que no. Insistiría en recrear una existencia paralela, un tránsito esencialmente novelesco en el que nunca había dejado de llamarse Ramón, de ser Ramón, de actuar como Ramón, tal vez lejos de su tierra y sus recuerdos, como tantos hombres de su generación, pero siendo siempre Ramón Mercader del Río, en cuerpo y, sobre todo, en alma. (42)
>
> (many times Ramón persisted in challenging himself to imagine what would have happened with his life had he said no. He would insist on re-creating a parallel existence, an essentially novelistic journey in which he had never ceased to be called Ramón, to be Ramón, to act like Ramón, perhaps far from his country and his memories, like so many men of his generation, but always being Ramón Mercader del Río in body and, above all, in soul. [26])

The novel narrates Mercader's frequent contemplation of his own "other novelistic possibilities," as in his repeated doubts about his role in the murder plot, or when he contemplates his brother's death at the gates of Madrid as a possible alternative destiny to his own (605). Iván—and Padura—both produce and reference additional novelized Mercaders, and in so doing gesture with a certain sympathy toward the restoration of a Mercader who could be recuperated, or ordered in narrative form and in narrative time, from among his many aliases and the silences surrounding his life. Padura has clear debts to the Spanish writer Jorge Semprún's *La deuxième mort de Ramón Mercader* (*The Second Death of Ramón Mercader*) (1969), the best-known novelistic treatment of Mercader, as well as to the 1990 biography of Mercader, *Ramón Mercader: Mi hermano: cincuenta años después* by Mercader's brother Luis and two co-authors. Within the novel's diegesis, Iván himself receives *Ramón Mercader: Mi hermano* in a mysterious package more than a decade after Mercader's death, and relies on its details to begin writing about Mercader's life.

However, there are additional literary intertexts that shape the text beyond its historical content. The first, from which the novel gets its title, is Raymond Chandler's "The Man Who Liked Dogs," one of the stories in the collection that Iván is reading on the beach when he first encounters Mercader and his two Russian borzois.[8] Like Mercader, Trotsky and Iván are also "men who like dogs"; as Emily Maguire has argued, the pet dogs that accompany each of the three main characters serve to expose each of the protagonists' most ethical version of themselves. For Gina Herrmann, the presence of dogs in literature by twentieth-century leftist Spanish exiles invokes the Western tradition linking dogs and homecoming as in *The Odyssey*; for the exiled, dogs thus become the repository of both the faithful memory of places (and, I would suggest, times) lost, and the site of mourning an impossible recuperation (154). Mercader and Trotsky demonstrate this pattern: each insists that their dogs accompany them in exile; and it is the dogs that help precipitate the fateful encounters among each of the protagonists.[9] Iván's dog accompanies him, conversely, through a process of insile, of internal estrangement from the public sphere, exacerbated not by physical distance, but by proximity; his dog Truco, as a final demonstration of fidelity, accompanies Iván in his death. Padura's reference to Chandler also suggests, in line with Birkenmaier's observation, the reformulation of the chronological organization of a traditional historical novel as a mystery or crime fiction. In Chandler's story, private investigator Ted Carmady tracks a missing young woman, and in the process uncovers an increasingly corrupt web of criminals, eventually taking down most of the police force of a small California town. Like Carmady, the origins of the dog in question—Carmady chases a police dog, while Iván admires Russian borzois—signal the source of a much more devastating corruption—either the police force or repressive Stalinist strategies—than that implied by the original crime. The novel's invocation of Chandler, therefore, is an apt signal for Padura's revisionary perspective on late-twentieth-century Cuban history. His revision of the structure of the historical novel similarly points to another intertextual figure of significance to Padura's work: Cuba's most renowned twentieth-century writer of historical fiction, Alejo Carpentier.

Hurricanes, Literary History and Historical Literature

When as a young student Iván experiences his first literary success, he ingenuously attributes his brief ascent to adjusting to the artistic demands and social utility of Cuba's revolutionary ideals: "había demostrado que era un escritor de mi tiempo" (103) ("I had proved that I was a writer of my time" [69]). Given Iván's subsequent censure for his next story about a doubting revolutionary, his banishment to a government post in a distant town, and his realization that his published book represented a simplistic "simian" failure at a lasting artistic accomplishment, Iván's declaration can be read as both an indictment of the "time" in which he is writing, the 1970s, as well as an ironic repetition of its referent. The sentence paraphrases the epitaph on Alejo Carpentier's tomb in Havana's Necrópolis Cristóbal Cólon: "Hombre de mi tiempo soy y mi tiempo trascendente es el de la Revolución Cubana" (I am a man of my time and my transcendent time is that of the Cuban Revolution). The epitaph is drawn from Carpentier's 1975 essay reflecting on his own literary trajectory, "Un camino de medio siglo," the title of which Padura repeats as the title of his own critical study of the marvelous real in Carpentier's work, drawn from his undergraduate thesis and published in 2002. Alejo Carpentier represents a constant presence in Padura's novels, not least, as Birkenmaier argues, as the prototypical intellectual architect of the *nueva novela latinoamericana* (new Latin American novel), whose history inflects Padura's own reconsideration of Cuba's place in twentieth-century history. Carpentier's most frequent subject, as myriad critics have noted, is History itself, and more particularly, the grand events—revolutions—that rupture history and embody its progression. Carpentier is concerned with the perspective of that history from the Americas: from the Haitian Revolution in *El reino de este mundo* (1949; *The Kingdom of This World*), to the French revolution in 1961's *El siglo de las luces* (*Explosion in a Cathedral*), to *La consagración de la primavera* (1978; *The Rite of Spring*) which tracks its characters through the October 1917 revolution, the Spanish Republican resistance and the triumph of the Cuban Revolution.[10]

The overlapping geographies but divergent temporalities of *La consagración de la primavera* and *El hombre que amaba a los perros*—a comparison that Casamayor-Cisneros has noted—point to Padura's deeper project of reconfiguring revolutionary time and historical memory through fictional narrative.[11] *La consagración de la primavera*, widely considered Carpentier's only novel of the Cuban Revolution, received mixed critical reviews in large part due to its socialist realist style. In a 2015 essay linking Carpentier's journalism in 1930s Spain to *La consagración*, Padura notes this aspect as a symptom of Carpentier being "a man of his time":

> *La consagración de la primavera* resulta una novela ideotemáticamente atrapada en el conflicto general que caracteriza el arte cubano de los años 1970 y hace evidente que ni la estatura artística del escritor ni su lejanía física del complicado ambiente cultural del país—por su condición de diplomático en París desde

1966—consiguieron liberarlo de los pesados lastres de la ortodoxia institucionalizada de ese período y de los dogmas estéticos entonces en boga. (*Yo quisiera* 81)

(*The Rite of Spring* ends up being a novel ideo-thematically trapped in the general conflict that characterizes Cuban art of the 1970s and makes evident that neither the artistic stature of the writer nor his physical distance from the complicated cultural environment of the nation—due to his position as a diplomat in Paris since 1966—were able to liberate him from the weighty ties of the institutional orthodoxy of the period and the aesthetic dogmas in fashion at the time.)

However, Padura also notes that there was historical information unavailable to Carpentier, uncovered in the final years of the twentieth century and the first decade of the twenty-first, that could have modified *La consagración de la primavera*'s univisionary, grandiose, and celebratory presentation of the historical future made manifest via its progression from Russia to Cuba. Beyond the details of the Moscow Trials, Padura discusses the evidence of the USSR's manipulation of divisions among the parties allied to the Republican cause in Spain as the likely cause of their ultimate disastrous loss. For Padura, these external pressures and historical absences register in the form of the novel; he notes that the effects of its ordered chronological succession through the first half of the twentieth century results in an excessive and ponderous text whose protagonists are mere witnesses to the events unfolding around them (83). These critiques suggest that *El hombre que amaba a los perros* can be read as a work in direct conversation with Carpentier's penultimate novel, both aesthetically and historically.

A number of other technical details link Padura's historical novels to Carpentier's. In his analysis of *El siglo de las luces*, Roberto González Echevarría argues that encoded in Carpentier's seemingly conventional style is a "highly complex experiment with history and the narrative" (*Alejo Carpentier* 233) which he identifies as a dialectical relationship between a future imagined as a past, where the novel functions as "a postponed presence that can only attain meaning in the future, a future that we read but whose meaning is suspended" (245). For the critic, this dialectical movement justifies Carpentier's repeated revisiting of revolutionary moments: his is "revolutionary writing in its etymological sense, in that it revolves around an absent axis that is constituted by the very movement of its periphery. If, in Hegel's famous dictum, world history is world judgment, in *Explosion in a Cathedral* history and judgment are one—writing is history" (253). We can observe a similarly dialectical relationship between Carpentier's and Padura's views of history: where Carpentier locates his characters at the center of revolutionary movements, both witnesses and *writers* of the historical future made manifest, Padura, looking back—rather than forward—in time, emphasizes the rupture between center and periphery. In this sense, *El hombre que amaba a los perros* shares with *El siglo de las luces* the precept that fiction has the capacity to make history legible. Padura's very reconsideration of this view of history serves, for some critics, as the evidence of its ongoing importance to Padura's work. Casamayor-Cisneros locates Padura as an inheritor of Carpentier's strain of utopian thought, though in her reading, rather than an absolute faith in the contours of history, she argues that Padura's characters evidence "tiredness" with history:

> Hoy, el humanismo moderno no les ha abandonado del todo, a pesar de la rabia y la frustración. Tal vez por eso prefieren hablar de un "cansancio histórico" (199), porque se resisten a quedarse sin certezas. Hay cansancio pero no desprendimiento absoluto de la Historia. Se sienten traicionados por ella, pero no se reconocen desprovistos del *telos* histórico. (124)[12]

> (Today, modern humanism has not abandoned them altogether, in spite of their rage and frustration. It is perhaps for this reason that they prefer to speak of "historical tiredness," because they resist an existence without certainties. It is tiredness but not detachment from History. They feel betrayed by it, but do not see themselves as devoid of a historical *telos*.)

We can thus read Padura's novel as introducing contingency to the Hegelian model to which Carpentier's historical imagination was so indebted, precisely because this legibility is so precarious. While Iván gains access to the Mercader archive, he fails to finish the text about Mercader before his death, leaving his notes for his friend Dany to find, organize, and write. Similarly, Padura's recuperation of Mercader and Trotsky does restore them to the historical *telos*, and yet it is not clear within the novel that this recuperation results in an inevitable dialectical movement forward through History. *El hombre que amaba a los perros* manifests disappointment in its contemplation of figures excavated from historical erasure but who may remain objects of melancholic contemplation, rather then re-invigorating the revolutionary cycle as Trotsky does for Hart Santamaría.

Iván's death due to his home's damage from Hurricane Ivan points to another link with Carpentier. The swirling power of the hurricane is cast as the natural incarnation of the upheaval of revolution in Carpentier's two most prominent novels that deal, respectively, with the historical impacts of the Haitian Revolution and the French Revolution in Latin America. The hurricane gives physical form to what for González Echevarría is a notion of history as "circular" in Carpentier's early novels, which cedes to history's "spiraling" movement forward in *El siglo de las luces* and Carpentier's subsequent works (232–33). Carpentier makes use of the cyclical recurrence of the natural phenomenon: Gabriela Pogolotti notes that in *El reino de este mundo*, both the rebellious ex-slave Mackandal and the narrator, Ti Noel, are swept away in the hurricane/Haitian revolution's power (70). Pogolotti also sees in the power of the hurricane that pounds Havana at the beginning of *El siglo de las luces* the metaphorical opening of "windows and doors" for the two young protagonists who first encounter the intoxicating ideas of the French Revolution as it arrives to the Caribbean (77). Other twentieth-century writers extend this trend, repeatedly invoking the hurricane in the context of the Cuban Revolution. Sartre's observational essays on Cuba's history and the changes brought by the revolution are titled in their Spanish translation *Huracán sobre el azúcar* (*Hurricane over Sugar*); Antonio José Ponte notes that compatriot Fernando Ortiz's 1947 history of the hurricane deploys the same metaphor to predict the turbulence of 1959 ("Carta de la Habana"107–08).[13] Padura replicates and adapts this trope: repeatedly, especially in the chapters told from Trotsky's perspective, the narrator refers to the revolutionary changes as "torbellinos," (whirlwinds) (73, 122), and uses the same word to describe Stalin's purges as a "torbellino de violencia" (whirlwind of violence) (138). However, whereas in the context of Carpentier's invocation of the revolution-as-hurricane the external forces of social and political upheaval sweep the characters along, Padura focuses on the edges of the storm—on three characters who, once at the center of revolutionary action, are now exiled or otherwise cast out. Each of the characters is introduced in the novel in the context of inclement weather: Trotsky, suffering the winter in the Kazakhstani steppe, receives the news of his expulsion from Soviet territory during "la más asoladora tormenta de nieve que jamás hubiera visto" (42) ("the most devastating snowstorm that he had ever seen" [23]). In the first chapter that features Mercader, the extreme cold of the Sierra de Guadarrama obliquely gestures toward Mercader's eventual encounter with Trotsky and the beginning of his own disenchantment and ideological exile, while the sounds and sights of the violent snowstorm are replaced with the cannon fire and aircraft engines of the surrounding Spanish Civil War (49). Most significantly, in the novel's first chapter, Iván prepares for the arrival of Hurricane Ivan to Cuba in 2004, the hurricane that most vividly demonstrates Padura's recasting of the storm not as the swirling force that ushers in the historical future, but one that unleashes the accumulation of a history that has passed Iván by, rather than, as in Carpentier's works, hastening progress toward an inevitable future.

In a reflection on the approach of the very same Hurricane Ivan to Cuba, Ponte juxtaposes the revolution's own adoption of the hurricane as the symbol of its impact with the stench of the receding waters and Havana's losses of power, gas, and telephones after Ivan largely bypasses the island ("Carta" 108). He elsewhere accuses the meteorological event as functioning as a sort of historical *deus ex machina* in *El hombre que amaba a los perros* and a technical cop-out that Padura employs to avoid the question of the Cuban government's own responsibility for the devastating consequences of its rapprochement with the Soviet Union ("El asesino" n/p). However, I think this assessment does not quite do justice to the consistency of how Padura's work employs the hurricane as a figure that is both fully Caribbean, and yet whose destructive force may extend far beyond a single island or the Caribbean region as a whole. As we have seen, it is evident that Padura, as Carpentier had done before him, deploys the metaphor of the hurricane to describe the impact of world historical events on a large scale. In one of the early chapters of Carpentier's *El siglo de las luces*, a hurricane passes through Havana, disrupting the comfortable bourgeois lives of the two protagonists, casting them out of their confinement on the island and their isolation from the revolutionary events that are arriving to their region from Europe. But progress is paired with devastation, signaling the direction of the revolution in the novel toward despotism and large-scale violence.

In Padura's reading of *El siglo de las luces*, the inevitable corruption of the revolution is a structural, generalizable feature that is represented by the novel's prologue, the only pages in the novel narrated in first person and out of chronological sequence. Citing Ariel Dorfman's observations that the beginning of the novel could belong to the eighteenth, nineteenth, or twentieth centuries, Padura argues that the anomalous prologue points to Carpentier's larger project of tracing the spiraling history of revolutions:

> los rasgos que asemejan a las revoluciones, durante los últimos tres siglos, son demasiado similares para que Carpentier perdiera tan propicia comprobación poética, y por ello, al leer la historia del fracaso revolucionario estamos leyendo también la Historia del Fracaso Revolucionario: oportunismo político, negación "dialéctica" de ideales, voluntarismo, incomprensión de la realidad, venganzas arribistas y la persistente excusa de la "razón revolucionaria" que lo justifica todo conducen a la inevitable pérdida de lo que fue "posible". De ahí, además, la persistente idea del caos y el apoc-

alipsis—simbólicamente resumido en el cuadro *Explosión en una catedral*—con que se identifican los procesos revolucionarios y que, en la novela, se suceden en Santo Domingo, París y Cayena, con la última derrota de Víctor Hughes. (*Un camino* 374)

(the features of revolutions that have been similar over the last three centuries are too similar for Carpentier to not have noticed such a favorable poetic corroboration, and therefore, when we read the history of revolutionary failure we are also reading the History of Revolutionary Failure: political opportunism, "dialectical" negation of ideals, voluntarism, incomprehension of reality, arriviste revenge, and the persistent excuse of "revolutionary reason" that justifies everything lead to the inevitable loss of what had been "possible." Hence, in addition, the persistent idea of chaos and apocalypse—symbolically rendered in the painting *Explosion in a Cathedral*—with which the revolutionary processes are identified and which, in the novel, take place in Santo Domingo, Paris and Cayenne, with the last defeat of Víctor Hughes.)

Padura goes on to note that despite his portrayal of the failures of the French Revolution in *El siglo*, Carpentier's technique of extracting it from its eighteenth-century context to comment on Revolutions writ large emphasizes the extent to which the French Revolution irrevocably changed the world. Thus, even Carpentier's novel of revolutionary disillusionment encodes an ideology that points to the inevitability of the next great event that will complete another turn in the spiral of history. Padura's novels introduce an important measure of contingency to this pattern that marks them as works of disappointment. Eduardo González, in his reading of the Mario Conde tetralogy, sees the hurricane as a contemplation of both Shakespeares's *The Tempest* and Retamar's anti-colonial essay *Calibán* (1971) in which the disruptive potential of the cyclone and Caliban's cursing Prospero the colonizer as a foundational revolutionary act has reached the end of its promise: "If one was taught how to curse by the other, by now and for the foreseeable future their common though disparately held stocks lie in the accursed share of arrest in growth and diminished Cuban dreams placed on hold" (204). In *El hombre que amaba a los perros*, the hurricane appears as a historical metaphor, but not for the revolutionary events that rupture history and occasion radical hope for the future. Rather, it signals the exhaustion of that telos, ushering in a profound alteration in the social and cultural fabric of the Cuban community without positing a concrete program of change in its wake.

The links between the hurricane and both devastation and historical exhaustion are explicit in Iván's alienation that begins in the 1970s and accompanies him until his death: "aquellas rachas de aire turbio eran parte de un huracán que recorría silenciosa pero devastadoramente la isla, por fin encarrilada en una concepción de la sociedad y la cultura adoptada de los modelos soviéticos" (102) ("those murky gusts of wind were part of a hurricane blowing silently but devastatingly across the island, bringing with them a concept of society and culture adopted from Soviet models" [69]). The hurricane has become, in Padura's imagination, the negative iteration of its function in Carpentier's revolutionary novels, as well as the devastating culmination of the revolutionary "whirlwinds" that follow Trotsky and Mercader in their respective sections of the novel. In Padura's work, as in Carpentier's, the hurricane symbolizes a disordering of history, a fracturing of historical temporality. What distinguishes the kind of historical disordering in Padura's novel from Carpentier, however, is the sense of a suspended future that freezes the present in a state of unresolved contingency. Derek Hook calls this state "petrified life," and among its multiple forms of expression is waiting. Hook is concerned with tracing how the seemingly monumental "eventness" of the end to apartheid in South Africa has nonetheless produced forms of temporality that provide continuity between the late-apartheid and post-apartheid eras; the result is a deferral of the historical reckoning that would release South African subjects from the anxiety and dread of how a not-yet-understood past might form a yet-unimagined future. That anxiety and dread are figured as historical deferral:

> I have in mind here Freud's notion of deferred action (*nachträglichkeit*), that is, the psychical temporality of the retroactive, which disrupts linear or chronological time. Historical events, from this perspective, remain latent, effectively incomplete, subject to the contingencies of later circumstances through which they might be reactivated in unexpected ways . . . Neither static nor consolidated then, the fragmentary residues of lingering histories themselves constitute latent modes of the present. What this ensures . . . is the virtual quality of the present which, underscored by an as-of-yet-indefinite past, remains itself precarious, open to further re-articulation. . . . We need to add to this . . . the prospect of the movement from the future to the past, the retroactive 'determination' of *what has been* by *what is to come* . . . Waiting thus is not merely an anxious state by virtue of how it relates to an indeterminate future; its anxiety is also the result of the as-of-yet-uncertain influence of *the past* on what is yet to come. (445)

Hook's notion of "petrified life," or the state that describes the anxiety-ridden waiting for the meaning of the past to take shape, characterizes Iván's existence both before and after 1989. Like the South African subjects of Hook's reading, Iván's waiting spans the "event" of the collapse of the socialist bloc and his faith in the Cuban present. Meanwhile the effects of the deferred access to the past are themselves figured as belated:

> Nada habíamos sabido de las represiones y genocidios de pueblos, etnias, partidos políticos enteros, de las persecuciones mortales de inconformes y religiosos, de la furia homicida de los campos de trabajo, del asesinato de la legalidad y la credulidad antes, durante y después de los procesos de Moscú. Muchos menos tuvimos la menor idea de quién había sido Trotski ni de por qué lo habían matado, o de los infames arreglos subterráneos y hasta evidentes de la URSS con el nazismo y con el imperialismo, de la violencia conquistadora de los nuevos zares moscovitas, de las invasiones y mutilaciones geográficas, humanas y culturales de los territorios adquiridos y de la prostitución de las ideas y las verdades, convertidas en consignas vomitivas por aquel socialismo modélico, patentado y conducido por el genio del Gran Guía del Proletariado Mundial, el camarada Stalin, y luego remendado por sus herederos, defensores de una rígida ortodoxia con la que condenaron la menor disidencia del canon que sustentaba sus desmanes y megalomanías. Ahora, a duras penas, conseguíamos entender cómo y por qué toda aquella perfección se había desmerengado cuando se movieron solo dos de los ladrillos de la fortaleza: un mínimo acceso a la información y una leve pero decisiva pérdida del miedo (siempre el dichoso miedo, siempre, siempre, siempre) con el que se había condensado aquella estructura . . . Y nosotros sin saber nada . . . ¿O es que no queríamos saber? (650–51)

> (We didn't know anything about the repressions and genocides of peoples, ethnicities, entire political parties, of the mortal persecutions of noncomformists and religious people, of the homicidal fury of the work camps, and the credulity before, during, and after the Moscow trials. Nor did we have the faintest idea of who Trotsky was or why they had killed him, or of the infamous subterranean and even the evident agreements of the USSR with Nazism and imperialism, of the conquering violence of the new Muscovite czars, of the invasions and geographic, human, and cultural mutilations of the acquired territories and of the prostitutions of ideas and

truths, turned into nauseating slogans by that model socialism, patented and led by the genius of the Great Guide of the World Proletariat, Comrade Stalin, and later patched up by his heirs, defenders of a rigid orthodoxy with which they condemned the smallest deviation from the canon that sustained their excesses and megalomania. Now, with great difficulty, we managed to understand how and why all of that perfection had collapsed like a giant meringue when only two of the bricks of the fortress were moved, a minimal access to information and a slight but decisive loss of fear (always that infamous fear, always, always, always) with which that structure had been placed together . . . And there we were, not knowing anything . . . or is it that we didn't want to know? [488–89])

The novel's explicit parallels between Stalinist violent repression and the iterations of that repression in the Cuban cultural sphere set up a retrospective historical vision that incriminates Iván and his generation by asking, from the vantage point of 2004: how could we not have known? Iván's waiting, or inability to assimilate that knowledge that had petrified his life, makes the belated avalanche of information both more devastating and deadlier when it finally arrives.

While Iván slowly overcomes his lack of access to information, the first of these two "bricks" of the fortress, he never truly overcomes his fear throughout the novel. He first announces his intent to write a novelistic version of Jaime López's story in 1996, but fails to complete it as of his death in the final pages of the novel in 2004. Similarly, *El hombre que amaba a los perros* slows the reader, who must assimilate a massive accumulation of narrative detail leading up to the inevitable deaths of each of the three protagonists. Stylistically, the text enacts this deferral in the way the passage above indicates: in long, multi-claused sentences that defer their own conclusions through lists and series of conjunctions. The time linking the two revolutionary spaces figured in the book—Cuba and the Soviet Union—is no longer one of futurity and messianic immanence, but one where the accumulating mass of information weighs Iván down and stretches time. As a sharp contrast to the historical events narrated in the chapters on Mercader and Trotsky, Iván *does* very little in the novel, accentuating his belated access to the histories that are narrated in parallel with his life.

Tracing Padura's use of the metaphor of the hurricane in the novel, it becomes evident how the novel's disappointment is figured in this deferral. The novel begins in 2004, recounting the arrival of Hurricane Ivan to Cuba and Iván's wife Ana's death; Iván's death is prefigured in Ana's fear that "el techo herido de nuestro apartamento no resistiría la fuerza del huracán" (22) ("The battered ceiling of our apartment would not withstand the force of the hurricane" [7]). However, his death does not occur until three months later, in December of the same year, via the collapse of the apartment ceiling, and is narrated in the final chapter of the novel. Iván's death from the crushing weight of the collapsed roof serves as a metaphor for the massive weight of information that overwhelms Iván and his generation during the post–Cold War transition. The book about Mercader that Iván never finishes is finally completed by his writer friend Dany after Dany finds Iván's body and his partially-completed notes and text. While the "cracks" in Iván's vision of his present begin with his first encounter with Jaime López and accelerate with *perestroika*, Iván does not live to see the full realization of its impact—that is, the novel that Dany/Padura complete. Thus we could also think of Iván, in addition, as suffering under the weight of all the words, pages, and texts that he never wrote as a result of the trauma of the *quinquenio gris*, as his writerly time stops in his youth and is deferred past the end of his life.

Jorge Fornet reads the hurricane that arrives at the end of Padura's fourth Mario Conde detective novel, *Paisaje de otoño* (1999) (*Havana Black*), as a metaphor for the events of 1989. Conde's only possible response is to close himself in and write:

> Al final, encerrado en su habitación, espera la llegada del huracán cuya cercanía se ha venido anunciando en toda la novela y al cual el Conde no se ha cansado de invocar. Y el anhelado huracán llega, barriendo con todo lo que encuentra a su paso. 'En realidad,' reconoce en un momento el narrador, 'la devastación había empezado mucho antes, y el huracán sólo era el rematador feroz enviado para concretar las condenas ya iniciadas. . . .' En ese instante, el protagonista se da cuenta de que sólo puede salvarlo la memoria, y se sienta ante la máquina de escribir, a 'contar la historia de un hombre y sus amigos, antes y después de todos los desastres: físicos, morales, espirituales, matrimoniales, laborales, ideológicos, religiosos, sentimentales y familiares . . .' [p. 227]. (16–17)

> (At the end, shut in his room, he awaits the arrival of the hurricane whose proximity had been announced throughout the novel, and which Conde has never gotten tired of invoking. And the longed-for hurricane arrives, sweeping away everything that it finds in its path. 'In reality,' the narrator recognizes at one point, 'the devastation had begun long before, and the hurricane was only the savage auctioneer sent to carry out the sentences already

begun . . .' At that moment, the protagonist realizes that only his memory can save him, and he sits down at the typewriter 'to tell the story of a man and his friends, before and after every kind of disaster: physical, moral spiritual, marital, work-related, ideological, religious, emotional and familial.')

This is strikingly similar to the scenes narrated in the first and last chapters of *El hombre que amaba a los perros*, with some important differences. In both of the cases of Conde and Iván, the "devastation had begun long before" the actual hurricane arrives. In this sense, the hurricane points to the immediate past, figured as the overwhelming cognition of the impact or meaning of the event that it lays bare. In Fornet's estimation, Conde embarks on a similar task as Iván: "para explorar, desde el crimen, los entresijos de la época" (17) (to expose, using crime, the hidden details of the era). Like Conde, Iván closes himself in his apartment to narrate Mercader's story, though in the months after the passage of the hurricane, emphasizing further the temporal deferral that characterizes *El hombre que amaba a los perros*. Conde is inspired to write, and survives the hurricane; Iván is frozen into inaction and suffocates under the weight of the history he has struggled to discover. The small-scale solidarity and sociability that Casamayor-Cisneros and De Ferrari observe among Padura's characters are the remnant of revolutionary values remain visible in the brotherly relationships that are the core of the act of narration (Conde's theme of "un hombre y sus amigos"; Dany who completes the text for Iván), but it is not clear that these values are reproducible or heritable for future generations. However, what the comparison also makes evident is Padura's enduring faith in narrative as the necessary, and perhaps unique, mechanism of that historical reckoning.

The historical paths that *El hombre que amaba a los perros* traces, including the cultural closure introduced by the *quinquenio gris* and the post–Cold War spiritual crisis that Iván's generation experiences, demonstrate Hook's sense of the frozen present in which the undetermined future will make legible the still-contingent past. I thus want to point back to Guevara's signaling of the multiple paths forward for global spaces emerging from colonial and colonialist paradigms. Theorists of colonial, postcolonial, and Global South spaces have explored how time is configured and experienced differently in different contexts, and these reconsiderations of temporality in the Global South can be a particularly productive approach for moving with but also against the sharp periodization that sees these various moments in Cuban history and its contexts as progressive or linear.[14] Padura's novel gives us one compelling model of how we can think about these questions without losing sight of how they are embedded in proximate and distant histories.

6

Post-Revolutionary Pastiche in Pepetela's Jaime Bunda Novels

Angolan novelist Pepetela's corpus spans the early years of revolutionary action in the mid-1970s to the present day, and has repeatedly interrogated the relationship between literary form and political form. His earliest literary success, for example, the 1980 novel *Mayombe*, dramatizes a Marxist dialectic in the debates of the guerilla independence fighter protagonists. Later historical works such as 1985's *Yaka* and 1989's *Lueji* are often read within the genre of nation-building novels that seek to replace colonial narratives of conquest with Angolan epics that trace resistance and national unity to African empires of the past. Other novels, such as *A Geração da Utopia* (*The Generation of Utopia*) and *Parábola do Cágado Velho* (*The Parable of the Old Tortoise*) record the author's increasing disillusionment with the late-twentieth-century political turns away from the idealistic drive of the early post-independence years to corrupt political organization and the seemingly interminable war. Pepetela's two Jaime Bunda novels, *Jaime Bunda, Agente Secreto* (2000) (*Jaime Bunda, Secret Agent* [2006]), and *Jaime Bunda e a Morte do Americano* (2003) (*Jaime Bunda and the Death of the American*), similarly take on the ideological demands of their social context, portraying contemporary Angola as a kleptocratic oligarchy. The protagonist of both novels is the comically inept "secret agent" of Angola's Serviço de Investigação Geral, (General Investigative Service) who acquires his nickname of "Bunda" due to his oversized backside, and his lowly junior position only due to the nepotism of a distant relative from the better-placed side of his once-prominent family. While both Bunda novels nod to the crime genre conventions of a central murder and a series of secondary crimes whose eventual solutions structure the plot, the wandering, tangled intrigue of government corruption, social disorganization, false leads, misinformation, and widespread ineptitude by the end of each novel remains unresolved.

Stephen Henighan argues that the worlds imagined in the Jaime Bunda novels are inseparable from the economic and political form of late capitalism, and therefore the novels also show how the project of national construction via politically engaged letters to which Pepetela had dedicated his early career is not only abandoned but inconceivable. For Henighan, the point of the novels is not the restoration of order disrupted by a crime, but the search for a form to understand the contemporary disorder of the Angolan capital as a microcosm of Angolan society ("Um James Bond" 148). In this chapter, I take up the question of how Pepetela probes the use of genre in both Jaime Bunda novels, in which the deformation of genre tropes is the repository of post–Cold War disappointment. This chapter therefore extends the examination of the legacies of empire in Soviet and post-Soviet Cuba addressed in chapter 5 by considering how literature of post–Cold War Angola addresses the contemporary politics of Angola's transition to globalized capitalism. An examination of the two Jaime Bunda novels with attention to genre shows how the recognizable forms and formulas of crime fiction in Pepetela's iteration operate as an analogy to the postcolonial state's reiterations of the forms of surveillance, kleptocracy, and repressive violence exercised by both its colonial predecessors and the contemporary neo-imperial powers. Whereas in classic detective fiction, there are often two crime plots that seem unrelated but ultimately interconnect, in the Jaime Bunda novels, the secondary plot does not help us to solve the primary crime. Rather, it reveals a larger trans-national crime or crisis that is every bit as problematic as the original murder and potentially more so. The conventions of the classic or hard-boiled detective genres and spy or secret agent fiction, which Jaime Bunda reads obsessively, adjust uncomfortably, inadequately, or comically to the crimes and social structures Jaime confronts. The Jaime Bunda novels use the penetration of English-language culture to critique the widespread embracing of global capitalist culture in twenty-first century Angola. Thus, like Padura, Pepetela exposes the ongoing existence of the terms and situations—underdevelopment and neocolonial exploitation—that motivated the development of south-south allegiances, and which reactivate their underlying anti-colonial politics in the postcolonial present.

In *Jaime Bunda, Agente Secreto*, the titular character, the laughingstock of his office, gets his big break when his boss recruits him to oversee the investigation of the rape and murder of a teenage girl. While Jaime finds it strange to devote police efforts to the case, as her family is neither politically nor socially prominent, it is his first chance to put into practice the investigative techniques he reads about in the English-language crime novels and films he favors. The murder is eventually solved by the regular police, who discover that the murderer is the son of a prominent congress member. Though Jaime fails to solve the crime, he does accidentally stumble upon an international counterfeit currency ring which leads to the apprehension of several of the participants, though the masterminds remain at large. Nonetheless, Jaime, distracted from his original mission and more concerned with his esteem in the office of the SIG and his access to a car and a gun, accepts his new reputation as a star, willing to accede to the version of the truth that puts him and his collaborators in favor with the bosses. He thus is initiated into a system of corrupt cronyism that in both novels has replaced the early revolutionary values of social responsibility and solidarity for those who hope to advance.

A similar concern for corruption and social decay dominates the second Jaime Bunda novel, though *Jaime Bunda e a Morte do Americano*, similarly to Padura's *El hombre que amaba a los perros*, posits the possible recuperation of historical truths by returning to the archive. In *Jaime Bunda e a Morte do Americano*, Jaime is called from the capital of Luanda to the city of Benguela to oversee the investigation into the death of an American engineer. While Jaime suspects suicide, he quickly learns that the central government's enthusiasm for offering the Americans a satisfactory ending—the discovery and imprisonment of a perpetrator—is at odds with the results of his investigation. The Benguela police are anxious to blame Júlio Fininho, the boyfriend of the last person to see the engineer alive, the beautiful Maria Antónia. However, Jaime discovers that Júlio has a strange alibi when he exacts Júlio's confession to being the infamous "Robin dos Comboios" (Robin of the Trains), a small-time thief who targets passengers of the Benguela railway, where he was engaged at the time of the engineer's death. Jaime, however, is unable to convince either the Benguela police or his superiors at the SIG of Júlio's innocence. Just as Jaime accidentally discovers the counterfeiter's ring in the first novel, in *Jaime Bunda e a Morte do Americano* he stumbles upon a child organ-trafficking operation, for which the Benguela police are nationally lauded when they take it down. The novel then presents us with two possible conclusions: one where Júlio Fininho and Maria Antónia are left in prison without vindication, though the narrator refuses to reveal whether they eventually are released; and a second, in a chapter labeled "Segundo epílogo possível" (Second possible epilogue), where Jaime secures a confession from the engineer's compatriot Elvis to committing the murder out of romantic jealousy. In this second version, Maria Antónia is freed, but Júlio dies in prison before he can be released.

Central to both Jaime Bunda novels are genre conventions of crime fiction, the act of imitation, and the role of counterfeiting. Imitation operates on at least two different levels: on the one hand, Pepetela's portrayal of a bungling but accidentally successful investigator registers a satire of a wide variety of aspects of contemporary Angolan society, including its rampant nepotism and a rising revolutionary elite-turned-bourgeoisie who, following the post-Cold War political winds, avidly consumes all things American. This imitation of the elite, including both their consumption of action-oriented crime novels and films and their corruption, is the key to Jaime's success. Second, however, Jaime Bunda also imitates the behaviors, investigatory techniques, and patterns of deductions drawn from his obsessive consumption of English-language crime fiction. In their constant references to crime and espionage fiction and films, the Jaime Bunda novels are clearly inserting themselves into the history of the crime genre. I also, therefore, read the Jaime Bunda novels as stylistic pastiches that reveal the two keys to Angola's neocolonial present: the replication of the abuses of its colonial past and its present subservience to the demands of the global marketplace.

Through frequent detailed descriptions, the two novels record the evidence of Angola's turmoiled recent history through a number of the narrative divergences, including descriptions of corrupt political cronyism, failing infrastructure, and illicit commerce of Angola's primary natural resources, diamonds and oil. The narrative logic works backwards against crime genres: rather than starting with a crime to whose solution a unified narrative voice guides us, Pepetela's works contain extensive "evidence" for many crimes that could be investigated, but few of which are resolved. As an extension of this technique, the use of four different narrators in *Jaime Bunda, Agente Secreto* functions like a rehearsal of different narrative logics, just in case one of the four manages to put the pieces together. The effect of this narrative abundance, therefore, serves to underline rather than challenge Jaime's lack of investigative prowess. In the twenty-first-century Luanda of the novel, where everyone is either hustling in order to survive or benefiting from ill-gotten luxuries siphoned from the state, it is virtually inevitable that Jaime stumbles upon a major crime; it is far less certain that he will manage to solve it. While the structure of the counterfeiting and organ-harvesting subplots certainly critique foreign exploitation of African resources, Pepetela does not let the Angolans off the hook. Imprisoning the perpetrators does nothing to restore the semblance of an ordered society, and nothing to interrupt the frantic pace of Angola's peripheral participation in global markets.

Genre Forms and Stylistic Satire

Pepetela points out in a 2005 interview that detective fiction is impossible in the Angolan context precisely because of its unpredictability: "Acho que num livro policial o autor sabe o fim desde o princípio. Ele encaminha o livro para o fim. Eu não sei o fim. Por isso é um pouco anti-policial (Wieser and Pepetela n/p). (I think that in a crime novel, the author knows what the ending will be from the beginning. He writes the book for that ending. I don't know the ending. That's why [the Jaime Bunda novels are] a bit anti-crime novels). In giving Jaime the title "secret agent," for example, the author's clear reference to James Bond's initials in Jaime Bunda's name ironically indicates that the sophisticated technological accessories that define James Bond's prowess are by definition absent from Jaime Bunda's "underdeveloped" world (*Jaime Bunda* 131; *Jamie Bunda e a Morte* 108). The name, Pepetela says, is the only point of contact between James Bond and Jaime Bunda (Weiser and Pepetela n/p). Critics, however, have noted a number of ways that the Jaime Bunda novels parody certain central elements of James Bond films and novels, noting Bunda's frustrated desire for the markers of James Bond's material wealth, membership among the social elite, and easy sexual conquests.[1] As Umberto Eco signals in his analysis of Ian Fleming's James Bond novels, both pre-Bond crime fiction and the Bond novels themselves capitalize on some combination of knowable characters and plot structures, even if the mysteries and events that take place are unexpected (*The Role of the Reader* 160). The unpredictability in the Jaime Bunda novels is located in precisely how they modify, or even deform, genre conventions through satire. The Jaime Bunda novels also incorporate spy fiction's portrayals of omnipresent conspiracies that extend beyond individual crimes and its sense of paranoia; these features suggest a filiation with a broader array of examples drawn from espionage fiction. In the first Jaime Bunda novel, Jaime's suspicion of an unnamed important suspect T., who turns out to be a higher-up at his own agency, has clear echoes of G.K. Chesterton's *The Man Who Was Thursday* (1908). Similarly, there are also elements to Jaime Bunda's character that have precedence in Joseph Conrad's Verloc, the protagonist of *The Secret Agent*, including his corpulent body and apparent ineptitude, as well as Conrad's use of satire of nineteenth-century espionage fiction (Attridge 129). The two novels also adapt and play with elements of the hard-boiled genre, particularly in its portrayal of flawed detectives and corrupt and decaying cities, classical detective fiction in portraying Bunda's observational and reasoning skills, and the police procedural, in which the "bureaucratic, industrialized enterprise" of police work is the central actor (Mueller 99). The effect of this genre montage is the primary locus for Pepetela's criticism of a tangled and corrupt postcolonial Angola.

While most critics have, rightly, focused on the elements of parody and exaggeration in the Jaime Bunda novels, pastiche—that is, satire of textual style per Gérard Genette—is one of the primary ways that Pepetela's two works encode its layered critiques. Both Linda Hutcheon and Fredric Jameson describe pastiche as a genre wholly or partially devoid of critical possibility because pastiche fails to transform the object of its imitation in the new iteration or loses sight of the object of imitation, reducing history to the historicity purely of style (Hutcheon 38; Jameson 20–25). In the context of portrayals of Angola's present, however, where the recent colonial past and the globalized present provide overlapping structuring logics—what we might call the inherent historicity of the postcolonial condition—pastiche can retain its critical edge. As I examine in the example of the nineteenth-century crime story *Mistério da Estrada de Sintra* (*The Mystery of the Sintra Road*), the use of pastiche in the Jaime Bunda novels inserts them into a history of pastiche as social critique rooted in the perceived social decline of nineteenth-century Portugal. In this sense, Genette's argument for the transformative capacity of pastiche remains relevant: "[a pastiche] becomes a new production—that of another text in the same style, of another message in the same code" (*Palimpsests* 84). In his study of pastiche, Richard Dyer argues that pastiche deforms the elements that it takes to be representative of the target of its imitation; it thus produces a noticeable discrepancy for the readers' or viewers' experience with the pastiche depending on their insider knowledge of the target of imitation (56–60). However, at the same time, pastiche has the potential to communicate what Dyer calls the feeling about the target of imitation that contemporary modes of criticism have largely placed in opposition to critical judgment. Dyer sees in pastiche, in particular, a reminder that culture shapes our affective reactions to texts, in addition to their forms. For Dyer, pastiche has unstable or uneven critical possibilities, evident in its capacity to admire as well as to judge, to displace satire away from the style imitated (178–80). This reminder is encoded in pastiche's historicizing gesture—suggesting that pastiche is a technique central to a feeling like disappointment.

Pepetela manifests the stylistic imitation central to pastiche in describing Jaime Bunda's approach to investigation, an approach drawn from a literary history of careful observation and logical deduction clearly rooted in detective fiction. However, Jaime's observations and deductions are often unrelated to solving any crimes in general, and the crimes to which he is assigned to investigate in particular. Early in *Jaime Bunda, Agente Secreto*, the narrator describes how, though he lacks the confidence of his bosses and coworkers, Jaime has honed his observational acumen through minute observations of the details around him: "nunca lhe davam ensejo de provar que era mesmo um craque, só mandavam ir comprar cigarros . . . Durante todos os meses que ali passava na sala, mais de vinte, aprendera a distinguir todas as moscas que entravam e saíam pelas janelas" (15) ("[they] never gave him a chance to prove that he could be an ace, only ordering him to go and buy cigarettes. . . . During all those months spent in that room, more than twenty, he learnt to distinguish all the types of flies which came in and out through the windows" [12-13]). The reader is left initially unsure whether Jaime's ability to distinguish among the flies is an allusion to Holmesian obscure or esoteric knowledge that may come into play later, or an example of his absurd inability to discern important observations from trivial ones. The novel nudges the reader's judgment toward the second interpretation when Jaime interrupts his boss's briefing on the details of the case, prioritizing over the murder the chance to deduce the reasons that the boss ended up with one brown shoelace and one black one. The narrator's style reveals a clear allusion to the step-by-step reasoned logic typical of Doyle's Sherlock Holmes or Poe's Auguste Dupin:

> Jaime Bunda levantou da cadeira postada à frente da secretária do chefe e deu a volta, para ficar ao lado dele. Até se abaixou para ver melhor e depois se ergueu com um sorriso triunfal. —É o que me parecia, chefe. De facto, os dois são castanhos. Só que um recebeu tinta preta, provavelmente quando engraxou os sapatos. É o chefe mesmo que o faz? Com aquelas bisnagas que têm uma esponja na ponta?—Exactamente—respondeu Chiquinho Vieira, espantado. . . . Jaime Bunda voltou a sentar confortavelmente à frente do responsável, o qual não parava de olhar para os sapatos e para o subordinado, completamente abuamado, diminuído na sua autoridade. (16-17)

> (Jaime Bunda got up from the chair in from of the chief's desk and walked round to the other side, to stand next to him. He even bent down to get a closer look, and then straightened up with a triumphant smile. "This is what I think happened, chief. Actually, both shoelaces are brown. Only one received some black polish, probably when you were shining your shoes. Did you do that yourself, chief? With one of those bottles with a little sponge at the tip? "Exactly," responded Chiquinho Vieira, amazed. . . . Jaime Bunda went back to sit comfortably in front of his superior who could not stop looking at his shoes and then at his subordinate, completely dumbfounded, his authority undermined. [14])

The joke, of course, is not just that Jaime exercises his considerable observational skills on exaggeratedly trivial matters, but that he is entirely unable to distinguish trivial or irrelevant observations from important clues. Before even beginning his investigation, he dramatically considers that he may well be dealing with "Um crime sem indícios. O crime perfeito? Nunca há crime perfeito" (27) ("A crime without clues. The perfect crime? There is no such thing as a perfect crime" [24]). However, it might well be said that if the crime is largely without clues that lead the readers to its conclusion, the novel is replete with clues (like the mismatched shoelaces) unrelated to any crime. This example thus evidences what Seymour Benjamin Chatman calls "direct" satire of style: "it is not the form that is satirized, but the content—by being put into that form" (31). A display of a similar kind of mis-match between style and content takes place early in *Jaime Bunda e a Morte do Americano*. Recently arrived in the city of Benguela to investigate the death of an American engineer, Jaime is assigned to work with a local investigator, Nicolau, who hopes to learn as much as he can from the big-city star. An exchange with Nicolau that starts off in the style of a rapid-fire questioning would, in other crime works, reveal the experienced investigator's prowess; for Jaime Bunda, however, it ends up revealing his imitation of the ruling political class, rather than a concern for the investigation at hand:

—Soube se já fizeram a autópsia?

—Negativo.

—Negativo quê? Não sabe ou não fizeram?

—Não sei. O chefe Aguinaldo Trindade está ocupado, não pôde receber-me...

—E esse comandante Aguinaldo, é? Estava ocupado a fazer o quê que não pôde recebê-lo?

—A ver televisão em casa. Está a dar o jogo que define o título de campeão de futebol em Portugal.

—Merda para isto!—disse Bunda...

—De facto, o comandante devia pôr o serviço à frente do futebol... -arriscou Nicolau, numa primeira crítica aos colegas da polícia.

—Claro, claro... Mas ajude-me a levantar, tenho que ir ao quarto. Espero que a televisão esteja a funcionar lá. Esqueci-me do jogo. (35)

(—Did you find out whether they already did the autopsy?

—Negative.

—Negative what? You don't know or they haven't done it?

—I don't know. The boss Aguinaldo Trindade is busy, he couldn't see me. . . .

—And this Captain Aguinaldo, eh? He was busy doing what that he couldn't see you?

—Watching tv at home. They're showing the game that'll decide the soccer championship in Portugal.

—Shit!—said Bunda . . .

—In fact, the captain should put service before soccer . . . risked Nicolau, his first criticism of his police colleagues.

—Of course, of course . . . But help me get up, I have to go to my room. I hope the tv is working. I forgot about the game.)

The deliberate unpairing of the detailed narration of the protagonist's observations and reasoning from the investigation of the crime and its clues is one of the primary deformations of the detective-novel style that appears throughout the two Jaime Bunda novels.

The mismatch between form and style, therefore, provides a code to the social context that the novels narrate. In *Mysteries and Conspiracies: Detective Stories, Spy Novels and the Making of Modern Society*, Luc Boltanski argues that detective fiction arose in the late nineteenth century together with a modern view of society. In Boltanski's analysis, detective fiction makes visible the rules that constitute social "reality" by subjecting those rules to a series of tests, via the mysteries—interruptions of the "normal"—that structure the plots (3). Boltanski distinguishes between the world, used in the Wittgensteinian sense of all possible actions and outcomes, and reality, which is "stabilized by pre-established formats that are sustained by institutions, formats that often have a legal or paralegal character . . . reality is presented as a network of causal relations that holds together the events with which experience is confronted" (3). Both the world and reality are founded on the natural sciences, and therefore are both logical and realistic, in their depictions of both the natural world and the social milieus they portray. In this sense, the causes of the mysteries are knowable through observation and deduction (5–6).

Boltanski analyzes in detail several literary models in which he argues that these notions of reality are formulated. Doyle's Sherlock Holmes stories are examples of a dynamic where the higher moral order of social good may come into conflict with the legal codes that govern his society. As a private detective, Sherlock Holmes never fails to correct the irregularities that interrupt social "reality," even though he operates as a substitute for the state; the detective takes those facts and actions that "threaten the logical consistency of reality and dissolves them as such. This operation allows the possibility of radical uncertainty to be reduced in favour of the providential banality that makes reality predictable—its criminal dimensions included—and thus governable" (56). Like Sherlock Holmes, Boltanski's second model, George Simenon's police superintendent Maigret, is charged with maintaining reality, this time not in parallel, or exception (per Agamben) to the state, but from within it via administrative bureaucracy (71). Investigations, in this model, enact the surveillance function of the distant, impersonal state in order to assert its absolute authorship of reality (110–11). In both cases, the predictability of the outcomes—the resolutions to the crimes—are linked to the stability of the reality guaranteed by the society in which the works are embedded. This second model of crime fiction echoes in the modern genre of the police procedural, where the protagonist is the collective apparatus of the state police, reflecting its sole authority—and ability—to redress wrongs; this moral authority is established through the text's verisimilitude, promising access to a "real world" of policing (Mueller 99; 106).

This relationship between social and literary form is deliberately undermined in the Pepetela novels. Jaime Bunda operates to some extent in both of Boltanski's models: though he is a state employee, he operates as part of a secret agency that is exempt from many of the restrictions that govern the regular police. Out of ignorance of the unspoken rules of his corrupt social milieu, he chases suspects and clues that would prove politically inconvenient to his superiors if they were linked to crimes. A prototypical example is his pursuit of the mysterious T., high up in the Bunker (slang for the presidential palace) whom Jaime suspects of the murder in the first novel. His boss prohibits Jaime from pursuing T., however, due to the potential political fallout of finding him implicated in a crime. As social and political order are never the starting premises of Jaime Bunda's world, Jaime must, in many cases, operate independently of the state bureaucracy; finding the perpetrators to discreet crimes frequently reveals larger conspiracies whose intellectual authors remain at large. In this sense, the Jaime Bunda novels fail to confirm the central premise that Mueller argues undergirds the police procedural: the validation of the state apparatus to maintain social order (99).

However, in another sense, Jaime Bunda's investigations do lead to his access to and validation of a different kind of social order. Another way to read Jaime Bunda's attention to details unrelated to the crimes he is investigating, therefore, is to examine how these details point to an obliquely signaled para-criminal network: the class-based patronage system that the petit-bourgeois Jaime Bunda longs to ascend. Fabrice Schurmans has observed that across the two novels Jaime Bunda does acquire, if not the detective skills that would back up his reputation as a "craque" (a whizz/ ace), the corrupt rules of social ascent in operation in Pepetela's portrayal of early twenty-first-century Angola (331–333).[2] The deductive style in Jaime Bunda's observations about his boss's shoelace and the soccer game in Portugal helps direct the reader toward this network: while the humor lies in the triviality of the objects of his observations, Jaime is, literally, closely observing both hierarchy and power. Throughout both Jaime Bunda novels, the figures of authority are, for the most part, some combination of corrupt and incompetent. The novels have frequent references to public servants' profligate spending, for example, as when the provincial governor who hosts Jaime Bunda for a lavish dinner in *Jaime Bunda e a Morte do Americano* remarks to his wife that "O que vale é que não somos nós a pagar, é o Estado" (96) (What matters is that the State is paying, not us). In *Jaime Bunda, Agente Secreto*, the narrator reveals that Jaime's girlfriend Florinda is married to a diamond trafficker, though Jaime "tinha que reconhecer que nem sabia se ainda era tráfico ilícito, pois tão generalizado estava. Além do mais, a kamanga era legalizada quando convinha politicamente ao governo . . . para logo a seguir voltar a ser criminalizada . . . Era com o dinheiro da kamanga que iam jantar esta noite" (53) ("would have to admit that he did not actually know if it was illicit trafficking because it had become so commonplace. Besides which, illegal diamond trading was legalized when it was politically convenient for the government . . . to be criminalized again shortly afterwards . . . It was with money from illegal diamonds that he was going to be taken out to dinner that evening" [49]). The novel thus signals to the reader, in a subtle way, both the crimes that lie beyond the murders central to both novels, and that the networks they implicate are much wider than those that the detective tracks. It is clear that the Jaime Bunda novels are imitations of various genres of crime fiction with comic effect, but the charge of the imitation helps elucidate the engagement the novels make with the broader Angolan social sphere, as well as the literary genealogy into which Pepetela inserts them. The novels' satire stems from narrating a range of uniquely Angolan, African, or postcolonial conditions in a literary style that, according to the texts, is poorly adjusted to their realities.

The Historicity of Style and Colonial Critique

Jaime Bunda is an avid reader as well as writer of crime fiction, and in fact, after sharing his affinity with the national police inspector whom he is helping, thinks to recommend to him "algumas leituras, a começar pelo Conan Doyle, é sempre por aí que se começa, não?" (*Jaime Bunda* 30) ("a few readings, beginning with Conan Doyle, that's always where one begins, isn't it?" [27]). However, the way that Pepetela satirizes both the detective's careful observations and the style in which the reader accompanies the acquisition of clues in Jaime's misplaced examinations also points to another point of origin that is not explicit in the Jaime Bunda novels. *Mistério da Estrada de Sintra* (*The Mystery of the Sintra Road*) (1870) predates Doyle's first Sherlock Holmes story, and is considered the first detective story written in the Portuguese language by Portugal's most famed satirical author, Eça de Queirós, with his friend Ramalho Ortigão. *Mistério da Estrada de Sintra* was a satirical literary hoax about the supposed accidental murder of a young Englishman by his Portuguese lover, delivered in a series of letters to the editor of the Lisbon newspaper *Diário de Notícias* (*Daily News*). The final letter, from the two authors, reveals that the case is not news of a real murder at all, but a literary fiction. *Mistério da Estrada de Sintra* narrates how a young doctor is kidnapped by a group of masked men in order to verify a young man's death by opium overdose, later revealed to be the English Captain Rytmel. The serial unfolds through competing points of view, as four additional letter-writers respond to fill in details of the story, correct the observations of the others, and reveal the details of the murder and its author, the unhappily married Countess of W., Luísa. Luísa, who has fallen in love with Rytmel and has been foiled in her attempt to abscond with him, doses him with opium in order to search for love letters from the innocent Miss Shorn, for whom Luísa is convinced that Rytmel has abandoned her. When Rytmel accidentally dies from the opium, her cousin and a group of friends dispose of the body, cover up the murder, and help Luísa turn herself in to a convent, where they are convinced she will suffer sufficient punishment for her misdeeds.

Mistério shares a number of formal characteristics with the Jaime Bunda novels. *Jaime Bunda, Agente Secreto* employs four different narrators, reflecting *Mistério da Estrada de Sintra*'s composition by five different authors of letters explaining their various roles in the murder and cover-up. In both the cases of Pepetela's and Eça's novels, the single woman narrator reveals details about the cases inaccessible to the other narrative voices: Luísa writes a letter explaining how Rytmel's death occurred, while Malika, the second narrator of *Jaime Bunda, Agente Secreto*, reveals details of the counterfeit plot. Both the 1870 work and *Jaime Bunda e a Morte do Americano*, in particular, draw constant attention to the role of the press in disseminating sometimes sensationalized news stories about salacious items, but also in cultivating particular popular tastes among its readership. As an example, an author's note at the end of the second Jaime Bunda novel claims that the work was inspired by piece of news about the murder of a Portuguese engineer from the 1950s, lost in the archives of Benguela's colonial newspapers. The Jaime Bunda novels and Eça and Ortigão's serial also use many of the same strategies, especially signaling their respective foreign sources, thus implicating the narrators, characters, and the readers as steeped in mass-market crime fiction. As one of the narrators remarks in *Mistério*,

> Principiei a ler, como quase toda a gente em Lisboa, as cartas publicadas na sua folha, em que o doutor anónimo conta o caso que essa redacção intitulou *O Mistério da Estrada de Sintra*. Interessava-me essa narrativa e segui-a com uma curiosidade despreocupada que se liga a um *canard* fabricado com engenho, a um romance à semelhança dos *Thugs* e de alguns outros do mesmo género com que a veia imaginosa dos fantasistas franceses e americanos vem de quando em quando acordar a atenção da Europa para um sucesso estupendo. (65)

> (In common with a large part of Lisbon's population, I have been reading the letters published in your paper, in which an anonymous doctor recounts the case that your editorial office has chosen to entitle *The Mystery of the Sintra Road*. This narrative intrigued me and I followed it with the idle curiosity with which one tends to read such ingeniously devised fables, the kind of tale occasionally used by imaginative French and American writers to bring to the attention of Europe some astonishing phenomenon, such as the Thuggees of India. [59–60])

The unnamed mysterious narrator, identified as "Z," appears as a participant in the cover-up in the anonymous doctor's first letter to the paper and then writes his own account of the story of Rytmel's death. In doing so, he reveals himself as a reader of both the French and American stories that the *Mistério* resembles, as well as a reader of the first part of the novel. As Isabel Oliveira Martins signals, Eça and Ortigão's stated intention with the hoax was to make fun of the "backward" literary tastes of the Lisbon elite, "to innovate, to provoke, to shake up the literary and moral situation, wishing to wake up 'in shouts' the mental inertia of Lisbon, which at the time was asleep and at the mercy of such authors as Ponson du Terrail or Octave Feuillet" (78).[3,4]

The self-aware stylistic pastiche in which the narrators of both Pepetela's and Eça's novels engage amplifies our awareness of their workings within the genre's conventions, and draw our attention to the ways in which they exaggerate and deform it.

The key to figuring out Eça and Ortigão's hoax is style. The authors accomplish their critique of Lisbon's literary tastes by employing what they see as new, modern, and revitalizing language drawn from the modern French poets such as Baudelaire and English-language narrators such as Edgar Allan Poe (whom they likely read in Baudelaire's translation). They juxtaposed new styles with tired sentimentalist tropes drawn from novels like Eugène Sue's *Les Mystères de Paris*, clearly invoked in the title to the Portuguese work. Like Jaime Bunda, Eça and Ortigão's first narrator, the young doctor, deploys an exaggerated observational capacity that points the reader to figures like Poe's Dupin. Dupin's process of "ratiocionation" models not only the modern kind of writing that Eça and Ortigão admire, but indicate to the readers-as-detectives the process that they should be applying to the text itself: looking for and identifying the markers of tired, sentimental fiction. After he is kidnapped and called upon to try revive the opium victim, the doctor begins to surreptitiously look for clues to the victim's death, and comes upon a single golden hair. He determines without hesitation, that "era o indício dum assassinato, duma cumplidade pelo menos!" (59) ("[It] was the clue to a murder or, at the very least, to someone's complicity in a murder!" [52]). The doctor's examination of the hair evidences an extravagant attention to detail, exaggerating the precision of its conclusions from a miniscule piece of evidence. Stylistically, features such as the inelegant chains of adjectives tip the reader off that the woman described is a hackneyed sentimentalist feminine type:

> A pessoa a quem [o fio de cabelo] pertencia era loura, clara, decerto, pequena, *mignonne*, porque o fio de cabelo era delgadíssimo, extraordinariamente puro . . . O carácter dessa pessoa deve ser doce, humilde, dedicado e amante . . . Devia ter gostos simples, elegantemente modestos a dona de tal cabelo . . . Teria sido talvez educada em Inglaterra ou na Alemanha, porque o cabelo denotava na sua extremidade ter sido espontado, hábito das mulheres do norte, completamente estranho às meridionais, que abandonam os seus cabelos à abundante espessura natural (59).

> (The person to whom [the hair] belonged was clearly blonde, doubtless of fair complexion, petite, *mignonne*, because the strand of hair was fine and extremely pure . . . By nature, this woman would be gentle, humble, devoted and loving. . . . The owner of

that hair would have simple elegantly modest tastes. . . . She had probably received her education in England or Germany because the tip of the hair showed that it had been cut, a custom among Northern women, but unknown to Mediterraneans, who allow their locks to grow to their full, abundant, natural length. [52])

While the doctor's observations do point the reader to discovering the eventual murderer—a fact that he himself never uncovers—the details that he gleans from the hair comply with the literary type of the tragic sentimental heroine.[5] Compounding the joke, another sentimentalist trope gets in the way of satisfactorily resolving the crime: all the young men determined to figure out what happened to Rytmel fall in love with the murderer, and thus end up helping her get rid of the body and retire to a convent rather than face justice. The association with mass-market distribution and with popular tastes is undoubtedly also a significant point of contact with Pepetela's citation of English-language crime fiction. Ofélia Paiva Monteiro's series of three articles on verisimilitude in Eça and Ortigão's novel examines how a series of meta-diegetic observations by the characters signal to the readers their own inscription within literary tradition, winking at those few astute readers who should read these moments as "tells" of the hoax. Meanwhile the masses, un-self-aware and accustomed to unoriginal tropes, remain unaware of the stylistic imitation—central to pastiche—that constitutes the satirical content of the novel. The comparisons between the Jaime Bunda novels and *Mistério da Estrada de Sintra* demonstrate not only the historicity of pastiche itself, but also the historicity of the style as deployed in crime fiction.

The technique of portraying characters as readers of their own genre is one that is shared between the Jaime Bunda novels and *Mistério da Estrada de Sintra*. As we have seen, in the nineteenth-century novel, the narrators and characters remark upon not only themselves as readers, but on the similarities between the story they are telling and the fiction that the authors mock via in their satire. In his first letter, the doctor dryly admits the absurdity of the story of his kidnapping: "puro Ponson du Terrail! dirá o Sr. Redactor. Evidentemente. Parece que a vida, mesmo no caminho de Sintra, pode às vezes ter o capricho de ser mais romanesca do que pede a verosimilhança artística. Mas eu não faço arte, narro factos unicamente" (29) ("pure pot-boiler fiction, worthy of Ponson du Terrail! But that is because life, even on the road from Sintra, can at times seem more like a novel than artistic verisimilitude can tolerate. But I am not creating art, I am recording facts" [17]). Paiva Monteiro explores how the authors' games expertly hinge on affirming the "verisimilitude" of the text, and then undermining it in moments when the characters refer to themselves as textual constructions or as novelistic readers of other parts of the story. Paiva Monteiro argues that the novel's fourth narrator, known by the initials A.M.C., corrects some of the misapprehensions of prior narrators and thus serves as Eça's mouthpiece for a modern, realist style of writing—but not through a portrayal of the *believability* of the story, but through what she calls the "scientificity" of the [new] novel. Responding to the exaggeratedly sentimental narrative of Luísa's tragic love story, Paiva Monteiro notes that A.M.C. moves suddenly between metadiegetic awareness of himself as reader/consumer of the romantic story and participant in the realist one (Paiva Monteiro 1987b 39). For Paiva Monteiro, the "novelistic character" of *Mistério da Estrada de Sintra* lies, therefore, not in the verisimilitude of the various stories, told through accumulation of details, corrections by subsequent narrators, suspense, and resolution. Rather, what makes it a novel is the very *inverisimilitude* that its satirical tone emphasizes. For, as Paiva Monteiro points out, A.M.C. himself falls victim to the "passions" of sympathy that the "tragic" figure of Luísa evokes. As he passes the narrative voice to her to allow her to explain her story, Paiva Monteiro signals that Luísa herself observes, "não sou uma mulher, sou um *romance*" (qtd. in Paiva Monteiro 42) (I am not a woman, I am a *novel*). Nonetheless, A.M.C. compromises his moral outrage at her adultery in order to help her escape, ceding narrative space and authority to her, even as he points out what he sees as the tired, anachronistic, and vacuous serial novel tradition in which she writes herself. Rather than providing continuity, the narrative disruptions and stylistic clashes necessarily introduce into the novel unresolved conflicts, facts that remain in dispute, and an unsatisfying ending where the murderer remains unpunished by official means. The textual limitations that the sentimental serial novel imposes on *Mistério da Estrada de Sintra* are the literary manifestations of a paucity of spirit, a lack of imagination that imprisons the "invioláveis liberdades do espírito" (*Mistério* qtd. in Paiva Monteiro 46) (inviolable liberties of the spirit).

There remains coded in Eça and Ortigão's novel, therefore, the narrative clash not just between the style the readers are accustomed to and the new style the authors want to promote, but between Portugal's peripheral position vis-à-vis European culture and the center of new, modern expression. The style and tropes that Eça and Ortigão mock are presented as an anachronistic narrative mode that by its very popularity and familiarity fails to adjust Portugal's artistic expression to its larger social surroundings. If *Mistério da Estrada de Sintra* serves as a possible intertext for Pepetela's two Jaime Bunda novels, this epistemic clash can be read as a structural point of contact between the two authors; it additionally constitutes the political context into which each of the works intervenes. One of the most prominent through-threads in Eça's literature is the decaying Portuguese empire, Portugal's fading global influence, and its peripheral cultural and political significance in nineteenth-century European and global spheres. This critique casts as an undercurrent to many of his novels the precarious imperial future of the former *império do mar* (empire of the sea). The decaying remnants of old and new empires permeate the urban and rural landscapes of Jaime Bunda's travels through Luanda and Benguela, and force a similarly unreconciled confrontation with Angola's neoimperial present.

These two elements—the unresolved crime and the satire of style—link the nineteenth-century Portuguese text with the twenty-first-century Angolan novels through the notion of counterfeiting. The "counterfeit news" in *Mistério da Estrada de Sintra* reappears in *Jaime Bunda, Agente Secreto* as a false conspiracy that Jaime conceives in order to deliver results to his bosses when he fails at solving the murder. He stages a raid on a drug ring he has invented, but to his surprise, discovers in the process actual criminals scheming to exchange counterfeit Angolan kwanzas for US dollars. "És um génio, Jaimito. Vais longe nos SIG" (225) ("You're a genius, Jaimey, you'll go a long way in the GIS" [197]), his partner tells him after Jaime reveals the plot. Jaime's genius in his "invention of stories" differs only in the details from the crime he actually discovers; the narrative structure is more or less the same. On the one hand, this conclusion certainly points to Pepetela's critique of corrupt public officials: Jaime invents a fake story that brings him success, but because the social milieu is so replete with crimes, he ends up solving a real one anyway. On the other hand, however, as readers we are called upon to recognize another kind of counterfeit: in explicitly attributing the sources of Jaime Bunda's style of investigation to English-language sources, the potential Portuguese origins of the satire are obscured. This mapping together of the acknowledged and unacknowledged sources is crucial.

For Eça and Ortigção's novel, the detective formula serves as a marker of literary modernity that both guides the astute reader to figure out the hoax and tricks the uniformed reader who fails to perceive the "clues." In the Angolan novels, the history of the crime genre referenced throughout the text has itself become the formulaic form and style that has to be adapted, at least as deployed through Jaime Bunda's lens, to grasp the complexity of the Angolan society in which it operates. In most crime fiction, the reader is also the detective, and the economy of the text provides the necessary clues for both to follow the logic. While Jaime can apply the narrative formula to the Luandan context, the intimate integration of the content and style falls apart. The layering of the English-language and Portuguese sources of literary styles operates as both critique and warning: if the revolution sought to cast off the vestiges of colonial occupation, replacing Portuguese political hegemony with American cultural hegemony leaves the fundamental colonial formulas intact. The old and the new colonial regimes float just above and just below the surface of Angolan reality. For Pepetela, and for Jaime Bunda's world, the key to the crimes remain illegible without both of them.

While in the crime literature that Jaime enjoys narrative details serve as clues to the resolution of the crime, the four different narrators in *Jaime Bunda, Agente Secreto* and the two different possible endings to *Jaime Bunda e a Morte do Americano* are additional incarnations in the form of the novels of the layered colonial and postcolonial histories visible in the portrayals of the cities of Luanda and Benguela. *Jaime Bunda, Agente Secreto* includes detailed descriptions of Luanda's various neighborhoods, cuisine, roads, family histories, explanations of Luandan and Angolan slang, and various character's personal and family backgrounds. These descriptions create the impression of the postcolonial urban palimpsest: the traces of Angola's rapid pace of transformation over the last quarter of the twentieth century leave visible and sometimes disorienting marks on the city. Roads, routes, and traffic are prominent topics of Jaime Bunda's conversations with his driver, suggesting an allegorical function for the urban landscape in deciphering Angola's recent history, as his driver's complaint indicates:

> Bernardo estava com pouca paciência para se meter no tráfego desgraçado da Avenida Hoji ya Henda . . . foi sempre rezingando, a mudança do nome é que provocou essas desgraças, no tempo do colono se chamava Avenida do Brasil e era boa de andar, larga, via rápida, alimentava o bairro do Rangel e o Cazenga. Depois a FNLA pôs ali a sede, começaram as confrontações e a FNLA prendeu e matou as pessoas do Eme, o povo lhe chamou Avenida dos Massacres. Começou então o massacre da avenida: candeeiros da luz a serem derrubados pelos carros a cem à hora, valas a serem abertas para procurar canos de água furados e que não mais eram tapadas, buracos que nasciam todos os dias. Depois criaram uma comissão para estudar a toponímia da cidade. Em vez de voltarem ao nome antigo, não. Estupidez, até porque o Brasil, país irmão, foi o primeiro a reconhecer a independência de Angola. (*Jaime Bunda* 99–100)

> (Bernard had little patience for entering the horrendous traffic on Hoji ya Henda Avenue. . . . [He] didn't stop grumbling, the change of name is what caused this disgrace, in colonial times it was called Brazil Avenue and it was good to drive along—wide, fast, feeding the suburbs of Rangel and Cazenga. After the FNLA . . . put their headquarters there, the confrontations began and the FNLA got

caught up in things and killed MPLA people, the people called it Massacre Avenue. That's when the massacre of the avenue began: streetlights knocked down by motorists going at a hundred miles an hour, ditches dug to find broken water pipes and never filled in again, potholes born every day. Then they created a commission to study the names of places in the city. Instead of reverting to the old name, no. Idiotic, especially because Brazil, a loyal friend, was the first to recognise the independence of Angola. [87–88])[6]

The decaying and corrupt city is a trope drawn from the hard-boiled and police procedural genres, in which cityscapes reflect the social ills that conduce to crimes both large and small. In Bernardo's recounting of Hoji ya Henda Avenue's renamings, the city of Luanda functions as a simultaneous monument to the colonial past and to the violence of the civil conflict of the post-independence era. The transformations themselves have a performative effect on the road: "the people called it Massacre Avenue. That's when the massacre of the avenue began." Similarly, *Jaime Bunda e a Morte do Americano* presents Jaime's view of the city of Benguela in terms of his admiration for all things American, starting with American detective fiction: "esticaram até o Bairro Benfica, talvez o mais célebre da urbe, todo formado por ruas paralelas com números, rua nove, rua dez, rua onze, como Nova Iorque, disse Bunda, encantado, descobrindo referências dos livros e filmes, embora as estreitas ruas do Benfica estivessem esburacadas e as pequenas casas fossem de um só piso" (92) (They continued to the Benfica neighborhood, perhaps the city's most famous one, composed of parallel streets with numbers, 9th Street, 10th Street, like New York Bunda said, delighted, discovering references made in books and films, even though the narrow streets of Benfica were full of potholes and the small houses were only one story.) The cities have dual projections—one gesturing toward the colonial past and the violence of the civil war; the other toward the neocolonial encroachment through English-language cultural products—that concretize the sites of Pepetela's critique.

This layered mapping of the cities is represented in the problem of pragmatics as well; both novels document the shifts in meaning of coded words such as "counter-revolutionaries" and "anti-Americans" as the ideological allegiances of the Angolan state shifted through the last decades of the twentieth century. The narrator of *Jamie Bunda, Agente Secreto* sarcastically notes that a dossier on a suspect reports that only the established order "pode levar-nos para o futuro radioso há muito prometido e ainda não atingido por acção dos contra-revolucionários ontem considerados contra o socialismo e hoje contra a democracia" (*Jaime Bunda* 195–96) ("could deliver the radiant future—a future not yet achieved due to action by the counter-revolutionaries who were viewed one day as being against socialism and the next against democracy" [172]). The novel is mocking the cynical use to which the state deploys the ideology of the moment: while the counter-revolutionaries, those who oppose the state, are accused of competing ideological interests, the power of the state to define right remains unquestioned.

Some critics, rightly, see in Jaime Bunda's enthusiasm for a particular body of detective fiction his epistemological colonization through United States literature and its implicit association with the faults and excesses of the globalized capitalist machine.[7] Jaime Bunda is enchanted to discover "a twin soul" in the local police chief Kinanga, who is also a fan of the crime genre, but Jaime is dismissive of Kinanga's admiration for European writers: "Kinanga, aquecido pela conversa e pelo uísque lembrou que Conan Doyle era inglês, logo europeu, mas logo Bunda arrematou, esse não conta, fala inglês, língua do gringo" (49) ("Kinanga, heated from the conversation and from the whiskey remembered that Conan Doyle was English, and therefore European, however Bunda cut him off, that doesn't count, he spoke English, the gringo's language" [44]). Later, discussing his concern that Jaime's frequent visits and conversations are a mode of surveillance from the national agency, Kinanga remarks that while Jaime seems to know well some detective literature, it is only the North American authors. "Claro," replies his subordinate, "é a moda no Bunker" (50) ("Obviously, that's just like the Bunker" [45]). Kinanga, educated in Cuba and the Soviet system in Bulgaria, is paranoid about being watched by those above, and suspicious of the direction of national politics in the post-1991 era toward embracing all things American. As a product of the old revolutionary education, he functions as a foil to Jaime's ingenuous pursuit of the American way, and it is he, at the end of the novel, who eventually solves the murder. However, Kinanga's success is presented as a brief footnote to Jaime's public acclaim and professional ascent. In *Jaime Bunda e a Morte do Americano*, Pepetela's ironic portrayal of Angola's pro-American shift is even more explicit. Jaime's shock at finding out that some older residents cheered the death of the American engineer—he asks how they could hate whoever made such fabulous action films and wrote the best crime novels (161)—points to one of the fundamental critiques that Pepetela's works offer. Jaime Bunda's haste to acclimate to the circles of influence and power are accompanied by his selective historical erasure, catalyzed by his immersion in literary models that he constantly finds are out of sync with his complicated present.[8]

Stephen Soitos argues in his study of African-American detective fiction that one of the defining features of this genre is the social milieu, or what he calls the "blackground," that often takes over the narrative and eclipses the primary crime plot. He notes that African-American crime writers often repurpose Conan Doyle's technique in *A Study in Scarlett* of the long digression "that reorients the basic foundation of the criminal and the crime in the removed historical past . . . suggesting African-American continuity with an African past" (50). The Jaime Bunda novels posit a similar historical view of the Angolan post-colony, rooting both the crimes that Jaime Bunda solves and those he doesn't solve in the pervasive corruption that spans both past and present. Critical examinations of crime fiction, including genres such as detective fiction and the "secret agent" novel, have interrogated both the complicity of imperial politics with the formulas of crime genres, as well as their systematic complication and dismantling in categories identified with modifiers such as "postcolonial," "trans-national," or "transcultural" crime fiction. In their introduction to *Postcolonial Postmortems*, for example, Christine Matzke and Susanne Mühleisen argue that postcolonial crime fiction often breaks the epistemological unity associated with classical detective fiction, for example, juxtaposing "other knowledges against the local or global mainstream," while the object of detection expands out beyond specific instances of criminality to examine larger social ills implicating colonial and neocolonial conditions (5; 8). In their criticism of Jaime's slavish application of tropes learned and imported from English-language detective fiction, Pepetela's novels are simultaneously serving up postmodernism and global capitalism's sense of the eternal present and incessant incorporation of any marketable idea or product to its readers, while signaling how its operations sometimes effect a new coloniality superimposed on the spaces of colonial and imperial histories. Jaime Bunda's narrative excesses—in the novels' detail and formal citations and the dozens of implied crimes that open up to dozens of new novels—lead us to examine both Angola's recent history and the narrative forms drawn on to explore it. The novels suggest that these exist in an analogic relationship, and thus an examination of the form of one necessarily implies understanding the form of the other. One of the important functions of pastiche in the Jaime Bunda novels, therefore, is to signal the split between the reader-as-detective and the detective protagonist. Pepetela accomplishes this split through narrative intrusion, selective dramatic irony, and the two epilogues in *Jaime Bunda e a Morte do Americano*. As the next section shows, it is in these stylistic devices that the novels locate their ethical gesture, offering a possible alternative path to critique that ends solely in cynicism and despair.

Jaime Bunda's Self-Awareness of Genre

As we have seen, Jaime Bunda and Kinanga, among other characters, are readers of the crime genres that the Jaime Bunda novels themselves adapt and sometimes deform. What the readers of Jaime Bunda experience as pastiche—stylistic repetition with a difference—becomes a source of consternation for Jaime, when he is put off to discover that his hours waiting outside the house of a suspect fail to provide immediately damning evidence: "nos livros, bastava o detective ficar umas horas a vigiar o suspeito que logo a acção estoirava como pipocas em panela de alumínio. Um só detective. Aqui não, era preciso uma batalhão de tipos para vigiarem todos os gestos e momentos. E não acontecia nada" (200) ("in the books, it was enough spend a few hours watching the suspect, for action to explode like popcorn in an aluminum pot. Just one detective. While here, a whole battalion of guys was necessary to keep watch over the movements and moments. And nothing happened" [176]). In its reference to "popcorn," a prop of a movie theater audience, this passage suggests a comparison between Jaime and the viewership and readership of crime works for mass consumption. The passage also both reproduces and makes fun of the conventions of the crime genres by constantly referring to them: it implies, for example, that the author of the two novels is inadequately adapting the plot to the expectations of its readership, just as Jaime's expectation of immediate action is unfulfilled in this passage.

This meta-textual awareness is additionally represented through intrusions from both the narrators and the pseudo-author.[9] Intrusions from the narrators tend to point out stylistic or plot features, expand on details the characters don't offer, or offer personal observations, while the pseudo-author comments on the composition of the novel itself. In *Jaime Bunda e a Morte do Americano*, these authorial intrusions point to possible sources for the novel, while in *Jaime Bunda, Agente Secreto*, the pseudo-author offers his reasons for dismissing narrators: the first is disposed of because the pseudo-author finds the narrator boring and monotonous, like a "tribo de quissonde a mudar de formigueiro" (140) ("a tribe of *quissonde* ants seeking a new nest" [122]); the second, the only intradiegetic narrator, only female voice, and only first-person narrator, is sent away because she might lead the story too far astray (a question I return to below); and the third narrator, who the author tells us is actually the return of the first, uses too many hunting metaphors, and thus for reasons of economy the pseudo-author must choose "outro, mais próximo dos cânones clássicos do género" (264) ("one closer to the classic canons of this genre" [230]). Structurally, these intrusions highlight a constant attention on the composition of the text, and its conformity (or not) with crime genres. In this way, these stylistic and structural elements can be seen as operating in analogy to the operations of power that Jaime's investigations partially expose. Tania Macêdo notes that by parodying detective fiction, Pepetela "acaba por gerar uma tensão na medida em que o texto, a partir da focalização das entranhas da burocracia, deixa entrever—sem contudo reveler totalmente—a face obscura e tenebrosa do poder" (193) (ends up creating tension insofar as the text, though its focus on the messy inner workings of bureaucracy, allows a glimpse—though without revealing it completely—of the dark and ominous face of power). The tension that Macêdo identifies between the glimpses of the operations of the state machine and the narrators' coy reticence to reveal them completely is doubled in the relationship that the pseudo-author establishes with both the narrators and the readers. The result is a structural allegory of political power, which Sharae Deckard sees as a representation of "uneven development" and "secondhand ideologies of neoliberalism implemented by neocolonial elites" (95; 105). Ricardo Soares de Oliveira, however, points out that the uniquely Angolan manifestation of the convergence of the wholesale privatization of state functions for profit-making and the consolidation of the influence and power of state patrons (123-32). The informal and partially visible presence of state patronage has a formal manifestation in Pepetela's texts through the pseudo-author.[10]

A number of examples from each of the novels demonstrate the repetition of textual strategies that the political machine employs *in* the novel and the pseudo-author deploys *on* the novel, particularly revealing or withholding information. Jaime Bunda, upon searching for the state police file on his primary suspect T., finds that no such file exists, even though "Nos arquivos do Bunker, as pessoas estavam classificadas de uma maneira muito própria: empresários, sacerdotes, intelectuais, dirigentes, funcionários, oposicionistas, etc." (79) ("In the archives of the Bunker, people had been classified in a very precise manner: businesspeople, priests, intellectuals, directors, functionaries, those in opposition" [71]). Though he eventually gets his hands on the suspect's secret dossier of political activity—which the narrator shares with the reader—it lacks appendices and an official stamp, thus undermining its credibility. Similarly, the pseudo-author withholds the suspect's name from the reader:

> É tão poderoso, tão poderoso, que nem o nome dele ouso mandar escrever. Ficará, pela minha covardia, apenas como senhor T ou simplesmente T. . . . Apenas saberemos que é conselheiro no Bunker e isso vai bastar também aos leitores, que mais dados não deixo revelar, pois ainda a pessoa em causa pode descobrir que a ela me refiro. Dirão vocês: gente dessa não lê literatura de segunda categoria. Pois não nem de terceira ou quarta. E da de primeira, ah, fogem dela como o Cristo da cruz. Mas sempre há algum caxico que lê e lhes vai zongolar. Nem na morgue de Luanda, lugar tenebroso e mal cheiroso por excelência, bom para perigosíssimas conspirações, deixo revelar dados sobre T, senão os estritamente necessários. (67)

(He is so powerful, so powerful, that his name cannot be written down. He will remain, thanks to my cowardice, merely Mr T or simply T. . . . All we know is that he is a functionary in the Bunker and that is also enough for the readers, for whom we cannot reveal any further details, because the person in question could find out that I had said something. I'm telling you all: people like that don't read second-rate literature. Of course not, nor third or fourth. And of first-rate, well, they run from it like Christ from the cross. But there is always some traitor who'll read it and then go snitch. Not even in the Luanda morgue, a dark and malodorous place *par excellence*, good for extremely dangerous conspiracies, would I reveal details about T, if it wasn't strictly necessary [61])

Though Jaime finds out the suspect's name, the readers never do; similarly, while the novel strongly suggests T.'s involvement in the web of organized crime of which the counterfeiting ring is a part, neither Jaime, his boss, nor the readers ever receive confirmation of such participation. The pseudo-author, therefore, operates like the mysterious bureaucratic authorities under whom Jaime Bunda serves: they protect those in power by withholding information from the public eye. They are thus by definition excluded from their own taxonomy of those under surveillance—businesspeople, intellectuals, priests, counter-revolutionaries, etc.—as the authors, like the author of the novel, of the social reality that the other characters inhabit. This power is exercised, at times, through the impression of freedom. Acknowledging a "technical error" of focalization at the end of the only chapter narrated from T.'s point of view, the pseudo-author shrugs off the error as belonging to the narrator, since "Eu é que não tenho nada com isso, sou apenas defensor das liberdades" (77) ("I have nothing to do with this, I am just a defender of freedoms" [70]). By appearing and then withdrawing from view, the pseudo-author creates the impression of autonomy, only to remind the narrators and readers that he is ultimately pulling the strings.

This authorial absolutism is challenged in two ways in the two novels: through the female narrator in *Jaime Bunda, Agente Secreto* and through the two possible epilogues in *Jaime Bunda e a Morte do Americano*. As an informed counterpoint to Jaime Bunda's ignorance and the previous narrator's missteps, Malika, the first-person narrator in *Jaime Bunda, Agente Secreto*, reveals substantial detail about her own life as well as clues about the international circulation of criminal goods and services. Malika, a belly dancer, escapes an abusive father and an arranged marriage in Algeria; she is contracted to travel to Angola and pose as the wife of the counterfeiter in order to bait T., who is attracted to unavailable women, into the scheme. The three short chapters she narrates, in fact, appear within the diegesis of the novel: we discover that her section is the confession she writes after she is arrested for her association with the counterfeiters. When at one point Malika undercuts her narrative style and thus her reliability as gendered female, her protestation reads as ironic. She tells the readers that "Os homens cultivam o pre-conceito de que as mulheres analisam as coisas com subjectivismo excessivo. É um estereótipo, muitas vezes sem corresponder à verdade, mas eu seria a confirmação objectiva dele" (174) ("Men cultivate the idea that women analyze things with excessive subjectivity. That's a stereotype, which often doesn't correspond to reality, but I would be the objective confirmation of it" [152]). Malika does, in fact, narrate events subjectively: her "subjectivity" is marked in her first-person voice, which serves as an explicit counterpoint to the assumed "objectivity" and associated "freedom" with which the pseudo-author characterizes the other three narrators. However, this proclaimed subjectivity only heightens the irony that she is, in fact, the more reliable narrator. Her observations reveal crucial details that contribute to the apprehension of the counterfeiters, such as the clue that her presumed husband Said and T. likely have a long-standing relationship. However, her narrative style also threatens the integrity of the detective genre.

When the pseudo-author dismisses the female narrator, he questions the adequacy of a particular genre and style to the text by signaling gender, racial, and cultural stereotypes and formulas, positing Malika as a narrator more suited to a text like the *Thousand and One Nights*. He thus emphasizes the novel's general critique of the Angolan readership's *taste* for American fiction (the question of aesthetics) as allegorically linked to its portrayal of Angolan society as hovering between the vestiges of a colonial past and neocolonial future. He warns:

> Se continuamos com ela, vamos provavelmente entrar pelos fabulosos harens de sultões e califas, dignos das Mil e Uma Noites. Sabemos que esteve no Marrocos e no Egipto. Daí até um califado do Golfo é só um salto, facilmente transponível pela ficção . . . mas perderíamos o espantoso Jaime Bunda e sua infatigável luta contra os horrendos crimes cometidos em Luanda, razão dos nossos propósitos. (179)

> (If we had stayed with her, we would probably have entered the fabulous harems of sultans and caliphs, mentioned in the *Thousand and One Nights*. We know she had been in Morocco and Egypt. From there to a Gulf caliphate is just a jump, easily crossed in fiction . . . but we would lose the amazing Jaime Bunda and his

indefatigable struggle against the horrendous crimes committed in Luanda, the reason for our interest. [156])

The text, here, sets up a false opposition between the markers of the detective genre—the typical masculinity of the hero, especially as narrated through his sexual conquests; the "objective" voice and reliance on scientific discourse; the textual economy that leads the reader to assemble the clues with the detective—and the markers of an exoticized, perhaps fantastic, female-narrated tale derived from the *Thousand and One Nights*. Breaches of genre conventions, the pseudo-author warns, are "easily crossed in fiction." However, it is precisely in the stylistic challenge to the other three narrators, who share the detective's perspective, that the novel locates its ethical core. In this sense, Jaime's repetition of Alexandre Dumas's clichéd phrase—"cherchez la femme" (30) (look for the woman) proves prophetic, though beyond Jaime's grasp. The interruption of Malika as narrator in the text, even though she is dismissed by the pseudo-author, offers another iteration of the tension between form and content that is central to the novel. If pastiche, in Genette's formulation, offers a different message in the same code, Malika's section of chapters offers a new stylistic and genre code that by definition communicates different messages. Her perspective threatens to break the hegemony of the pseudo-author's genre code, pointing to another narrative possibility in the author's analogous realm of the political.

While the two novels' caustic tone toward the powerful and the would-be powerful dominates the texts, Pepetela treats many of the economically and socially marginalized characters sympathetically. The unfortunate Júlio Fininho in *Jaime Bunda e a Morte do Americano* is a prime example: he has a secret identity as "Robin dos Comboios" (Robin of the Trains) who rides the Benguela railroad, stealing from the first-class passengers to give to the poor. While he is imprisoned for theft at the end of the novel and scapegoated for the murder, the two endings to *Jaime Bunda e a Morte do Americano* offer, separately, two aspects of the crime fiction genre conventions. In the first epilogue, the true murderer is never discovered and the falsely accused Fininho languishes in prison and, though the narrator declines to reveal his future. Júlio thus fulfills the prophesy offered by a practitioner of magic to Júlio's girlfriend, who requests that he be "preso a *mim* para toda a vida" (*my* prisoner for life)—except that the practitioner fails to hear the possessive, interpreting Júlio's girlfriend's words as "prisoner for life" (100; my emphasis). The narrator then undermines this destiny by reminding the readers of their expectations of a happy ending: "nem sempre as profecias se cumprem e neste caso, temos de convir, há profecias a mais, pode ser que se confundam e anulem umas às outras, conduzindo o caso para o férico *happy-end* tão do gosto americano" (275) (prophesies don't always come true and in this case, we have to agree, there are too many prophesies, it's possible that they confuse each other and some annul other ones, leading to the magical happy ending that is so fitting to American tastes). Júlio might remain imprisoned by the state until his death, or he may, in fact, be imprisoned by the genre and American tastes for a happy ending—creating the possibility for his release from the physical prison where he ends up. In the second epilogue, which the pseudo-author tells us is in his own words, rather than those of the narrator, the engineer's American companion Elvis is discovered to be the murderer, thus complying with another reader expectation that the crime is solved in crime fiction. However, in this case the happy ending is definitively denied, in that the hero Júlio Fininho does in fact, die in prison.

The structural allegory of power in the second Jaime Bunda novel more explicitly implicates the Angolan elite's willful accommodation to American expectations in the pursuit of economic and political gains, though the varied possible endings suggest a fissure in the unity of this power. The parallel plotting of politics of convenience and the composition of the novels is evident in the two endings. As the governor of Benguela makes clear to Jaime Bunda as the detective begins his investigation, "o embaixador americano já fala de terrorismo. Isso é péssimo para o país" (the American ambassador is already talking about terrorism. That's terrible for our country). The narrator echoes his concern: "Não era nada conveniente que os americanos voltassem agora a ter medo de vir para Angola. Sobretudo os seus capitais que, afinal, eram as notas verdes mais procuradas do mundo" (61) (It wasn't at all convenient for the Americans to go back to being afraid to come to Angola. Especially their capital which, after all, were the most sought-after green notes in the world). In *Jaime Bunda, Agente Secreto*, the pseudo-author himself readily admits to his own implication in the economic global order, after the narrator modestly passes over some details that the "intelligent readers" can glean for themselves: "Reparem que obriguei o narrador a fazer um cumprimento à vossa inteligência? Foi apenas com o intuito de agradar ao leitor e incitá-lo a recomendar este livro aos amigos" (102) ("Do you remember I requested the narrator to compliment you on your intelligence? It was only for the purpose of pleasing the readers and encouraging them to recommend this book to their friends" [89]). The pseudo-author makes explicit his accommodation to the readers in order to sell more books. However, at the end of *Jaime Bunda e a Morte do Americano*, by opening the range of possibilities for concluding the plot to the reader, the pseudo-author involves those same readers in the ethical implications of such accommodation to American "tastes" in both the political and aesthetic realms.

For Pepetela, this ethical possibility opened by handing over a measure of authority to the readers is, at its heart, a function of literature. The potential recasting of events by the multiple narrators in *Jaime Bunda, Agente Secreto* is similar to those opened by the central role of the news press in *Jaime Bunda e a Morte do Americano*, both intradiegetically and extradiegetically. Throughout the novel, competing newspapers reveal details of the cases the novel tracks—both the murder and the thefts on the train. Large sections of the novel take place in the bar Flor Morena, and recount the conversations about current and past events among a group of longtime residents of Benguela, including the murder of a Portuguese engineer in the 1950s and the subsequent capture of a thief who robbed trains. Like the case of Robin dos Comboios, in the 1950s, the thief died in prison, and the Portuguese engineer's murder was never solved. In response to the reporter Gouveia's request for permission to cite the conversation to write about the similarity of the case, the writer Raul argues that the facts aren't his to offer: "Mas elas foram descritas . . . Não pertencem a ninguém. Consulte os arquivos, existem os jornais da época, é só saber procurar" (112–13) (But they've already been described. . . . They don't belong to anyone. Check the archives, the newspapers of the time are there, you just need to know to look for them). The author's note after the two epilogues presents the reader with almost exactly the same charge:

> É rigorosamente verdade que nos anos 50, na cidade de Benguela, faleceu um engenheiro português nas circunstâncias aqui reveladas pelo personagem Raul Dândi, bem como a morte na cadeia de um assaltante de comboios, acusado de ser o autor do assassinato do engenheiro, com a cumplicidade da sua amante. Os factos foram acompanhados minuciosamente pelos dois jornais da terra, *O Intransigente* e o *Jornal de Benguela*. Ainda há poucos anos se encontravam exemplares desses jornais na biblioteca municipal. Ultimamente já não encontrei os que se relacionavam directamente com o caso, fruto do tempo e de algum desleixo de quem os compulsou anteriormente. Mas em alguma parte do mundo esses jornais existirão. (291)

> (It is absolutely true that in the 1950s, in the city of Benguela, a Portuguese engineer died under the circumstances revealed here by the character Raul Dândi, as is the death in jail of a train robber who was accused of the murder of the engineer with his girlfriend as an accomplice. The two local newspapers, *The Intransigent* and the *Benguela Journal*, reported on the facts of the cases in great detail. Just a few years ago there were issues of these newspapers in the municipal library. Recently I was no longer able to find the ones that reported directly on the case, a question of time and the negligence of whoever consulted them last. But in some part of the world these newspapers probably still exist.)

The novels' criticisms of the repetition of political forms of control between the colonial past and the kleptocratic present are cast as fictionalized repetitions of historical facts. The implicit charge to the reader to verify the facts in copies of the newspapers that must exist somewhere in the world implies a similar charge to the reader to examine and acknowledge the parallel historical and fictional plotting of colonialist tropes—as the narrator, pseudo-author, and author do in speaking directly to the reader. Genre deformation through satire and pastiche results not only in the consciousness-raising that many readers have come to expect from authors in places of former colonization, but in an injunction to the reader to take charge of the course of the narrative future.

Pepetela's Jaime Bunda novels register their post–Cold War disappointment in the overlapping citation of pre-revolutionary texts and styles and the post-1990s influx of American and English-language cultural products, signaling a repetition of the terms under which third-world revolutionary transformation was imagined and enacted. Much of the evidence of these past stages of horizontal solidarities remains blunted or invisible in the novels—as in the details of the Cuban-educated Inspector Kinanga's past—in favor of Jaime Bunda's enthusiasm for the material evidence of the new, global, capitalist order. Both Pepetela's and Padura's examinations of these new incarnations of imperial pasts, in their calls to return to the historical archive, are also oblique calls to re-expose these histories and potentially open the possibility of new kinds of solidarities in and from the Global South in the future.

Epilogue

At Cuba's 2013 International Book Fair in Havana, Angola was the Invited Country of Honor. Included among the literary and cultural events was a film series about the war in Angola, featuring *O Herói* and the Cuban films *La guerra en Angola* (1976) (*The War in Angola*), *Angola, victoria de la esperanza* (1976) (*Angola, Victory of Hope*), *Cabinda* (1977), *Caravana* (1988) (*Caravan*), *Kangamba*, and *Sumbe* (2011). At every showing I attended at the Multicine Infanta, there were apparent veterans in the audience, often commenting out loud to each other about their memories of weapons, aircraft, places, and people. One important Cuban film was absent from the series, however, though it is the one that Juan Antonio García Borrero argues had the most "international resonance" among films about Cuba's internationalist missions (110). It is a film that captures the dissonance between the official narratives of heroic sacrifice and the ambiguity that the island community often felt about the missions abroad, especially the families of those who served.

Emilio Óscar Alcalde's *El encanto del regreso* (1991) (*The Enchantment of Return*) won the 1991 Caracol Prize for best film from the UNEAC at its only public showing in Cuba (García Borrero 110). In *El encanto del regreso*, Roberto, an internationalist soldier who has been serving abroad, returns home to many familial disappointments: his son has dropped out of college and spends his time repairing motorcycles, his daughter attempts suicide after Roberto throws her boyfriend out of the house, his father seems more interested in his pet cat than in the family, and his wife works tirelessly to keep the household running with little help from the others. Roberto's one-on-one encounters with his family members suggest a constellation of dissonances as he struggles to reintegrate into domestic life. In one emblematic scene, we see Roberto and his wife Teresa seated at the family dining table as the camera recedes from the table to a higher-angle shot while the son, daughter, and grandfather, rather than sitting to eat together, come and go from the table, in and out of the frame. Intimate and close-up shots of the family members and their small and large conflicts dominate the film. The effect the director creates by building the film around the interlinked series of encounters among different family members, almost entirely inside the family home, is one of suffocation and miscommunication, as much as intimate familiarity. This style functions as a formal counterpoint to the grandiose narratives told about the internationalist missions and Cuba's central place in global decolonization and third-world revolution that dominated print, television, and film media.

El encanto del regreso thus relies on a series of contextual histories that remain implicit in the film: Cuba's internationalist missions in Angola and elsewhere between the 1960s and the 1980s, the news and entertainment that arrive to people in their homes through the media's one-way transmission, the way that Cubans experienced the war in Africa at home on the island, and the perspective of women and the intimate space of the home as a counterpoint to the virile socialist New Man, the model of the ideal revolutionary. In fact, we could see the film as systematically de-heroicizing the internationalist hero. The film accomplishes this effect by simultaneously humanizing Roberto as a hypercritical, frustrated father who loves his family but struggles to understand them, and by focusing on the other family members in their own personal battles. This critical lens, in Juan Antonio García Borrero's estimation, is the likely reason that the film was suppressed and has never been distributed (111).

Late in the film, again at the dinner table, the family's frustrations explode as Roberto laments his "hija loca" (crazy daughter) and his "hijo delincuente" (delinquent son), the reality of which he accuses his wife of having kept out of the letters she has sent him, "¡cartas mentirosas, cartas de mierda!" (letters that lie, bullshit letters!). The scene ends when Roberto receives a phone call informing him that he will soon be mobilized, leaving his family once again. Roberto's foreshadowed departure, rather than resolving the family's tensions, threatens to reproduce the processes of disconnection and estrangement. The film's staging of representation—the "letters that lie"—draws our attention to the many ways in which the layered mediation brings forward the characters' frustrated communication and memories and experiences that are impossible to transmit. The film's formal techniques emphasize historical and affective disjunctions emblematic of the disappointment that predominates the post–Cold War period, but also how these works often propose ethical gestures of empathy. *El encanto del regreso* thus demonstrates how the legacies of Cuba's south-south solidarities are fundamental to understanding the broader patterns of post-Cold War culture.

I have not been able to see the end of *El encanto del regreso*. I know of no publicly available copies of the film in libraries or other institutions, and am unaware of any public screenings of the film since 1991. The director,

Emilio Alcalde, most generously supplied me with a DVD copy when I wrote him about this project. The DVD was somehow damaged, and my university's dedicated digital media and library staff was able to recover all of the film except the final six minutes. Alcalde summarized the final scene to me in an email, in which Roberto leaves for his next mission, but "se queda pensativo, dudoso" (remains pensive, doubting) ("Re: Pregunta").

What is striking to me is the way in which the unexpected technological failure of the DVD has indefinitely suspended the cultural activity of sense-making of this period of transition by deferring my *visual* access to the film's conclusion. My frustrated visual access to the final scene has been dis-appointed from the director's narration of it: the damaged DVD becomes an unexpected reverberation on a personal level of the feeling that pervades the film. *El encanto del regreso* is a film that reveals the intimate dimensions of familial disappointments as a result of the internationalist missions. It was suppressed at a time when Cuba was still reeling from the public shock of Arnaldo Ochoa's confession and rapid execution, and Cuba's sudden "disappointment" from its Global South leadership role as withdrawal of all Cuban personnel from Angola was enforced as a stipulation of the US-brokered cessation of hostilities with South Africa. I thus read the damaged DVD as an apt figure for the deferral of a publicly accessible representation of this other side of the internationalist missions, a parallel on a miniscule scale to the film's suppression and the larger disillusionment and disappointments that, for example, prevent Iván in Padura's *El hombre que amaba a los perros* from bringing to completion his own text of historical reckoning. This inadvertent moment of suspended legibility is an unexpected symptom that can help us read the more pervasive public silences around this aspect of the period of Global South solidarities.

The Cuban and Angolan novels and films I have analyzed in this book reveal how the literary and cinematic techniques and forms of disappointment continue to register the residue of past enthusiasm for third-world solidarity and shared leftist political projects in the Global South. The forms of the works I have considered are shaped by figures of doubling and multiplicity—allegory, pastiche, satire, and irony. The feeling of disappointment is discernable in the differences among iterations, citations, and displacements inherent to these devices. However, these figures of multiplicity also open new sites of meaning-making for literature and film. Authors and filmmakers who create narratives of disappointment thus posit a range of political positions arising from historical disenchantment and the historical fact of living through the crises of the post-1989 eras. These narratives in turn avoid characterizing contemporary Cuba and Angola solely in terms of unmitigated postcolonial and postsocialist catastrophe. Instead, they search for new sites of meaningful social transformation, seek reconciliation among divided communities, insist on the acknowledgment of historical silences, and propose a return to the archive as among the ethical possibilities of literature in the contemporary era.

One outcome of this study is a new sense for the variety of techniques that writers and filmmakers employ as they interrogate the legacies of third-world solidarity and anti-colonial allegiance in narratives published between the end of the twentieth century and the beginning of the twenty-first. These texts implicitly reference aesthetics, figures, and works associated with revolutionary enthusiasm and anti-colonial ideologies in order to signal the gaps between dreamed and lived realities. These works thus also highlight the reproduction of pre-revolutionary colonial exploitation and censorship, and the ongoing effects of war and social violence. Cardoso's two novels enlist two kinds of silences: first, the MPLA's collective refusal to acknowledge and reckon with the catastrophic purges following Nito Alves's failed coup attempt in 1977 and the fracturing of the social body as the civil war extended into three decades; and second, the silences and secrets signaled but not revealed in the literary text that mark knowledge guarded among the people. Cardoso's novels celebrate the creative multiplicity of Angolan Portuguese and simultaneously enact textual reticence as two interlinked strategies of reckoning with the collective trauma of the past. The implied multiplicity of pasts, presents, and futures inscribed through these textual forms suggest, therefore, the plasticity of narrative as an answer to the open question of how to deal with these disappointments.

Angolan and Cuban directors and writers make other uses of techniques of doubling and restaging. In film, familial doublings make visible the urge to mourn the loss of revolutionary solidarity. In *O Herói*, they signal the breach between national leadership and the masses, while in *Kangamba*, citation of early revolutionary cinematic styles and the staging of the revolution's charge to document its social transformations reveal that these forms no longer register the revolutionary feelings in the 2000s that they did in the 1960s and 1970s. The Cuban film thus manifests its disappointment not internally to its diegesis, but rather through its poetics and between the context of collective disillusionment with the war and the film's redemptive gesture of reestablishing a message of collective sacrifice and solidarity. Eliseo Alberto's *Caracol Beach* and J. E. Agualusa's *O Ano em que Zumbi Tomou o Rio* each search for techniques by which to reconcile the deep social fractures that have resulted from post-revolutionary political divisions. Alberto's exiled protagonist imagines his impossible return to the island through the ritual devotion to the orisha Babalu Ayé, while Agualusa's Francisco helps to restage Angola's incomplete revolution in Rio de Janeiro's favelas, seen as racialized internal colonies. For both Alberto and Agualusa, the interpenetration of other literary texts, artistic styles, genres, and voices strategically perform ideological and aesthetic heterodoxy, and enact Alberto's call to "clemency" through their eclectic textual excess.

As we have seen, Alberto and Agualusa's typically postmodern textual exuberance establishes the basis for a broader and more heterogeneous literary archive from which to build an understanding of the disappointments of war and political fracturing. Padura and Pepetela explicitly call for a return to the historical and the archive as a way of addressing the historical asynchronicity of the Global North and the Global South. They thus remind us of the relevance of the terms under which Cuba and Angola's horizontal solidarities were forged in the mid-twentieth century. Padura's *El hombre que amaba a los perros* examines the implications of the two rhetorical foundations for Cuba's allegiance with the Third World—its colonial history and its economic marginality—in its relationship with the Soviet Union, ultimately casting Cuba as the victim of Soviet coloniality. For Padura, excavating the historical and literary archives reveals the destructive nature of this past complicity. Pepetela calls for the reader to return to the pre-independence archive to untangle the mutual instantiation of Angola's pre- and post-independence ruling class, and the oligarchical elite's concomitant reproduction of the exploitive practices of both Angola's colonial past and its globalized present. These Angolan and Cuban narratives thus encode a more complex and nuanced understanding of the Cold War as experienced in the Global South in order to understand cultural expression since 1989. Importantly, post–Cold War literature and cinema is not coded solely with the politics of Cuba and Angola's vertical relationships to Europe and the United States, but also through interlinked horizontal relationships and collectively experienced disappointments that are only recently coming into public conversation.

Recent literary works by younger Cuban and Angolan writers emphasize the necessity of understanding this interlinked history. Their texts continue to evidence the residue of Global South solidarities and resultant disappointment, although they often also encode alternative affective relationships to these pasts. These works tend to decenter the experience of the wartime veteran and revolutionary hero to focus instead on how the war was experienced at home, especially by the families and children of internationalist soldiers and workers. In this sense, they extend Alcalde's suppressed portrayal of the war at home in *El encanto del regreso*, and thus also occupy a space between Cardoso's evocation of the people living on the periphery of the war and Pepetela's caustic criticism of the historical amnesia of the opportunistic present. Angolan Ondjaki (Ndalu de Almeida; b. 1978) and Cuban Karla Suárez (b. 1969), have both written about Cuba and Angola's entangled histories from the perspective of children who lived its consequences. Ondjaki's autobiographical novel *Bom dia camaradas* (2001) (*Good Morning Comrades*), narrated from the perspective of a school-age child, takes place in the final year before Cuba withdrew from Angola and portrays the protagonist's Cuban teachers with fondness and appreciation for the model of generosity and solidarity they represent to their students. Suárez's *El hijo del héroe* (2017) (*The Son of the Hero*), published as I finished drafting this book, vacillates between the protagonist's past as a child in Havana during the 1970s and 1980s and his present in Lisbon, beginning from the day he receives the news that his father has been killed in Angola.[1] In these two paradigmatic portrayals of the second generation to live through the consequences of the war, the two protagonists accompany the ideological and political unmooring of the post-1989 transition from the perspective of young people who are not able to make sense of what they have seen, heard, and experienced. Emilio Alcalde's film from 1991 prefigures these two novels' strategies of highlighting the clash between official narratives of wartime action and the perspectives of those who are at its center.

Ondjaki's *Bom dia camaradas* and Karla Suárez's *El hijo del héroe* use different strategies to continue the conversation that Alcalde's film initiates, addressing the public silences around precisely the transition from the 1980s to the post–Cold War world and offering new affective engagements with this past. Ondjaki's novel makes use of a child first-person narrator named Ndalu, a perspective which functions as a counterpoint to various protagonists' and narrators' perceptions in the other novels and films I have analyzed in this book: those disillusioned with the past or complicit in its erasure. However, Ondjaki also portrays Ndalu's simplified understanding of the complex political world which he inhabits, his affection for his Cuban teachers and his family, as well as the solidarity built among his neighbors and schoolmates as an artifact of a fleeting period of faith that the dreamworlds of the independence period might still be realized. As the author has repeatedly pointed out in interviews, he was born in an Angola already independent: independence is, for him, literally and figuratively a "family legacy" since his parents met fighting the Portuguese (Santillán Sábado). His observation elsewhere that the child narrator also has an allegorical function for a young nation implies, nonetheless, a double perception that echoes the pathos of Cardoso's young character Hermínio, disappeared in 1977 for suspected factionism. In *Bom dia camaradas*, the children's enthusiasm for the ideals of solidarity and equality serves equally to indict the cynicism and opportunism of a political class that has already abandoned the project of constructing a society that practices those values. As Ondjaki notes in 2006, "Eu acho que nós, os miúdos que estavam na escola e que participavam nos comícios, nas actividades políticas, ouvíamos certas coisas em que acreditávamos e que as pessoas que nos diziam já não acreditavam" (Henighan "Uma entrevista" 368) (I think that we, the children who studied in school and participated in rallies, in political activities, we heard certain things that we believed, and that the people who were telling them to us no longer believed).

In this way, *Bom dia camaradas* forms a continuity with the project in which writers of prior generations engage: that of capturing the overlapping structures of enthusiasm and disappointment, which in Ondjaki's incarnation characterizes the Cuban teachers' presence and final departure as a metaphor for the wholesale historical transition of the early 1990s. In Phillip Rothwell's analysis of the novel, the Cubans represent the last vestiges of possibility for the transformations of socialism that disappear with them: "The effective expulsion of Cubans from Angola embodied the death of the revolution, and the nation's capitulation to Western interests" ("The Authenticity" 244). Nonetheless, Ondjaki refuses to characterize his own political position as one of disillusionment. Rather, he insists on "incerteza," (uncertainty), even in later novels that are more critical of the Angolan underclasses' precarious survival (Henighan "Uma entrevista" 368). This sense of uncertainty about both the past and the present also permeates Suárez's *El hijo del héroe*. Like *Bom dia camaradas*, Suárez's novel portrays the generation growing up in the 1980s as one trapped in a period of historical contingency. This generation, born after the first decade of Cuba's transformation, does not feel indebted to the revolution as their parents had been, but, like Alberto's Beto and Padura's Iván, has internalized its values. For the novel's protagonist Ernesto, whose father disappears in Angola when Ernesto is a child, it is these values that are placed in crisis, not directly by the conflict itself, but by the collective process of silencing public discourse about Cuba's internationalist missions.

Suárez's project is similar to Ondjaki's: one of breaking the silence, of documenting the internationalist missions and the inheritances of third-world solidarity from the perspective of the youths who experienced it from the island. Virtually none of Suárez's novel is set in Angola; Angola appears only indirectly through the memories and dialogue of other characters who reveal scattered snippets of information that as an adult Ernesto takes upon himself to collect as part of a blog. Rather, like Padura's tracking of Trotsky and Mercader on the margins of the Soviet empire, Ernesto retraces the disparate geographies that are at once peripheral and central to Angola's past: from his childhood in Havana, he moves to Berlin and then to Lisbon, before the novel ends as he is aboard a plane destined for Luanda. A conversation in Berlin among Ernesto and his Cuban friends in 2002, the year of UNITA leader Jonas Savimbi's death and the subsequent end of the Angolan civil war, rehearses the centrality and yet precarity of this palimpsestic history in the memories and archives of the international community:

En un momento, me pregunté en alta voz para cuánta gente en Berlín aquella noticia de la mañana, aquel nombre, Savimbi, significaba algo.

—Y sin embargo—dijo Felipe—, en esta ciudad Europa se repartió África en el siglo diecinueve.

—Y aquí tumbaron el muro de la guerra fría—agregó Baby Ranger.

—¿Y pa' qué los cubanos se metieron en esa guerra, a ver?— comentó el Vlado.

—¿Y por qué coño no nos retiramos antes?—dije yo, antes de pasar la botella para seguir bebiendo mientras contemplábamos el despertar de un Berlín calmado y frío. (237)

(In that moment, I asked myself out loud how many people in Berlin that morning had heard the news, that name, Savimbi, and it meant something.

—Even though—Felipe said,—it was in this city that Europe divided Africa up in the nineteenth century.

—And where they brought down the cold war wall—added Baby Ranger.

—And I wonder why the Cubans ever got involved in that war? Vlado remarked.

—And why the fuck we didn't get out sooner?—I said, before passing the bottle so we could keep drinking while we contemplated Berlin waking up calm and cold.)

Throughout the novel, the characters identify various "ends" to the Cold War history in which the Cuban and Angolan revolutions, the two nations' allegiances and antagonisms, and the movement of their texts and people have been inscribed: Cuito Cuanavale, the decisive 1988 battle in Angola where South Africa admitted defeat, the fall of the Berlin Wall, and in the final paragraphs of the novel, the reestablishment of diplomatic relations between the United States and Cuba in 2015 (263; 237; 339). However, the novel—like the analysis presented in this book—suggest that these "ends" are also gestures of opening. The structures of feeling that accompany the transitions away from these "ends" point to new paths of historical and affective reckoning.

Similar to Ondjaki's refusal to identify with disillusionment, the feelings that Suárez's novel offers in response to this history are compassion and relief, rather than cynicism or fatalism. For Ernesto, these "ends" also release him from an obsession with interrogating the past when he discovers that his father has been living in Luanda since his presumed death: "A mi padre en realidad lo mataron y no sé cómo será el que voy a encontrar allá abajo, lo único que espero, al menos, es que su nariz se parezca a la mía. Lo demás son recuerdos, esa mole invisible de imágenes que te aplasta y que, al final, son la vida que pasó. Pero después de cada cosa siempre nos queda el futuro. Así que allí vamos. Al futuro" (340) (In reality they killed my father, and I don't know what the one I'm going to meet down there will be like, the only thing I hope for, at least, is that his nose looks like mine. The rest is memories, that invisible mass of images that crushes you and, in the end, are life gone by. But after everything we are always left with the future. So there we go. To the future). In order to arrive at this moment where Ernesto releases his future from the prison of the past, he must systematically investigate, interview, and order whatever information he can find about his father's disappearance and the wider conflict that claimed him. It is this process of accumulation and organization which makes this history legible to him, and, through Suárez's duplication of that process in the novel, for the reader. This strategy of legibility, however, is only one among many that authors who employ techniques of disappointment use to claim the narrative text as a privileged site for negotiating the contested legacies of south-south solidarities during and after the Cold War.

Each of the texts of disappointment analyzed here ends with a similar gesture of opening to Ernesto's call to move onward toward an undefined future. Their figures of doubling and multiplicity invite us to participate in the work of the imagination, as a project both for redressing the silences and violences of the past and for escaping from singular narratives of post–Cold War capitulation and postcolonial catastrophe. These narrative forms capture the feelings of disappointment that characterize an era of transition, when the past and the present are still coming into view, and thus open to the possibility of many futures that could be constructed from these pasts. Tracing the axis between Cuba and Angola demonstrates the wider implications of this example of Global South solidarity for understanding literature of the post–Cold War world, beyond and between narratives of superpowers and empires.

Notes

Introduction

1. MPLA: Movimento Popular para a Libertação de Angola (Popular Movement for the Liberation of Angola).

2. *Na Cidade Vazia* was the first Angolan film produced after the Angolan state film initiatives introduced under the revolutionary one-party government in the 1970s were shuttered after only a few years, discussed in more detail in chapter 2. I therefore see the use of the two media as explicitly evocative of two different historical and ideological moments.

3. Of course, Angola was not Cuba's first mission in support of African independence movements. It had offered strategic support to revolutionaries in Algeria during the early 1960s, and Guevara's failed mission in the Congo took place in 1965.

4. Though the text of the agreement signed by the presidents of the two writers' unions promises publication of literature by authors from the other nation, Don Burness has found that during the 1970s and 1980s, Angola displayed more interest in publishing Cuban writers than vice versa (60–61).

5. The notion of revolution as a contagion has its origins, of course, in the eighteenth-through-nineteenth-century Age of Revolutions. It is in the twentieth century, however, that this discourse acquires a renewed fervor: Guevara's "one, two, many Vietnams" ("Mensaje al Tricontinental") is seen as articulating a theory of iterability of revolution posited as the positive and inevitable outcome of revolutionary enthusiasm; conversely, as Buck-Morss notes, the "threat" of the "spread" of Bolshevism and communism was a mainstay of the United States' and its allies' rhetoric and interventionist foreign policies in the post-WWII era (2–7).

6. Casamayor-Cisneros argues that "uncertainty" is perhaps the most universal factor linking post-Soviet Cuban literature, locating in this literature a postmodern "reencantamiento" with chaos and irrationality that stems from the failure of politics to continue inspiring strong feelings among some of the most recent Cuban authors (35–36).

7. See especially Brian Massumi's *Parables for the Virtual*, where Massumi defends this distinction (28), and Rei Terada's *Feeling in Theory*, in which Terada argues that all emotions are subjectless (3).

8. In his examination of the "erotics of disappointment" in the work of Hong Kong filmmaker Wong Kar-wai, Abbas analyzes the features of asynchronicity and of repetition as central to a visual poetics of disappointment. For Abbas, layering together visual symbols of different "historical grids" results in a cultural landscape where "the multiple meanings do not cohere or support each other. We never find synesthesia, but always disjunction, dissemination, fugue . . . The image . . . misses its appointment with meaning" (44–45). Abbas is interested in uncovering a particular politics of coloniality in films, and a filmmaker, seen as decidedly apolitical. The context of the Angolan and Cuban works, however, is different. Rather than apolitical, they might be seen as suffering from the over-determination of the histories of revolutionary politics on critical receptions of their work in the international sphere. Thus, formal techniques that signal "missed appointments with meaning" in the novels and films analyzed here are responsive to, and frequently subversive of, reductive framings of their encoded politics.

9. My use of "emergent" means both recent histories that contemporary writers and filmmakers are beginning to interrogate, and, following Abbas, refers to the global circulation of these cultural products beyond their respective national and often linguistic spheres. There has been an increasing interest in Angolan authors among Portuguese and Brazilian writers during the turn of the twenty-first century, as well as some limited translation of their works into other languages, including English. While, of course, Cuban authors had been included in the mid-twentieth-century Boom of Latin American literature, due to the legal limitations that the revolutionary authorities placed on Cuban artists and writers during the first three decades of the revolution, the legalization of foreign publishing contracts during the Special Period resulted in what Whitfield calls a "new Cuban Boom" as Cuban literature found market success among international readers.

10. In his analysis of African novels, Kwame Anthony Appiah, for example, argues that postcolonial works are incommensurable with the relativism of postmodernism, and postmodernism's tendency to reduce its delegitimation of Western rationality to an aesthetics. For Appiah, postcolonial works cannot be postmodern because they maintain a position of political engagement with a universal ethics. Similarly, Cuban critic Margarita Mateo Palmer argues that "hay, en efecto, más de un rasgo característico de la cultura latinoamericana, derivado de su condición colonial y dependiente—y no exactamente de las influencias recibidas en la segunda mitad de este siglo—, que podría considerarse posmoderno en la actualidad. Desde esta perspectiva, la recepción europea y norteamericana de los modelos supuestamente posmodernista de la literatura latinoamericana . . . resulta insuficiente, desde el punto vista epistemológico, para la literatura latinoamericana" (127) (there is, in fact, more than one characteristic feature of Latin American culture, derived from its colonial and dependent condition—and not exactly from influences received in the second half of this century—that could currently be considered postmodern. From this perspective, the European and Latin American reception of supposedly postmodern models of Latin American literature . . . turn out to be insufficient, from an epistemological standpoint, for Latin American literature).

11. Lyotard extrapolates the possibility of an enthusiasm-like glimpse of the sublime (which he calls a "communitarian sense") initiated in a diversity of different politico-aesthetic events. Like Kant, who expressed horror at the violence of the revolution and ensuing terror, Lyotard grapples with how to make sense of horrifying events at a time when the teleologies and accompanying metanarrative language that allows linkages among the Ideas suggested by these events are no longer possible, noting as examples the horrors of Auschwitz, the Soviet gulags, or the Prague Spring: "The occasions for this highly cultivated 'communitarian sense' would be called: Auschwitz, an abyss opened up when an object capable of validating the phrase of the Idea of human rights must be presented; Budapest 1956, an abyss opened up before the phrase of the Idea of the rights of peoples; Kolyma, an abyss opened up before the phrase of the (illusory) speculative concept of the dictatorship of the proletariat; in 1968, an abyss opened up before the phrase of 'democratic' illusion, which hid the heterogeneity between power and sovereignty" (63). As a philosopher of the postmodern, he is concerned with how to link the "phrases," or units of communication, in the absence of the metanarratives (especially in *The Differend*, where the ideas presented in *Enthusiasm* are developed more fully), and thus how to adjudicate concepts of justice and ethics.

12. Guevara's text theorizes the socialist New Man, the new socialist subject whose intellect would be free of the "sins" of the bourgeois and colonial past. In Guevara's essay, Rojas attributes to Sartre the thesis of United States neocolonialism in Cuba, and to Fanon the notion of the public spectacle of violence as a mechanism of decolonization. Similarly, he locates the idea of the Cuban Revolution as the historical mechanism that would pull Cuba out from underdevelopment to Charles Wright Mills's *Listen, Yankee: The Revolution in Cuba* (1960).

13. In 1898, Spain lost Cuba and Puerto Rico, its last American colonies, after nearly a century of independence wars in Latin America; Cuba was established as an independent republic in 1902. As the international tolerance for direct colonial occupation of Africa soured in the decades after WWII, Portugal came under increasing international scrutiny for its ongoing occupation of Angola and the other Lusophone African colonies, at a time when other African countries were winning their own independence through the 1950s and 1960s.

14. Douglass Wheeler and René Pélissier report that UNESCO estimated the illiteracy rate in Angola at 97 percent in 1958, three years before the anti-colonial war against the Portuguese began (199). David Birmingham outlines the many ways in which colonial policies destabilized social relations and local economies before independence (Chabal and Birmingham 137–48).

15. Portugal's colonial bureaucracy kept detailed archives on Cuba's activities in Africa, including both firsthand reports by informants and published media. For example, one informant for Portugal's colonial intelligence service writes in 1967: "É grande por demasiado evidente, o interesse de CASTRO, principalmente depois da Conferência Tricontinental, pelo continente africano. Este interesse segue o padrão da revolução mundial comunista. A maior parte dos enviados cubanos são negros, constituindo este factor, para CUBA, uma enorme vantagem. Isto elimina qualquer preconceito racial que possa haver por parte dos africanos, e tal pode conceder

primazia aos cubanos sobre chineses e sobre russos" (*Política em relação a África*). (Though excessively obvious, Castro's interest in the African continent is great, principally after the Tricontinental Congress. This interest follows the pattern of world communist revolution. The majority of the Cubans sent are black, constituting an enormous advantage for Cuba. This eliminates any racial prejudice that there could be on the part of the Africans, and thus could concede superiority to the Cubans over the Chinese and the Russians).

16. The full title of the congress was "Congreso Cultural de La Habana: Reunión de intelectuales de todo el mundo sobre problemas de Asia, África y América Latina" (Cultural Congress of Havana: Meeting of Intellectuals from the whole world about the problems of Asia, Africa and Latin America). See Andrade's essay "Culture et Lutte Armée," published in the journal *Révolution Africaine* after the 1967 preparatory seminar for the 1968 Congress, as well as his remarks delivered at the Congress, "Culture et independence nationale/Culture et lute armée."

17. This is the thesis of Retamar's 1971 essay *Calibán*.

18. FNLA: Frente Nacional de Libertação de Angola (National Liberation Front of Angola): UNITA: União Nacional para a Independência Total de Angola (National Union for the Total Liberation of Angola).

19. Henighan argues that because of the Soviet preference and support for the coup, Alves's uprising "would have represented a victory of European imperialism, in the guise of Soviet communism, over political structures created in response to local conditions in the Caribbean and Africa" ("Cuban Fulcrum" 238).

20. Fernando Arenas cites the numbers of those killed at twenty-eight thousand, with another three thousand disappeared by the MPLA in the aftermath of the coup attempt (170); Dalila Cabrita Mateus and Álvaro Mateus arrive at a similar estimate of thirty thousand though they note that the numbers vary wildly, with some sources asserting as many as eighty thousand people killed and disappeared.

21. The exiled Cuban journalist and writer Norberto Fuentes has made explosive charges implicating the upper echelons of revolutionary leadership in the scandal and portrays Ochoa as a scapegoat in his *Dulces guerreros cubanos* (1999) while Christine Hatzky calls Ochoa's trial a "show trial" (310 n. 76).

22. Suárez's 2017 novel *El hijo del héroe* deals with the Cuban generation of who were children during the war, while Yoss has repeatedly criticized the war as a source of generational trauma for the *novísimos*, the generation of writers coming of age in the 1990s.

23. Both Fornets are also concerned with bridging the divide among Cuban writers living on and off the island.

Chapter 1

1. See, for example, Mata, "*Maio, Mês de Maria*: as águas da memória em movimento"; Secco, *A Magia das Letras Africanas*; Olimpia dos Santos, *A Alegórica "Mãe, Materno Mar" Angolana*; Cesar, "*Kuatiça O Ngoma!*, and Kandjimbo, "O social e o religioso em dois romances de Boaventura Cardoso."

2. The designation of *assimilado* was not purely a social designation; it was a legal distinction offered to those few African colonial subjects who could demonstrate cultural, religious, and linguistic "assimilation" to Portuguese values and customs. It was accompanied by access to educational and employment opportunities not available to the majority of the colonized, though, as João Segunda's metaphorical last name indicates, these privileges did not erase the rigid racial and cultural hierarchies of colonizer and colonized.

3. Our Lady of Fátima is the name given to the apparitions of Mary to three Portuguese children in Fátima, Portugal in 1917. Three secrets were entrusted to the children to be revealed later; while in the 1940s, one of the children revealed the first two, concerning visions of hell and the ends of world wars, the Vatican held the third secret until 2000. The revelation that the third secret involved the persecution of Christians did not solve the controversy; some believers continue to doubt that the account entrusted to the Vatican contains the entire prophecy revealed to the children.

4. Rancière opposes his use of the "people" to Michael Hardt and Antonio Negri's "multitude," as developed in *Empire* (2000) and *Multitude* (2005). Rancière argues that the idealized concept of multitude fails to escape the traditional Marxist conceptualization of political subjectivity as arising from economic identifiers and, in its assertion of universalism, fails to account for political contestation and refusal. He critiques the concept of "multitude" as a manifestation of "metapolitics," or the interpretation of a political subjectivity from the vantage point of the existing order, rather than imagining the grounds for a new order.

5. Rancière uses the example of nineteenth-century French philosopher Pierre-Simon Ballanche's rewriting of Livy's account of the withdrawal of the plebs. In Rancière's reading, Ballanche draws out the performative capacity of speech in generating a political situation through which the people can enact greater equality: "Politics exists because those who have no right to be counted as speaking beings make themselves of some account, setting up a community by the fact of placing in common a wrong that is nothing more than this very confrontation, the contradiction of two worlds in a single world: the world where they are and the world where they are not, the world where there is something 'between' them and those who do not acknowledge them as speaking beings who count and the world where that is nothing" (27).

6. In an interview from 2011, Pepetela speaks of the aftermath of the coup in a way that exemplifies this reticence: he refutes the interviewer's suggestion that he was involved in the detention and torture of victims and says he does not like to speak of the coup, as only the MPLA—and not him—knows the whole truth. Though he was a part of the MPLA leadership in 1977 he points out that there was insufficient information available to him and others: "Não se sabia . . . Havia zunzuns, havia muitos presos, era o que se sabia. Pensava que ia haver um julgamento, como tinha havido para os mercenários. Afinal não houve julgamento nenhum . . . Toda a gente devia ter sabido mais. E parado imediatamente os abusos que houve (" 'Não se festeja a morte de ninguém' " n/p) (No one knew . . . There was buzz, there were a lot of prisoners, that was what was known. I thought there would be a trial, as there had been for the mercenaries. In the end there was no trial. . . . Everyone should have known more. And immediately stopped the abuses that were taking place.)

7. Translations are my own. Though I have done my best to suggest in the English examples the type of linguistic innovation and typically Angolan language use that Cardoso captures in his prose, because of the complexity of his novelistic language, my translations have privileged comprehensibility for English-speaking readers.

8. Peres discusses Vieira's refusal during many years to provide glossaries or translations of the Kimbundu language that appears in his works; his English-language translator notes that "he wrote his estórias for the very people whose language he used, adding that ignorance of musseque speech was the problem of the Portuguese colonizer, not his" (qtd. in Peres 38).

9. Here, I am referring to both the novel's portrayal of the João Segunda's sudden indoctrination into the postcolonial system, and to the MPLA's official policies of universal equality and anti-tribalism. Opposing parties and particularly UNITA, however, accused the MPLA of reinforcing the racialized system of privilege forged under the colonial regime, due to its center of power in the capital and its leadership drawn from the educated upper echelons of Angolan society. As historian David Birmingham notes, "After independence, the colonial niceties of race, pedigree, language, education, and ambition were to haunt the MPLA as it struggled to create a stable ruling establishment in the capital city. . . . The educated minority also had a political edge over the people of the far interior—whether in the south or the north—when it came to bargaining over the future of Angola. Language was power in postcolonial African politics and it was the assimilated class which spoke Portuguese, the language of command" (*A Short History* 85).

10. Nito Alves was owner of the Sambizanga soccer club (a working-class neighborhood in Luanda), and the soccer club was known as a site for discussions of Alves's ideas.

11. The theoretical contours of the critique of postcolonial reproduction of the forms and styles of colonial domination are well established. Fanon's chapter on national culture in *The Wretched of the Earth* points precisely to this phenomenon as a characteristic of the postcolonial bourgeoisie; Mata notes that the political form that this reproduction takes in *Maio, Mês de Maria* is precisely that of revolutionary "oligarchy of bureaucracy" ("*MMM*: as águas" 149).

12. In these parallel perspectives on the youths' reappearance, there are echoes of the techniques of the Latin American marvelous real and magical realism. For example, in Alejo Carpentier's 1949 novel *El reino de este mundo* (*The Kingdom of this World*) the death of the slave Mackandal is perceived in two different ways, narrated simultaneously. The white slave owners see Mackandal burned at the stake, while the slaves forced to watch the public execution see him transform himself and fly away.

13. Batucada is traditional drumming; canjica is a dish made with corn and palm oil.

14. Of course, many of the criticisms of the MPLA have focused precisely on its regional and urban appeal. Sousa Jamba's novel *Patriots* (1990) centers its critique of Angola's postcolonial wars in part on the regional, ethnic, and linguistic allegiances that defined party affiliation for many Angolans.

15. Portugal has made many of the archives from the period of the Estado Novo dictatorship available to the public, permitting a complex view into the organizations,

individuals, and information considered threatening or worthy of surveillance, including prophetic movements. A report on the Tokoist church between 1961 and 1965, for example, warns of the Tokoists' politically subversive messages in invoking the exile and enslavement of the Jews to describe their own situation under Portuguese control. Other documents warn of the capacity of prophetic and other Protestant churches to act as cover for revolutionary activities, or to siphon money to anti-colonial subversives.

16. Blanes and Sarró point out that the anti-religious climate of the period of MPLA single-party rule has changed since the post-1990 transition in Angola, and that in the last decade of the twentieth century and the first decade of the twenty-first, charismatic and other African Christian churches have occupied an increasing public and political role and offer an African-centered alternative to the Catholic church (60–61).

17. Jeyifo sees this impasse as rooted in a number of approaches to contemporary African culture that reify racial thinking: the notion of the radical otherness of African culture, the notion of a clash between Africa and the West, and the idea of culture as the only possible bulwark against Africa's insuperable developmental lag when compared to the West. He finds in Achebe, Fanon, and Cabral a valuable series of challenges to these approaches.

Chapter 2

1. I have not been able to confirm whether Cuito Cuanavale, the third film of the trilogy mentioned in press materials at the time of the releases of *Sumbe* and *Kangamba*, will be another fictional film. At the time this chapter was composed, no such film has been listed as a coming release or as "in production" on the website of the ICAIC. A documentary and multimedia project, "Cuito Cuanavale: Una gesta más allá del tiempo," directed by Olivia Marín Álvarez and Susana Pérez Gil, is available online and was shown following *Kangamba* by the Cuban Embassy in India in Delhi on May 11, 2014 (CubaMINREX).

2. For a thorough discussion of Cuba's film history, including films made about movements in Latin America, Africa, and elsewhere in the world during the 1960s and 1970s, see Chanan's *Cuban Cinema* and Ambrosio Fornet's "Apuntes para el cine cubano de ficción."

3. For more on Cuban internationalism, see Krull, Díaz-Briquets, and Huish and Blue.

4. A similar episode takes place in París's *Caravana*.

5. There are interesting differences between the portrayals of UNITA soldiers in *Kangamba* and in París's 1990 *Caravana*. While in *Caravana* Savimbi and the UNITA soldiers are vilified as murderous and violent, in *Kangamba* the portrayal of the opposition party is much more neutral, even approaching sympathy, in casting them as unfortunate puppets of a cruel South African regime.

6. I cannot say with any certainty whether there are direct references to specifically Angolan cinema in *O Herói*. As Moorman indicates, the limited tradition of post-independence Angolan film is largely unavailable to the public.

7. Sarah Maldoror (Sarah Ducados), born to Guadeloupean parents in 1938, was heavily involved in the anticolonial and revolutionary movements of the 1960s and 1970s, and her large body of work is consistently dedicated to questions of race and injustice, as well as celebrating significant cultural figures of African descent.

Chapter 3

1. *Caracol Beach* was awarded the Premio Alfaguara (Alfaguara Prize) in 1998.

2. The term "hyper-real" is coined in Jean Baudrillard's *Simulacres et Simulation* (*Simulacra and Simulation*) (1981), and further developed in Umberto Eco's "Il costume di casa" ("Travels in Hyperreality"). Baudrillard posits the hyper-real as the postmodern condition, where the simulated image delivered through mass media portends the end of politics as understood in the modern era—those founded around ideology, class, etc. Martin Weiss argues that in Baudrillard's thought, power (here, the state) must grasp simulations—the components of hyper-reality, that is, media representations that replace external reality—and make them real in order to sustain itself (Weiss n/p). This dynamic clearly inflects Guerra's reading of state-produced hyper-real images of the Revolution.

3. As *Caracol Beach* has a published translation under the same title, page numbers will be listed for the quotes from each of the Spanish and English editions following their respective selections.

4. Thanks to David Bordwell for this insight.

5. In the English translation, Edith Grossman changes Alberto's "la defensa de Leningrado" to "The defense of Stalingrad." Both "The Siege of Leningrad" and "The Defense of Stalingrad" are episodes of the Soviet miniseries *The Unknown War* (1978); however, as the soldier's time in Angola is to begin in 1976, the series may not in fact be the referent that Alberto intended. The Soviet film *The Battle of Stalingrad*, directed by Vladimir Petrov, was released in 1949, and Robert Bird names at least five films about the Siege of Leningrad produced by the Soviet studio Lenfilm between 1944–1973 (88). *The Great Patriotic War* (1965) is a documentary directed by Roman Karmen, about the Soviet involvement in WWII.

6. Guillén Landrián was the nephew of the famed poet Nicolás Guillén, for whom he was named.

7. See, for example, the films *Guardafronteras* (1981), *Caravana* (1990), and *Kangamba* (2004) where the scene of the fallen revolutionary is staged in a manner similar to Alberto's description.

8. Pico Turquino is the highest point in Cuba. One of the tasks set to the youth brigades (Brigadas Juveniles de Trabajo Revolucionarias [BJTR]) charged with 1960's literacy campaign, among other tasks, was to climb the Pico five times as a test intended to approximate the physical demands of the revolutionaries in the Sierra Maestra.

9. The poetry citation is from Martí's poem "XLVI," in *Versos sencillos* (1891).

10. "¡Al poeta dispídanlo! /. . ./ Pero no hay / quien lo haga abrir la boca, / pero no hay / quien lo haga sonreír / cada vez que comienza el espectáculo / y brincan /

los payasos por la escena; / cuando las cacatúas / confunden el amor con el terror / y está crujiendo el escenario / y truenan los metales / y los cueros / y todo el mundo salta, / se inclina, / retrocede, / sonríe, / abre la boca / 'pues sí, / claro que sí / por supuesto que sí . . .' / y bailan todos bien, / bailan bonito, / como les piden que sea el baile." (Padilla 1, 28–50). (The poet, kick him out! . . . But no one can make him open his mouth, no one can make him smile, every time the show begins, and the clowns burst onto the scene; when the old hags confuse love with terror and the stage is creaking and the brass and the drums are booming and the whole world jumps, leans forward, back, smiles, opens their mouths, 'yes, of course, of course . . .' and they dance so well, so pretty, exactly how they are told to dance.)

11. At different time seen as dangerous "black magic" or retrograde popular belief before the Revolution, Santería was outlawed for most of the twentieth century, until it was legalized and embraced by the state as "popular folklore" in the 1990s, seen as a source of much-needed tourist dollars.

Chapter 4

1. For a discussion of Palmares as a historical regression to savagery and a threat to civilization's tenuous hold in Brazil, see Rodrigues. Historian M. M. de Freitas anticipates contemporary interpretations in citing various Portuguese and Dutch sources to argue in his 1954 history that the cities of Palmares were idyllic recreations of African civilizations that were lost or deformed by contact with European slave traders. Both Freitas and, more recently, Flávio Gomes insist on the relevance of Angolan challenges to Portuguese imperial encroachment as a fundamental but ignored element of Palmares's development and success.

2. For a summary of historical and cultural sources on Zumbi and Palmares, see J. França and Ferreira.

3. "Cazumbi" is a diminutive of "nzumbi," or "zumbi," a Kimbundu word for a spirit or ghost that has the capacity to kill.

4. Euclides is both gay and an *anão*, a term for a person of short stature. David Brookshaw interprets the character's multiple marginalizations—in his stature, his sexual orientation, and his political views—as a criticism of the limited power of the press in postcolonial Angola ("Race Relations" 166). Yet, now outside of Angola, it is Euclides who plays a primary role in shaping the international reception of the conflict, its actors and their motivations.

5. For discussions of Agualusa's engagement with the concepts of diaspora and *lusofonia*, or transnational communities built through a shared Portuguese language, see Brookshaw "Race Relations," McNee, and Melo.

6. All English translations are my own.

7. The terms "*mestiçagem*" and "*crioulidade*," the latter used especially in Angola, refer not only to the racial, linguistic, and cultural mixing that resulted from Portuguese colonial projects in the Americas and Africa, but grow out of specific ideologies that characterized Portuguese colonialism as a gentler, more open interaction with

the peoples it colonized than that of other European powers. While these ideologies were implicated in nineteenth- and twentieth-century notions of "whitening" people of color to improve their race, as well as in eugenics and scientific racism, they have sometimes (controversially) been reclaimed by more recent authors as part of counter-colonial discursive strategies. For further analysis of *mestiçagem* in Brazil see especially Freyre's *Casa-grande e senzala* (*The Masters and the Slaves*), discussed elsewhere in this chapter. For a discussion of *crioulidade* in Angola, see especially António. For a critique of these ideologies as applied to Lusophone Africa, see Andrade's "Cultura Negro-Africana e Assimilção."

8. The collection brings together a wide variety of Sousa Santos's writing on the ideas of "epistemologies of the South" written in several languages, including English and Portuguese. The translations here from Spanish to English are my own.

9. The essay "Más allá del pensamiento abismal" ("Beyond Abysmal Thought") signals a number of ways that colonial knowledge continues to organize contemporary life via a line between the "here"—that which can be known, organized, and free—and the colonial zone or abyss. Those areas that most directly apply to an analysis of *O Ano em que Zumbi Tomou o Rio* demarcate, for example, urban ghettos or slums that are read as lawless zones of violence that must be contained and are interpreted as belonging to a prior point in development or civilization (the non-contemporaneousness of the colonial world).

10. The full name of the PIDE in Portuguese is the Polícia Internacional e de Defesa do Estado (International Police and Police for the Defense of the State).

11. Freyre defends not only racial mixture's presence in Brazil but also its advantage: "It is true that, acting always upon all these clashing antagonistic forces, deadening the shock or harmonizing them, have been certain conditions peculiar to Brazil that have made for fraternization and vertical mobility: miscegenation; the dispersal of inheritances; the possibility of a frequent and easy change of profession and of residence; frequent and easy access to public office and to elevated political and social positions on the part of mestizos and natural sons; the lyric character of Portuguese Christianity; the spirit of moral tolerance; hospitality to strangers and intercommunication between the different parts of the country" (*The Masters and the Slaves* 80).

12. The term "morro" or "hill/slope," when used in the context of Rio de Janeiro, refers to the peripheral spaces in the hills above the confines of the city where the city's slums, commonly known as *favelas*, have developed.

13. The most current estimates by the Trans-Atlantic Slave Trade Database (slavevoyages.org) place the total number of enslaved Africans who were shipped to Brazil at approximately 5.4 million ("Estimates"). The number of enslaved who embarked from ports spanning the area from present-day Gabon to Angola—the area known as West Central Africa—was about 5.7 million according to the same source; Douglass Wheeler suggests that around 4 million of those were sent from present-day Angola (73).

14. "Comando Negro" is certainly additionally a reference to the Comando Vermelho, one of the infamous favela-based criminal organizations in Brazil, whose

origins were fictionalized and sensationalized in Paulo Lins's *Cidade de Deus* (*City of God*) and its later film adaptation, as well as in the 2004 film *Quase dois irmãos* (*Almost Brothers*).

15. In a lecture, Pedro Pereira has traced the ideology of Portugal's "humane" approach to slavery and to colonialism at least as far back as Hegel's *Lessons on the Philosophy of History* (1837).

16. Carlos Diegues's 1984 film *Quilombo* has been critiqued as one example of this kind of portrayal of Palmares.

17. Thanks to Eli Carter for this suggestion.

18. The prototypical example of this type of critical reading of favela narratives surrounded Carolina Maria de Jesús's *Quarto de despejo* (1960) (*Child of the Dark*), a personal narrative about the author's daily struggles in extreme poverty.

19. When I wrote an earlier version of this chapter, published in 2014 in *The Global South*, I had only had access to a poor-quality scanned version of Knopfli's text. I subsequently mis-read and mis-transcribed "acocorado" ("squatting") as "acordado" ("wakened"); this is one of the challenges of a US-based scholar working in libraries where Lusophone African works are not always readily available.

20. "The Squatting Scribe" is an Egyptian statue from between 2620–2325 BCE, currently housed at the Louvre.

21. Knopfli's poems are (certainly deliberately) selectively quoted from non-contiguous verses (Knopfli 1–2, 27–28, 42–45).

Chapter 5

1. The term "quinquenio gris" is somewhat disputed, as a number of Cuban intellectuals argue that the period of most rigid enforcement of social realist models in literature extended at least through the end of the 1970s. Padura himself, in a 2015 essay, refers to the "decenio negro," the black 10 years (*Yo quisiera ser Paul Auster* 13).

2. By narrative time, I am referring to what Paul Ricoeur calls "narrative emplotment," or the mediating internal organization of time that structures the narrative.

3. Loss explores how the view of the Soviet Union as a colonizing power is a contested reading of its influence in Cuba, noting that nostalgic memories of Soviet products, evocations of solidarity, and justifications for Stalin's methods are important aspects of post-Soviet memory in Cuba. See in particular the Introduction (3, 12–13) and chs. 3 and 5 of *Dreaming in Russian*.

4. The NKVD, the People's Commissariat for Internal Affairs, was one of the Soviet police organizations between 1934 and 1946; it was reorganized as part of the KGB in 1954.

5. In the discussion following a reading from *El hombre que amaba a los perros* in 2015 in Portland, Oregon, Padura remarked that after the publication of the novel in Cuba (he cited the scarce number of 4000 copies) people had come up to him on the street or written to thank him for providing access to a history that had been largely silenced through the end of the twentieth century in Cuba. This notion

of literature as a historical revision is evident in the formal characteristics of the novel as well, particularly in Padura's choice, across his corpus, of adopting both the crime novel and the historical novel, two of the genres most closely associated with socialist realism.

6. Padura's text refers to Trotsky throughout by his given name, Liev Davídovich, perhaps to distinguish the fictionalized narrative of his personal exile from the flattened historical figure vilified by Stalin and Stalin-allied figures through the mid-twentieth century.

7. Ponte continues that he sees this absence as an accommodation to the publishing climate in Cuba, where a more stringent criticism of Cuba's sovietization may have prevented the book from coming out on the island at all. Padura has addressed his ethical commitment to being a Cuban writer who lives in Cuba and publishes in Cuba in the introductory essay to his 2015 collection *Yo quisiera ser Paul Auster*, among other outlets.

8. The Spanish translation of Chandler's "The Man Who Liked Dogs" changes the "liked" of the English original to "amaba," or "loved." While this was likely a choice made for grammatical expediency, it also introduces what I think is an important shift in emotional intensity in the context of Padura's novel. In Chandler's short story, we have little evidence that the primary criminal does indeed "like dogs" beyond a single comment by one of his accomplices. However, in Padura's novel, the protagonists' affection for dogs has a more significant humanizing register.

9. As I have noted, Iván's admiration for Mercader's two Russian borzois initiates their encounters. Similarly, Mercader gains entry to Trotsky's compound in part by admiring Trotsky's grandson's dog.

10. There has been extensive critical debate about the political significance of Carpentier's views of revolutions in general, and the Cuban Revolution in particular, following the publication of *El siglo de las luces*. *El siglo* examines the impact of the French Revolution on the Caribbean, including the disillusionment as the Cuban protagonists witness the violence and betrayal of the revolution's precepts of liberty and equality. Despite Carpentier's insistence that the novel was completed in 1958, some critics have been intent on seeing it as Carpentier's intentional allegory for the Cuban Revolution (González Echevarría 215). González Echevarría, however, has asserted that the manuscript was unlikely to have changed in response to the early revolutionary years, since it was published before the revolution had effected its most profound changes to the political sphere (215).

11. Casamayor-Cisneros has made a similar observation about Padura's indebtedness to Carpentier, and specifically about the possibility of reading *El hombre que amaba a los perros* as "un intento de Padura por superar lagunas históricas y políticas de *La consagración de la primavera*, que recalcaba ya en su artículo del 2008 "La consagración de la primavera y la Guerra Civil española" (125 n. 2) (an effort by Padura to overcome the historical and political lacunae of *La consagración de la primavera*, which he stresses in his 2008 article "La consagración de la primavera and the Spanish Civil War").

12. The quote and page number internal to Casamayor-Cisneros's passage refer to Padura's novel *La neblina de ayer* (2005) (*Havana Fever*), in which a disillusioned

Mario Conde leaves his detective job in favor of selling secondhand books, and attempts to solve the mystery of the destiny of 1950s bolero singer Violeta del Río.

13. Ponte was reflecting on the very same hurricane, Iván, with which *El hombre que amaba a los perros* begins and ends.

14. There is a large body of work that rethinks the Eurocentric proposition that colonial spaces arrive belated to futures already experienced in the metropolis, considering both the extension and fulfillment of ideas of liberation only partially imagined in Europe, as well as atrocities and violence that are first enacted and perfected in the colonies. Particularly relevant to the histories of revolution and liberation that underwrite the experiences traced in this book are works such as C. L. R. James's *The Black Jacobins* and Susan Buck-Morss's *Hegel, Haiti and Universal History*, both of which argue that the revolutionaries of the 1804 Haitian Revolution imagined a more radical notion of Enlightenment freedom than that conceived in Europe; Césaire's assertion that the atrocities of the Holocaust had been rehearsed in the colonies, mentioned in the introduction to this book; Sousa Santos's examination of zones of abjection, examined in chapter 5; or a more recent extension of Césaire's thesis in the era of globalization in Comaroff and Comaroff's *Theory From the South*, which argues that the effects of the world-capitalist system take hold first in the Global South.

Chapter 6

1. See, for example, Gomes, Henighan, Mantolvani, Schurmans, and Secco.

2. Schurmans specifies: "Jaime Bunda assimilou bem as regras que regem uma certa classe social: deseja enriquecer a todo o custo, detesta a ambiguidade da sua situação social, encara o grau de inspetor unicamente como acesso a certas regalias, não hesita em infringir as leis e em contratar sicários para satisfazer os seus projetos pessoais. Por outras palavras, é por ter percebido o modo de funcionamento de um determinado Estado pós-colonial—o que funciona só para uma minoria em detrimento da maioria . . . que Bunda procura as vias que lhe permitirão, pelo menos é o que espera, subir socialmente" (333) (Jaime Bunda has assimilated quite well the rules that govern a certain social class: he wants to enrich himself at any cost, he detests the ambiguity of his social situation, he sees the rank of inspector solely as a means of access to certain privileges, he doesn't hesitate to violate laws or contract hit-men to take care of his personal plans. In other words, it is because he has perceived the way that a particular postcolonial state functions . . . that Bunda looks for the means that will allow him, or so he hopes, to climb the social ranks.)

3. The two French authors cited are associated not only with the sensational, melodramatic serial novel that Eça and Ortigão were mocking. The title of *Mistério da Estrada de Sintra* is also an overt reference to the French novelist Eugène Sue's 1842–43 melodramatic serial *Les Mystères de Paris*, which inspired countless imitations, including by Ponson du Terrail.

4. Eça and Ortigão explained their motives in the introduction they published with the second edition of the novel fourteen years after its initial publication in the *Diário de Notícias*.

5. Luísa's hair has a clear filiation with the orangutan's hair that leads Dupin to discover the culprit in "The Murders in the Rue Morgue," as does the detective's interest in the crime via the press.

6. Hoji-ya-Henda was a FNLA fighter killed by the Portuguese in the anti-colonial war in 1968; he is recognized as a national hero.

7. See Deckard; Gomes; Henighan; Schurmans.

8. Henighan notes: "Pepetela's point seems to be not that scrambling the chronology of Western culture in some way 'subverts' the West's stranglehold on Angola, but on the contrary, that the barrage of Western culture that pours into the country with the post-1990 intensification of globalization prevents Angolans from perceiving the facts of their own national history" (143).

9. The narrators' interventions are placed in parentheses, while the pseudo-author's are italicized and bracketed. These graphic indicators allow the reader to distinguish between the narrative and pseudo-authorial voices.

10. Roberto González Echevarría has observed a similar effect in his analysis of nineteenth-century Latin American dictator novels, where the author is allegorized with the dictator (*Voice of the Masters* 65–85). Like some of the more recent African and Latin American dictator novels, Pepetela's critique is not concentrated on a single representative figure, but on a disperse system, making the allegory of a genre, rather than a single figure, appropriate.

Epilogue

1. The Spanish version of the novel was released in December, 2017, though Suárez's novel was published in Portuguese earlier in 2017 with the title *Um Lugar Chamado Angola* (*A Place Called Angola*).

Works Cited

Abbas, Ackbar. "Dialectic of Deception." *Public Culture*, vol. 11, no. 2, 1999, pp. 347–63.
———. "The Erotics of Disappointment." *Chinese Cinema*, unknown, pp. 216–32.
Agualusa, José Eduardo. *A Conjura*. Caminho, 1989.
———. *José Eduardo Agualusa, No ritmo da escrita*. Interview by Ramon Mello. Saraiva.
———. *Nação Crioula: A Correspondência Secreta de Fradique Mendes*. Gryphus, 1997.
———. *O Ano em que Zumbi Tomou o Rio*. Chá de Caxinde, 2002.
———. *Teoria Geral do Esquecimento*. Dom Quixote, 2012.
Alberto de Diego García Marruz, Eliseo. *Informe contra mí mismo*. Alfaguara, 1997.
———. *Caracol Beach*. Alfaguara, 1998.
———. *Caracol Beach*. Translated by Edith Grossman, Vintage International, 2001.
Alberto, Paulina L. *Terms of Inclusion: Black Intellectuals in Twentieth-Century Brazil*. University of North Carolina Press, 2011.
Alcalde, Emilio Oscar. *El encanto del regreso*. Point of View Productions, 1991.
———. *Re: Pregunta re: El encanto del regreso*. 12 July 2018.
Andrade, Mário Pinto de. "Cultura Negro-Africana e Assimilação." *Antologia da Poesia Negra de Expressão Portuguesa*, Pierre Jean Oswald, 1958.
———. *Culture et independence nationale / Culture et lutte armée*. Arquivo Mário Pinto de Andrade, Fundação Mário Soares, 04336.003.009.
———. "Reflexions Autour du Congres Culturel de La Havane." *Revolution Africaine*, no. 261, de Fevereiro de 1968, pp. 40–41. Fundação Mário Soares—Arquivo Mário Pinto de Andrade, Pasta 10202.001.002.
António Fernandes de Oliveira, Mário. *Luanda, "Ilha" Crioula*. Agência-Geral do Ultramar, 1968.
Appiah, Kwame Anthony. *In My Father's House*. Oxford University Press 1993.
Arenas, Fernando. *Lusophone Africa Beyond Independence*. University of Minnesota Press, 2012.
Arrufat, Antón. *Los siete contra Tebas*. UNEAC, 1968.
Assunção, Matthias Röhrig. "Angola in Brazil: The Formation of *Angoleiro* Identity in Bahia." *African Heritage and Memories of Slavery in Brazil and the South Atlantic World*, edited by Ana Lucia Araujo, Cambria, 2015, pp. 109–48.

Attridge, John. "Two Types of Secret Agency: Conrad, Causation, and Popular Spy Fiction." *Texas Studies in Literature and Language*, vol. 55, no. 2, Summer 2013, pp. 125–58.
Baudrillard, Jean. *Simulacra and Simulation*. Translated by Sheila Faria Glaser, Michigan University Press, 1994.
Beliso-De Jesús, Aisha M. *Electric Santería. Racial and Sexual Assemblages of Transnational Religion*. Columbia University Press, 2015.
Benítez Rojo, Antonio. *La isla que se repite*. Casiopea, 1998.
Benjamin, Walter. *The Origin of German Tragic Drama*. Translated by John Osborne, NLB, 1977.
Bird, Robert. "Lenfilm." *A Companion to Russian Cinema*, edited by Birgit Beumers, Wiley, 2016. Wiley Online Library.
Birkenmaier, Anke. "Leonardo Padura and the 'New' Historical Novel." *A Contracorriente*, vol. 13, no. 1, Fall 2015, pp. 13–25.
Birmingham, David. *A Short History of Modern Angola*. Oxford University Press, 2015.
Blanes, Ruy Llera, and Ramón Sarró. "Prophetic Diasporas: Moving Religion Across the Lusophone Atlantic." *African Diaspora*, vol. 2, 2009, pp. 52–72.
Blue, Sarah A. 2013. "Internationalism's Remittances: The Impact of Temporary Migration on Cuban Society," *International Journal of Cuban Studies*, vol. 5, issue 1, pp. 41–60.
Boltanski, Luc. *Mysteries and Conspiracies*. Translated by Catherine Porter, Polity, 2014.
Boym, Svetlana. *The Future of Nostalgia*. Basic Books, 2001.
Brignole, Francisco. "Biculturation and Beyond: Exile and Cuban-American Identity in Eliseo Alberto's *Caracol Beach*." *South Atlantic Review*, vol. 78, no. 3/4, 2013, pp. 75–89.
Brookshaw, David. "Race Relations in Brazil from the Perspective of a Brazilian African and an African Brazilian: José Eduardo Agualusa's *O Ano em que Zumbi Tomou o Rio* and Francisco Maciel's *O Primeiro Dia do Ano da Peste*." *Research in African Literatures*, vol. 38, no. 1, 2007, pp. 163–171. Project Muse.
Brown, Wendy. "Resisting Left Melancholy." *Boundary 2: An International Journal of Literature and Culture*, vol. 26, no. 3, 1999, pp. 19–27. JSTOR.
Buck-Morss, Susan. *Dreamworld and Catastrophe. The Passing of Mass Utopia in East and West*. MIT Press, 2000.
Buck-Morss, Susan. *Hegel, Haiti and Universal History*. University of Pittsburgh Press, 2009.
Buckwalter-Arias, James. "Poetic Prose and Useless Fictions: Political Ideology and Literary Form in Eliseo Alberto's *Informe contra mí mismo*." *Cuban Studies*, vol. 35, 2004, pp. 24–44. Project Muse.
Burness, Don. *On the Shoulder of Martí. Cuban Literature of the Angolan War*. Three Continents, 1996.
Burton, Julianne. "Film and Revolution in Cuba. The First Twenty-Five Years." *New Latin American Cinema*, edited by Michael T. Martin, vol. 2, Wayne State University Press, 1997, pp. 123–42.
Cabral, Amílcar. *Documentário. Textos Políticos e Culturais*. Edited by António E. Duarte Silva, Edições Cotovia, 2008.

Cardoso, Boaventura. *Maio, Mês de Maria*. Campo das Letras, 1997.
———. *Mãe, Materno Mar*. Campo das Letras, 2001.
———. "Entrevista." Chaves et al., pp. 23–29.
———. *Noites de Vigília*. União de Escritores Angolanos, 2012.
Carpentier, Alejo. *El siglo de las luces*. Revolución, 1965.
———. *La consagración de la primavera*. Castalia, 1998.
———. *El reino de este mundo*. Seix Barral, 2004.
Carpentier, Alejo, et al. *Un camino de medio siglo: setenta aniversario de Alejo Carpentier*. Orbe, 1976.
Casamayor-Cisneros, Odette. *Utopía, distopía e ingravidez. Reconfiguraciones cosmológicas en la narrativa postsoviética cubana*. Iberoamericana/ Veuvert, 2012.
Castro Ruz, Fidel. "Discurso pronunciado por Fidel Castro Ruz, Presidente de La República de Cuba, en el acto central por el XV aniversario de la victoria de Girón y la proclamación socialista de nuestra Revolución, celebrado en el Teatro "Carlos Marx," el 19 de abril de 1976, "año del XX aniversario del Granma." Government of the Republic of Cuba, 19 Apr. 1976, http://www.cuba.cu/gobierno/discursos/1976/esp/f190476e.html.
———. Castro Ruz, Fidel. "Discurso pronunciado por el Comandante Fidel Castro Ruz, Primer Ministro del gobierno revolucionario y Secretario del PURSC, como conclusión de las reuniones con los intelectuales cubanos, efectuadas en la biblioteca nacional el 16, 23 y 30 de junio de 1961." Government of the Republic of Cuba, 30 June 1961, http://www.cuba.cu/gobierno/discursos/1961/esp/f300661e.html.
Césaire, Aimé. *Discourse on Colonialism*. Translated by Joan Pinkham, Monthly Review Press, 2000.
Cesar, Rafael. *Kuatiça o Ngoma! Movimentos de linguagem, história e memória em obras de Boaventura Cardoso*. Terceira Margem, 2012.
Chabal, Patrick, and David Birmingham. *A History of Postcolonial Lusophone Africa*. Indiana University Press, 2002.
Chandler, Raymond. *Collected Stories*. Alfred A. Knopf, 2002.
Chanan, Michael. "The Changing Geography of Third Cinema." *Screen*, vol. 38, no. 4, 1997, pp. 372–88.
———. *Cuban Cinema*. University of Minnesota Press, 2004.
Chatman, Seymour Benjamin. "Parody and Style." *Poetics Today*, vol. 22, no. 1, Spring 2001, pp. 25–39. *Project Muse*.
Chaves, Rita, et al., editors. *Boaventura Cardoso, a escrita em processo*. Alameda/ União de Escritores Angolanos, 2005.
Chesterton, G. K. *The Man Who Was Thursday, and Related Pieces*. Edited by Stephen Medcalf, Oxford University Press, 1996.
Cortázar, Octavio. *Guardafronteras*. ICAIC, 1980.
Conrad, Joseph. *The Secret Agent*. Edited by David Price (transcribed), Project Gutenberg eBook.
Covington-Ward, Yolanda. *Gesture and Power. Religion, Nationalism, and Everyday Performance in Congo*. Duke University Press, 2016. E-book oapen.org.
Cristóvão, Aguinaldo, and Isaquiel Cori. *Pessoas com Quem Falar*. União de Escritores Angolanos, 2004.

CubaMINREX/ Embacuba-India. *Embajada de Cuba presenta* Kangamba *y* Cuito Cuanavale *en el Instituto Cervantes de Nueva Delhi.* Ministerio de Relaciones Exteriores de la República de Cuba, 12 May 2014, http://www.cubadiplomatica.cu/india/ES/Inicio/tabid/20344/ctl/Details/mid/31311/ItemID/40219/Default.aspx.
Curbelo, José. *"Sun Sun Babae," Live at the China Doll in New York*, Blue Moon, 1998.
da Cunha, Euclides. *Os sertões*. Edited by Alfredo Bosi, Cultrix, 1973.
Dávila, Jerry. *Hotel Trópico: Brazil and the Challenge of African Decolonization, 1950–1980.* Duke University Press, 2010.
De Ferrari, Guillermina. *Community and Culture in Post-Soviet Cuba.* Routledge, 2014.
de Jesús, Carolina Maria. *Quarto de despejo.* 5th ed., Livraria F. Alves, 1960.
de la Hoz, Pedro. "*Kangamba* u otra dimensión de la épica." *Cubacine*, vol. 12, no. 2, http://www.cubacine.cult.cu/revistacinecubano/digital12/cap02.htm.
de la Nuez, Iván. "De la tempestad a la intemperie. Travesías cubanas en el poscomunismo." *Paisajes después del muro. Disidencias en el poscomunismo diez años después de la caída del Muro de Berlín*, edited by Iván de la Nuez, Ediciones Península, 1999, pp. 163–75.
Deckard, Sharae. "Postcolonial Genre and Peripheral Modernity in Mabanckou and Pepetela." *Locating Postcolonial Narrative Genres*, edited by Walter Goebel and Saskia Schabio, Routledge, 2013, pp. 92–107.
Díaz-Briquets, Sergio. *Cuban Internationalism in Sub-Saharan Africa.* Duquesne University Press, 1989.
Diegues, Carlos. *Quilombo.* New Yorker Films, 1991.
dos Santos, Olimpia Maria. *A alegórica "Mãe, Materno Mar" angolana.* Caetés, 2008.
Dyer, Richard. *Pastiche.* Routledge, 2007.
Eça de Queiroz, José Maria, and Ramalho Ortigão. *Mistério da Estrada de Sintra.* Edited by A. Campos Matos, Parceria A. M. Pereira, 2005.
———. *The Mystery of the Sintra Road.* Translated by Margaret Jull Costa and Nick Phillips, Dedalus, 2013.
Eco, Umberto. *The Role of the Reader. Explorations in the Semiotics of Texts.* University of Indiana Press, 1979.
———. *Travels in Hyper Reality.* Translated by William Weaver, Harcourt Brace Jovanovich, 1986.
El-Tahri, Jihan. *Cuba, Une Odyssée Africaine.* Arte Video/ Facets, 2007.
Espinosa, Julio García. "Por un cine imperfecto." *Cine Cubano*, vol. 120, 1987, pp. 65–70.
———. Espinosa, Julio García. "For an Imperfect Cinema." *Jump Cut*, translated by Julianne Burton, no. 20, 1979, pp. 24–26.
"Estimates." *The Trans-Atlantic Slave Trade Database*, http://slavevoyages.org/assessment/estimates. Accessed 17 July 2018.
Fanon, Frantz. *The Wretched of the Earth.* Translated by Richard Philcox, Grove Press, 2004.
Fellini, Federico. *La Strada.* Ponti-De Laurentiis, 1954.
Ferreira, Carolin Overhoff. "Ambivalent Transnationality: Luso-African Co-Productions After Independence (1988–2010)." *Journal of African Cinemas*, vol. 3, no. 2, 2011, pp. 221–45.

Flatley, Jonathan. *Affective Mapping. Melancholia and the Politics of Modernism.* Harvard University Press, 2008. Ebook Central Academic Complete.
Fleitas, Miguel. *La guerra en Angola.* ICAIC; Fuerzas Armadas Revolucionarias; Movimento Popular para a Libertação de Angola, 1976.
Fornet, Ambrosio. "Apuntes para el cine cubano de ficción." *Temas,* vol. 27, 2001, pp. 4–16.
———. "La Crítica bicéfala: un nuevo desafío." *La gaceta de Cuba,* no. 1, 2002, pp. 20–25.
———. "El quinquenio gris: revisitando el término." *Narrar la nación. Ensayos en blanco y negro.,* 2nd ed., Letras Cubanas, 2011, pp. 379–403.
Fornet, Jorge. "La narrativa cubana entre la utopía y el desencanto." *Hispamérica,* vol. 32, no. 95, Aug. 2003, pp. 3–20. JSTOR.
França, Jean Marcel Carvalho, and Ricardo Alexandre Ferreira. *Três vezes Zumbi: a construção de um herói brasileiro.* Três Estrelas, 2012.
Freitas, M. M. *Reino negro de Palmares.* Americana, 1954.
Freyre, Gilberto. *Casa-grande e senzala.* Olympio, 1961.
———. *The Masters and the Slaves.* Translated by Samuel Putnam, Alfred A. Knopf, 1966.
Fuentes, Jorge. *Cabinda.* ICAIC, 1988.
Fuentes, Norberto. *Dulces guerreros cubanos.* Seix Barral, 1999.
Gamboa dos Passos, Zézé (José Augusto Octávio). *Dissidence.* Fábrica d'Imagens; Garance Production; RTP, 1998.
———. *O Herói.* David & Golias, 2004.
———. "'Como Angola Está, Eu Não Podia Fazer um Filme Alegre,' Zezé Gamboa." Interview by Paulo Spranger, 2 Feb. 2005, http://www.angonoticias.com/Artigos/item/3874.
———. *O Grande Kilapy.* David & Golias; Raíz Produções Cinematográficas; Gamboa & Gamboa, 2012.
———. "Entrevista: Zézé Gamboa. Um Golpe Entre Angola e Paraíba." Interview by Ivonete Pinto, No 2013, http://orson.ufpel.edu.br/content/04/artigos/entrevistas/ivonete_pinto.pdf.
Ganga, Maria João. *Na Cidade Vazia.* Global Film Initiative, 2004.
García Borrero, Juan Antonio. *Otras maneras de pensar el cine cubano.* Editorial Oriente, 2011.
García Marruz, Constante Alejandro de Diego. *El corazón sobre la tierra.* ICAIC, 1982.
Genette, Gérard. *Palimpsests: Literature in the Second Degree.* Translated by Channa Newman and Claude Doubinsky, University of Nebraska Press, 1997.
George, Edward. *The Cuban Intervention in Angola, 1965–1991: From Che Guevara to Cuito Cuanavale.* Frank Cass, 2005.
Gleijeses, Piero. *Visions of Freedom. Havana, Washington, Pretoria, and the Struggle for Southern Africa, 1976–1991.* University of North Carolina Press, 2013.
Goldberg, David Theo. *Racist Culture. Philosophy and the Politics of Meaning.* Blackwell, 1998. EPUB.
Gomes, Flávio. *Palmares.* Contexto, 2005.

Gomes, Miguel. "Maria João Ganga." *Rede Angola*, 11 July 2016, n/p.
González, Eduardo. *Cuba and the Tempest. Literature and Cinema in the Time of Diaspora*. The University of North Carolina Press, 2006.
González Echevarría, Roberto. *The Voice of the Masters: Writing and Authority in Modern Latin American Literature*. University of Texas Press, 1985.
———. *Alejo Carpentier. The Pilgrim at Home*. University of Texas Press, 1990.
Granma, 27 Nov. 2016, pp. 1–16.
Guerra, Lillian. "The Reel, Real and Hyper-Real Revolution. Scripts and Counter-Scripts in Cuban Documentary Film." *Scripting Revolution. A Historical Approach to the Comparative Study of Revolutions*, edited by Keith Michael Baker and Dan Edelstein, Stanford University Press, 2015, pp. 267–86.
Guevara, Ernesto "Che." "El socialismo y el hombre en Cuba." *Textos Revolucionarios*, Txalaparta, 1997, pp. 95–112.
———. "Mensaje a los pueblos del mundo a través de la tricontinental." *Textos revolucionarios*, Txalaparta, 1997, pp. 247–62.
Guillén Landrián, Nicolás. *Desde La Habana ¡1969!* ICAIC, 1971.
Guimarães, António Sérgio Alfredo. "Racial Democracy." *Imagining Brazil*, edited by Jesse Souza and Valter Sinder, Lexington, 2007, pp. 119–40.
Gutiérrez Alea, Tomás. *Guantanamera*. New Yorker Video; Lion's Gate, 2000.
Hamilton, Russell G. *Literatura Africana, Literatura Necessária*. Vol. 1, INALD/ Edições 70, 1981.
Hardt, Michael, and Antonio Negri. *Empire*. Harvard University Press, 2001.
———. *Multitude. War and Democracy in the Age of Empire*. Penguin, 2004.
Harrow, Kenneth W. *Trash: African Cinema From Below*. University of Indiana Press, 2013.
Hart Santamaría, Celia. "Aniversario del asesinato de León Trotsky. Apuntes al margen del crimen." *Escritos Políticos 2003–2008*, Nuevo Socialismo, 2009, pp. 39–51.
Hatzky, Christine. *Cubans in Angola. South-South Cooperation and Transfer of Knowledge, 1976–1991*. Translated by Christine Hatzky, University of Wisconsin Press, 2015.
Henighan, Stephen. "'Um James Bond Subdesenvolvido': The Ideological Work of the Angolan Detective in Pepetela's Jaime Bunda Novels." *Portuguese Studies*, vol. 22, no. 1, 2006, pp. 135–52. JSTOR.
———. "Uma entrevista com Ondjaki." *Hispanic Research Journal*, vol. 7, no. 4, 2006, pp. 365–71. Academic Search Premier.
———. "The Cuban Fulcrum and the Search for a Transatlantic Revolutionary Culture in Angola, Mozambique and Chile, 1965–2008." *Journal of Transatlantic Studies*, vol. 7, no. 3, 2009, pp. 233–48.
Hernández Salván, Marta. "Out of History: The Cuban Postrevolution." *Revista Hispánica Moderna*, vol. 64, no. 1, 2011, pp. 81–96.
———. *Mínima Cuba. Heretical Poetics and Power in Post-Soviet Cuba*. SUNY Press, 2015.
Herrmann, Gina. *Written in Red: The Communist Memoir in Spain*. University of Illinois Press, 2010.
Hook, Derek. "Petrified Life." *Social Dynamics*, vol. 41, no. 3, 2015, pp. 438–60. tandfonline.com.

Huish, Robert, and Sarah A. Blue, editors. *International Journal of Cuban Studies*, vol. 5, no. 1, 2013.
Hutcheon, Linda. *A Theory of Parody: The Teachings of Twentieth-Century Art Forms*. Methuen, 1985.
Izquierdo, Jaisy. "Para que zumbe en la memoria." *Juventud Rebelde*, Digital, 16 July 2011, http://www.juventudrebelde.cu/cultura/2011-07-16/para-que-zumbe-en-la-memoria/?page=2.
Jamba, Sousa. *Patriots*. Viking, 1990.
James, C. L. R. *The Black Jacobins. Toussaint L'Ouverture and the San Domingo Revolution*. Second, Vintage, 1989.
Jameson, Fredric. *Postmodernism. Or, the Cultural Logic of Late Capitalism*. Duke University Press, 1991.
Jeyifo, Biodun. "An African Cultural Modernity. Achebe, Fanon, Cabral and the Philosophy of Decolonization." *Socialism and Democracy*, vol. 21, no. 3, 2007, pp. 125–41.
Johnson, Randal. "The Romance-Reportagem and the Cinema: Babenco's 'Lúcio Flávio' and 'Pixote'." *Luso-Brazilian Review*, vol. 24, no. 2, 1987, pp. 35–87. JSTOR.
Kandjimbo, Luís. "O Social e o Religioso em Dois Romances de Boaventura Cardoso." Chaves et al., pp. 161–66.
Kant, Immanuel. *Immanuel Kant: Observations on the Feeling of the Beautiful and the Sublime and Other Writings*. Edited by Patrick R. Frierson and Paul Guyer, Cambridge Univeersity Press, 2011.
Karmen, Roman. *The Great Patriotic War*. Central Documentary Film Studios, 1965.
Knopfli, Rui. *O Escriba Acocorado*. Moraes Editores, 1978.
Krull, Catherine, editor. *Cuba in a Global Context: International Relations, Internationalism, and Transnationalism*. University Press of Florida, 2014.
Kurosawa, Akira. *Seven Samurai*. Janus Films/ Criterion, 2006.
Lahaye Guerra. "La posesión simbólica en la santería." *Catauro*, vol. 7, 2003, pp. 79–87.
Laranjeira, José Luís Pires. "José Eduardo Agualusa. Vale Tudo?" *Jornal de Letras*, Print, 26 June 2002, p. 23.
———. "A Intentona Fracassada de 27 de Maio de 1977." Chaves et al., pp. 167–71.
Lins, Paulo. *Cidade de Deus: Romance*. Caminho, 2003.
Llarena, Alicia. "Claves para una discusión: el 'realismo mágico' y 'lo real maravilloso americano.'" *Inti: revista de literatura hispánica*, vol. 43, no. 1, pp. 21–44. http://digitalcommons.providence.edu/inti/vol1/iss43/4.
Loss, Jacqueline. *Dreaming in Russian. The Cuban Soviet Imaginary*. University of Texas Press, 2013.
Lyotard, Jean-François. *The Differend: Phrases in Dispute*. Translated by Georges Van Den Abbeele, University of Minnesota Press, 1988.
———. *Enthusiasm. The Kantian Critique of History*. Translated by Georges Van Den Abbeele, Stanford University Press, 2009.
Macedo, Jorge. "Compromisso com a Língua Literária na Escrita de Boaventura Cardoso." Chaves et al., pp. 47–60.
Macêdo, Tania. *Luanda, Cidade e Literatura*. UNESP, 2008.
Maguire, Emily. "It's a Dog's Life: Canine Ethics in Leonardo Padura's *El hombre que amaba a los perros*." *A contracorriente*, vol. 13, no. 1, Fall 2015, pp. 26–45.

Mahler, Anne Garland. "Beyond the Color Curtain: The Metonymic Color Politics of the Tricontinental and the (New) Global South." *The Global South Atlantic*, edited by Kerry Bystrom and Joseph Slaughter, Fordham University Press, 2017, pp. 99–123.

———. *From the Tricontinental to the Global South. Race, Radicalism, and Transnational Solidarity.* Duke University Press, 2018.

Maldoror, Sarah. *Sambizanga*. Isabelle Films, 1972.

Mandela, Nelson. "We Will Ensure That the Poor and Rightless Will Rule the Land of Their Birth." *How Far We Slaves Have Come! South Africa and Cuba in Today's World*, Pathfinder, 1991, pp. 17–28.

Mantolvani, Rosangela Manhas. "*Jaime Bunda, Agente Secreto*: A Paródia do Mito." *Portanto . . . Pepetela*, edited by Rita Chaves and Tania Macêdo, Ateliê, 2009, pp. 329–35.

Margarido, Alfredo. "A Literatura e a Consciência Nacional." *Antologias de Poesia da Casa dos Estudantes do Império 1951–1963*, edited by A. Freudenthal et al., vol. 1, Associação Casa dos Estudantes do Império, 1994, pp. 9–23.

Martí, José. "XLVI." *Obras completas*, vol. 16, Editorial Nacional de Cuba, pp. 125–26.

Massip, José. *Angola, victoria de la esperanza*. ICAIC, 1976.

Massumi, Brian. *Parables for the Virtual. Movement, Affect, Sensation.* Duke University Press, 2002.

Mata, Inocência. "*Maio, Mês de Maria*: as Águas em Movimento." Chaves et al., pp. 145–59.

———. "Under the Sign of a Projective Nostalgia: Agostinho Neto and Angolan Postcolonial Poetry." *Research in African Literatures*, vol. 38, no. 1, 2007, pp. 54–67. JSTOR.

Mateus, Dalila Cabrita, and Álvaro Mateus. *Purga em Angola. Nito Alves/ Sita Valles/ Zé Van Dunem. O 27 de Maio de 1977.* 10th ed., Texto, 2009.

Matthews, Sean. "Change and Theory in Raymond Williams's Structures of Feeling." *Pretexts: Literary and Cultural Studies*, vol. 10, no. 2, Nov. 2001, pp. 179–94. Academic Search Premier.

Matzke, Christine, and Susanne Mühleisen. "Postcolonial Postmortems: Issues and Perspectives." *Postcolonial Postmortems: Crime Fiction from a Transcultural Perspective*, Rodopi, 2006, pp. 1–17.

Mbembe, Achille. *On the Postcolony*. University of California Press, 2001.

McNee, Malcolm K. "José Eduardo Agualusa, and Other Possible Lusofonias." *Luso-Brazilian Review*, vol. 49, no. 1, 2012, pp. 1–26. ProjectMuse.

Melo, Francisco José Sampaio. "Personagens Diasporizadas de José Eduardo Agualusa em *O Ano em que Zumbi Tomou o Rio*." *Letras de Hoje*, vol. 41, no. 3, 2006, pp. 159–68.

Méndez Rodenas, Adriana. "Identity and Diaspora: Cuban Culture at the Cross-Roads." *Cuba. Idea of a Nation Displaced*, edited by Andrea O'Reilly Herrera, SUNY Press, 2008, pp. 143–60.

Mercader, Luis, and Germán Sánchez. *Ramón Mercader: mi hermano: cincuenta años después*. Espasa-Calpe, 1990.

Michelena, José Antonio. *(A)cercando a Leonardo Padura*. Capiro, 2014.
Millar, Lanie. "Aguas inquietas: La Kianda en la ficción angoleña contemporánea." *Revolución y cultura*, no. 1, 2013, pp. 16–22.
Mills, C. Wright. *Listen, Yankee: The Revolution in Cuba*. Ballantine, 1960.
Monteiro, Ofélia Paiva. "Um Jogo Humorístico com a Verosimilhança Romanesca. *O Mistério da Estrada de Sintra*. I." *Colóquio: Letras*, no. 86, July 1985, pp. 15–23.
———. "Um Jogo Humorístico Com a Verosimilhança Romanesca: *O Mistério da Estrada de Sintra* II." *Colóquio: Letras*, no. 97, May 1987, pp. 5–18.
———. "Um Jogo Humorístico Com a Verosimilhança Romanesca: *O Mistério da Estrada de Sintra* III." *Colóquio: Letras*, no. 98, July 1987, pp. 38–51.
Moorman, Marissa. "Of Westerns, Women, and War: Re-Situating Angolan Cinema and the Nation." *Research in African Literatures*, vol. 32, no. 3, 2001, pp. 103–22. JSTOR.
Moya, Eduardo. *Sumbe*. ICAIC, 2011.
Mueller, Eddy Von. "The Police Procedural in Literature and Television." *The Cambridge Companion to American Crime Fiction*, edited by Catherine Ross Nickerson, Cambridge University Press, 2010, pp. 96–109.
Murat, Lúcia. *Quase dois irmãos*. Taiga Filmes, 2004.
Navarro, Desiderio. "In Medias Res Publicas: On Intellectuals and Social Criticism in the Cuban Public Sphere." Translated by Alessandro Fornazzari and Desiderio Navarro, *Boundary 2*, vol. 29, no. 3, Fall 2002, pp. 187–203. Project Muse.
Ngai, Sianne. *Ugly Feelings*. Ebook, Harvard University Press, 2007. Ebook Central Academic Complete.
Oliveira, Emanuelle K. F. *Writing Identity. The Politics of Contemporary Afro-Brazilian Literature*. Purdue University Press, 2008.
Oliveira Martins, Isabel. "'What Has Occurred That Has (Never) Occurred Before': A Case Study of the First Portuguese Detective Story." *Poe's Pervasive Influence*, edited by Barbara Cantalupo, Lehigh University Press/ Rowan & Littlefield, 2012, pp. 75–90.
Ondjaki (Ndalu de Almeida). *Ondjaki: "Mi lugar está demasiado dentro de mí."* Interview by Juan Santillán Sábado, 7 Feb. 2009, http://laventana.casa.cult.cu/noticias/2009/02/07/ondjaki-mi-lugar-esta-demasiado-dentro-de-mi/. Casa de las Américas, La Ventana.
———. *Bom Dia Camaradas*. 1st Brazilian, Editora Schwarcz, 2014.
Ortiz, Fernando. *El huracán: su mitología y sus símbolos*. 2nd ed., Fondo de Cultura Económica, 2005.
Padilla, Heberto. *Fuera del juego*. Ediciones Universal, 1998.
Padura Fuentes, Leonardo. *La Puerta de Alcalá y otras cacerías*. Olalla, 1998.
———. *Paisaje de otoño*. Tusquets, 1998.
———. *Adiós, Hemingway*. Unión, 2001.
———. *La novela de mi vida*. Tusquets, 2002.
———. *Un camino de medio siglo. Alejo Carpentier y la narrativa de lo real maravilloso*. Fondo de Cultura, 2002.
———. *La neblina de ayer*. Tusquets, 2005.

———. *El hombre que amaba a los perros*. Tusquets, 2009.
———. *Herejes*. Tusquets, 2013.
———. *The Man Who Loved Dogs*. Translated by Anna Kushner, Farrar, Straus and Giroux, 2014.
———. *Yo quisiera ser Paul Auster. Ensayos Selectos*. Verbum, 2015.
Palmer, Margarita Mateo. "Literatura latinoamericana y posmodernismo: una visión cubana." *Temas*, no. 2, June 1995, pp. 123–34.
Paranguá, Paulo Antonio. "Cuban Cinema's Political Challenges." *New Latin American Cinema*, edited by Michael T. Martin, vol. 2, Wayne State University Press, 1997, pp. 167–92.
París, Rogelio. *Caravana*. ICAIC; Laboratório Nacional de Cinema, 1990.
———. *Kangamba*. ICAIC; MINFAR, 2008.
——— and Cecilia Crespo. "Rogelio, Aprendiz . . ." *Revista Cine Cubano*, vol. 18/19, 2010, http://cubacine.cult.cu/sitios/revistacinecubano/digital1819/index.htm.
Pepetela (Artur Maurício Pestana dos Santos). *Mayombe*. Edições 70, 1980.
———. *Yaka*. 2nd ed., Dom Quixote, 1992.
———. *Parábola do Cágado Velho*. Dom Quixote, 1996.
———. *As Aventuras de Ngunga*. Dom Quixote, 2002.
———. *Lueji: O Nascimento dum Império*. 4th ed., Dom Quixote, 2003.
———. *Jaime Bunda, Secret Agent*. Translated by Richard Bartlett, Aflame, 2006.
———. "'Não Se Festeja a Morte de Ninguém,' Entrevista a Pepetela." Interview by Rita Silva Freire, 30 Dec. 2011, http://www.buala.org/pt/cara-a-cara/nao-se-festeja-a--morte-de-ninguem-entrevista-a-pepetela. *Buala*, 16 January, 2012.
———. *A Geração da Utopia*. 12th ed., Dom Quixote, 2014.
———. *Jaime Bunda, Agente Secreto*. 11th ed., Dom Quixote, 2014.
———. *Jaime Bunda e a Morte do Americano*. 6th ed., Dom Quixote, 2014.
Pereira, Pedro. "Hegel, Portugal, and the Transatlantic Grammar of Portuguese Exceptionalism." Iberian and Latin American Transatlantic Studies Symposium, University of Oregon, Eugene, OR, 2 Nov. 2013.
Peres, Phyllis. *Transculturation and Resistance in Lusophone African Narrative*. University Press of Florida, 1997.
Pérez, Rafa. "Leonardo Padura: 'La cifra de cubanos muertos en Angola es ridículamente baja.'" *CiberCuba*, 16 Mar. 2018, https://www.cibercuba.com/noticias/2018-03-16-u73624-e73624-s27061-leonardo-padura-cifra-cubanos-muertos-angola-ridiculamente.
Peters, Christabelle. *Cuban Identity and the Angolan Experience*. Palgrave McMillan, 2012.
Petrov, Vladimir. *The Battle of Stalingrad*. International Historic Films, 2008.
Phaf-Rheinberger, Ineke. "Myths of Early Modernity: Historical and Contemporary Narratives on Brazil and Angola." *The New Centennial Review*, vol. 7, no. 3, Winter 2007, pp. 103–29.
Poe, Edgar Allan. *Collected Works of Edgar Allan Poe*. Edited by Thomas Olive Mabbott, Belknap Press of Harvard University Press, 1969.

Pogolotti, Graziella. "La España de *El siglo de las luces*." *Alejo Carpentier y España: actas del seminario internacional, Santiago de Compostela, 2-3 marzo de 2004*, edited by José Antonio Baujín et al., Universidade de Santiago de Compostela, 2005, pp. 70-85.
Policia Internacional e de Defesa do Estado (PIDE). *Aliança Evangélica de Angola*. 1970. Arquivo Nacional Torre do Tombo, PT/TT PIDE/ DGS Pinf No. de Proc. 13.13A UI 1983.
———. *"Tocoismo": Religião da Estrela*. Arquivo Nacional Torre do Tombo.
Política em Relação a África. Boletim de Difusão de Informações No. 35/1967, Arquivo SCCIM, Serviços de Centralização e Coordenação de Informações de Moçambique, no. 670.
"Presidente de Angola agradece a La Habana su apoyo militar." *Cubaencuentro.com*, Online, 9 Sept. 2007.
Ponte, Antonio José. "Carta de La Habana: al paso del huracán." *Cuadernos Hispanoamericanos*, vol. 667, 2006, pp. 105-08.
———. "El asesino de Trotski, en una feria de La Habana." *Diario de Cuba*, 28 Mar. 2011, n/p.
Preminger, Otto. *Laura*. 20th Century Fox, 2004.
Quinney, Laura. *The Poetics of Disappointment. Wordsworth to Ashbery*. University of Virginia Press, 1999.
Rancière, Jacques. *Disagreement. Politics and Philosophy*. Translated by Julie Rose, University of Minnesota Press, 1999.
———. *Dissensus. On Politics and Aesthetics*. Edited and Translated by Steven Corcoran, Bloomsbury, 2015.
Retamar, Roberto Fernández. *Todo Calibán*. CLASCO, 2004.
Ribeiro, Raquel. "Cuba e Angola à procura dos seus heróis." *Público*, Online, 10 Mar. 2017, https://www.publico.pt/2017/03/10/culturaipsilon/noticia/cuba-e-angola-a-procura-dos-seus-herois-1764160.
Ricoeur, Paul. *Time and Narrative*. Translated by Kathleen Blamey and David Pellauer, University of Chicago Press, 1988.
Rodrigues, Nina. *A Tróia negra (Erros e lacunas da história de Palmares)*. Progresso, 1954.
Rodriguez, Besenia. "'De la esclavitud yanqui a la libertad cubana': U.S. Black Radicals, the Cuban Revolution, and the Formation of a Tricontinetal Ideology." *Radical History Review*, vol. 92, 2005, pp. 62-87.
Rojas, Rafael. "Anatomía del entusiasmo. La revolución como espectáculo de ideas." *Encuentro de la cultura cubana*, vol. 45/46, 2007, pp. 3-15, http://www.cuba-encuentro.com.
———. *El estante vacío*. Anagrama, 2009.
Rosales, Guillermo. *La casa de los náufragos*. Siruela, 2003.
Rothwell, Phillip. "The Authenticity of Smell: Contenting Civilization in the Angola of Ondjaki's *Bom Dia Camaradas*." *Bulletin of Hispanic Studies*, vol. 83, no. 3, 2006, pp. 241-48. ProQuest.
———. *A Canon of Empty Fathers. Paternity in Portuguese Narrative*. Rosemont, 2007.

Rui, Manuel. *Quem Me Dera Ser Onda*. Caminho, 2007.
Ryan, Connor. "Regimes of Waste: Aesthetics, Politics, and Waste from Kofi Awoonor and Ayi Kwei Armah to Chimamanda Adichie and Zeze Gamboa." *Research in African Literatures*, vol. 44, no. 4, 2013, pp. 51–68.
Sá, Ana Lúcia. *A Ruralidade na Narrativa Angolana do Século XX: Elementos de Construção da Nação*. Kilombelombe, 2012.
Sabine, Mark. "Rebuilding the Angolan Body Politic: Global and Local Projections of Identity and Protest in *O Herói/ The Hero* (Zezé Gamboa, 2004)." *Journal of African Cinemas*, vol. 3, no. 2, 2011, pp. 201–19.
Salgado, Maria Teresa. "O direito à angústia e à felicidade em *Luuanda*." *SCRIPTA*, vol. 19, no. 37, 2015, pp. 167–76.
Sarduy, Severo. *Escrito sobre un cuerpo*. Sudamericana, 1969.
———. *Written on a Body*. Translated by Carol Maier, Lumen Books, 1989, pp. 91–116.
Sartre, Jean Paul. *Huracán sobre el azúcar*. Ministerio de Relaciones Exteriores de la República de Cuba, Departamento de Asuntos Culturales, 1960.
Schurmans, Fabrice Aimé Fernand. *O Trágico do Estado Pós-Colonial. Pius Ngandu Nkashama, Sony Labou Tansi e Pepetela*. Dissertation, Universidade de Coimbra, 2012.
Schweizer, Harold. "Penelope Waiting." *Soundings: An Interdisciplinary Journal*, vol. 85, no. 3/4, Fall/ Winter 2002, pp. 279–99. JSTOR.
Secco, Carmen Lucia Tindó. "Entre Mar e Terra: Uma Polifónica Viagem pelo Universo 'Mágico-Religioso' de Angola." *Mãe, Materno Mar*, Campo das Letras, 2001, pp. 11–31.
———. *A Magia das Letras Africanas*. 2nd ed., Quartet, 2007.
Semprún, Jorge. *La deuxième mort de Ramón Mercader*. Gallimard, 1969.
Soares, Francisco. "A Inquietação das Águas: Um Comentário a *Mãe, Materno Mar* de Boaventura Cardoso." Chaves, et al., pp. 139–44.
Soares de Oliveira, Ricardo. *Magnificent and Beggar Land: Angola Since the Civil War*. Oxford University Press, 2015.
Soitos, Stephen. *The Blues Detective. A Study of African American Detective Fiction*. University of Massachusetts Press, 1996.
Solanas, Fernando, and Octavio Getino. "Towards a Third Cinema: Notes and Experiences for the Development of a Cinema of Liberation in the Third World." *New Latin American Cinema*, translated by Julianne Burton and Michael T. Martin, vol. 1, Wayne State University Press, pp. 33–58.
Someillan, Yamile Regalado. "Visual Culture and the New Cuban Man: Examining a Core Force of the Cuban Revolution, 1959–1963." *International Journal of Comic Art*, no. Fall, 2006, pp. 164–97. EBSCO.
Sommer, Doris. "Resisting the Heat. Menchú, Morrison, and Incompetent Readers." *Cultures of United States Imperialism*, edited by Amy Kaplan and Donald E. Pease, Duke University Press, 1993, pp. 407–32.
Sousa Santos, Boaventura de. *Refundación del estado en América Latina: perspectivas desde una epistemología del sur*. Siglo XXI; Plural; Siglo del Hombre, 2010.

———. *Una epistemología del sur*. Edited by José Guadalupe Gandarilla Salgado, Siglo XXI; CLASCO, 2012.
Suárez, Karla. *El hijo del héroe*. Editorial Comba, 2017.
———. *Um Lugar Chamado Angola*. Translated by Helena Pitta, Porto Editora, 2017.
Sue, Eugène. *Les Mystères de Paris*. Éditions Hallier, 1977.
Terada, Rei. *Feeling in Theory. Emotion After the Death of the Subject*. Harvard University Press, 2001.
The Unknown War, Sovinfilm, 1978.
Thornton, John K. "Les États de l'Angola et La Formation de Palmares (Brésil)." *Annales. Histoire, Sciences Sociales*, translated by Valentine Leys, vol. 63e Année, no. 4, Aug. 2008, pp. 769–97.
Traverso, Enzo. *Left-Wing Melancholia*. Columbia University Press, 2016.
Valente, Luiz Valente. "Brazilian Literature and Citizenship: From Euclides Da Cunha to Marcos Dias." *Luso-Brazilian Review*, vol. 38, no. 2, pp. 11–27. JSTOR.
Vieira, Luandino (José Vieira Mateus da Graça). "Nota de Censura Póstuma." *Maio, Mês de Maria*, Campo das Letras, 1997, pp. 9–10.
———. *Luuanda*. Caminho, 2014.
Weiss, Martin. "Reality, Simulation and Hyperreality: An Essay on Baudrillard." *The International Journal of Baudrillard Studies*, vol. 8, no. 2, 2011, n/p.
Weppler-Grogan, Doreen. "Cultural Policy, the Visual Arts, and the Advance of the Cuban Revolution in the Aftermath of the Gray Years." *Cuban Studies*, vol. 41, 2010, pp. 143–65.
Wheeler, Douglas, and René Pélissier. *História de Angola*. Translated by Pedro Gaspar Serras Pereira and Paula Almeida, Edições Tinta-da-China, 2009.
Whitfield, Esther. *Cuban Currency. The Dollar and "Special Period" Fiction*. University of Minnesota Press, 2008.
Wieser, Doris, and Pepetela. "O Livro Policial É Pretexto." *Espéculo*, no. 30, 2005, n/p.
Williams, Raymond. *Marxism and Literature*. Oxford University Press, 1977.
Winant, Howard. "Rethinking Race in Brazil." *Journal of Latin American Studies*, vol. 24, no. 1, 1992, pp. 173–92. JSTOR.
———. "'The Other Side of the Process': Racial Formation in Contemporary Brazil." *On Edge: The Crisis of Contemporary Latin American Culture*, edited by George Yúdice et al., Minnesota University Press, 1992, pp. 85–113.

Index

A Conjura (The Conspiracy) (Agualusa), 85
A Rainha Ginga e de Como os Africanos Inventaram o Mundo (Queen Nzinga and how Africans Invented the World) (Agualusa), 105
A Vida Verdadeira de Domingos Xavier (Vieira), 43
Abbas, Ackbar, xv, xx, xxii, xxiii, xxviii, 180*nn*8-9
Achebe, Chinua, 185*n*17
Adiós, Hemingway (Padura), 110-11
Adorno, Theodor, xxi
affect, xxi, 28
Agualusa, J. E.: *A Conjura (The Conspiracy)*, 85; *A Rainha Ginga e de Como os Africanos Inventaram o Mundo*, 105; background of, 85; Brazilian state perspective on, 84; *Nação Crioula*, 85; *Teoria Geral do Esquecimento*, 7, 89-90. See also *O Ano em que Zumbi Tomou o Rio*
Alberto, Eliseo, 53; background of, 55; *Informe contra mí mismo*, xxxii, 59, 68-69, 70-71. See also *Caracol Beach*
Alcalde, Emilio Óscar, *El encanto del regreso*, 169-71, 173, 174
Alea, Tomás Gutiérrez, *Guantanamera*, 55
Algeria, 179*n*3

allegory: in *Bom dia camaradas*, 174; in *Kangamba*, 27-28, 31-32, 36; in *Mãe, Materno Mar*, 17-18, 20, 24-25, 174; in *O Herói*, 27-28, 38, 40
Álvarez, Olivia Marín, 185*n*1
Alves, Nito. See Alves coup
Alves coup, xxxi, 7, 12, 13-14, 82, 182*n*19, 184*n*10. See also MPLA post-coup purges
American influences. See global marketplace
Andrade, Mário Pinto de, xxvii, xxviii, xxxi, 115
Angola, victoria de la esperanza (Angola, Victory of Hope) (Massip), 32, 57, 169
Angolan anticolonial revolution, xvii, xxx, 83, 104, 105
Angolan civil war: accords (1988 and 1991), xxxi-xxxii; Alves coup, xxxi, 7, 12, 13-14, 82, 182*n*19, 184*n*10; exiles from, 82; and historical revisiting/revision, 93, 97, 104; and intercultural translation, 98; Ochoa scandal, xxxii-xxxiii, 30, 46, 171, 182*nn*21-22; overview, xxxi; parties in, xxxi, 182*n*18; silence about, xxxii-xxxiii, 6, 7, 9, 13, 30, 36, 172, 183*n*6; South African invasion, xxxi, 29, 34-35. See also Cuba's Angola mission; MPLA post-coup purges

Angolan state film initiatives, 179*n*2
anticolonialism: Angolan civil war as failure of, 104; and concepts of revolution, 83, 105; and Global South solidarity, xvii, xxx, 93; hurricane images of, 133; importance of cinema to, 45; and linguistic authority, 8–10, 184*n*8; and Palmares, 81–82; and religion, 21–22, 184–85*n*15; and silence, 10, 25. *See also* post-independence colonial reproduction; post-independence transitions
Appiah, Kwame Anthony, xxiii, 180*n*10
Arenas, Fernando, xxxi, xxxiii, xxxv–xxxvi, 182*n*20
Arrufat, Antón, xxv; *Los siete contra Tebas*, 66
As Aventuras de Ngunga (The Adventures of Ngunga) (Pepetela), xiv, 35–36
assimilado status, 4, 10, 12, 183*n*2
Assunção, Matthias Röhrig, 93
asynchronicity, xv, xxix, 110, 173
Attridge, John, 143

Ballanche, Pierre-Simon, 183*n*5
The Battle of Stalingrad (Petrov), 186*n*5
Baudelaire, 152
Baudrillard, Jean, 186*n*2
belatedness, 115, 117–18, 191*n*14
Beliso-De Jesús, Aisha, 76, 77–78
Benítez Rojo, Antonio, xxiii, 71, 72
Benjamin, Walter, 17, 27–28, 36
Besenia, Rodriguez, 115
Bicesse Accords (1991), xxxi, xxxii
Bird, Robert, 186*n*5
Birkenmaier, Anke, 111, 112, 127, 128
Birmingham, David, xxxi, 181*n*14, 184*n*9
Blanes, Ruy Llera, 185*n*16
Boltanski, Luc, 147–48
Bom dia camaradas (Good Morning Comrades) (Ondjaki), 173–75
Boym, Svetlana, 73
Brazil. See *O Ano em que Zumbi Tomou o Rio*
Brignole, Francisco, 74

Brookshaw, David, 95, 98, 102, 187*n*4
Brown, Wendy, 113
Buck-Morss, Susan, xxix, 113, 118–19, 179*n*5, 191*n*14
Buckwalter-Arias, James, 71
Burness, Don, 179*n*4

Cabinda, 169
Cabral, Amílcar, xviii–xix, xxvii, 115, 185*n*17
Cadernos Negros, 94
Calibán (Retamar), xxiv, 133, 182*n*17
"Un camino de medio siglo" (Carpentier), 128
capitalism: and corruption, 140; and Global South solidarity, 37; and post-independence colonial reproduction, 43, 142; and religion, 18, 19–20, 22, 24. *See also* global marketplace
Caracol Beach (Alberto), 53–80; award for, 186*n*1; cinematic tropes in, 54, 55, 58–59, 60, 63–64, 78; clemency in, 54, 173; condemnation of novel in, 65–66; creative production in, 63, 75; doubling in, 64–65, 73, 76; eclectic form in, 54; enthusiasm in, xxviii; exile in, 72–74, 79, 172; historical elision in, 59–60; and hyper-real, 56–57, 61, 66, 69, 71–72, 79, 80; imaginative potential in, 75–76; and magical realism, 58, 74; male characters in, 74–75; multiplicity in, 71; nostalgia in, 73; plot of, 54, 58; and postmodernism, xxiii, 173; repetition in, 70–71; Santería in, 76–80; settings in, 71–73; slogans in, 68–70; tattoos in, 67–68, 77; transmediatic texture in, 54, 66, 172–73; and war film genre, 59; writing process, 57–58
Caravana (París), 29, 37, 46, 169, 185*nn*4–5
Cardoso, Boaventura: background of, 4, 7. See also *Mãe, Materno Mar*; *Maio, Mês de Maria*

Carpentier, Alejo: "Un camino de medio siglo," 128; *La consagración de la primavera*, 128–29, 190n11; and Padura, 112, 128–31, 132, 134, 190n11; *El reino de este mundo*, 128, 131, 184n12; *El siglo de las luces*, 128, 129–30, 131, 132, 190n10
La casa de los náufragos (Halfway House) (Rosales), 73–74
Casamayor-Cisneros, Odette, xx, xxxvi, 124, 128, 130, 179n6, 190–91nn11–12
Castro, Fidel: *Caracol Beach* on, 71; and Global South solidarity, xvii–xviii, xxvii; Meeting of Cuban Intellectuals speech, 56; militarized images of, 51; and Soviet invasion of Prague, xxv, 117
Castro, Raúl, 30
Césaire, Aimé, xxx, 191n14
Cesar, Rafael, 6, 25
Chanan, Michael, 30
Chandler, Raymond, "The Man Who Liked Dogs," 127, 190n8
Chatman, Seymour Benjamin, 146
Chesterton, G. K., *The Man Who Was Thursday*, 143
Cidade de Deus (City of God) (Lins), 189n14
citation, xxxiv; in *O Ano em que Zumbi Tomou o Rio*, 102, 103–4, 172–73; and repetition, xxx; and writing, 127
clemency, 54
Cold War, xxxi, 109. See also post–Cold War transition
collective/plurivocal narration: in Cardoso's post-independence novels, 5, 8, 11–12, 13, 14–17, 22–24, 25–26; and magical realism, 184n12
colonialism: and belatedness, 191n14; church as instrument of, 8; Cuban revolutionary missions as threat to, xxvii, 181–82n15; and economic policies, xxvii; and epistemology, 87, 188n9; and Global South solidarity, xvii–xx, xxvii; and racial mixing, xxvii, 85, 90, 94, 101, 187–88nn7, 11, 189n15. See also anticolonialism; postcolonialism
colonized time, xxix–xxx, 118–19
Comando Vermelho, 188–89n14
Comaroff, Jean, 191n14
Comaroff, John L., 191n14
community-building, xxxvi, xxxvii, 39–40
Congo, 179n3
Congreso Cultural de La Habana (Cultural Congress of Havana) (1968), xxvii, 182n16
Conrad, Joseph, *The Secret Agent*, 143
La consagración de la primavera (The Rite of Spring) (Carpentier), 128–29, 190n11
El corazón sobre la tierra (Heart Above the Land) (Rapi), 55
Cruz, Viriato da, xxxi
Cuba: Soviet influence on, xxxiv, 110, 117, 118, 124–25, 132, 136, 173; Special Period in Times of Peace, xxxiii, 111, 114. See also Cuban Revolution; Cuban revolutionary missions
Cuba: une odyssée africaine (Cuba: An African Odyssey), 46
Cuban Revolution: as decolonizing event, xxiv–xxvii, xxx, 114–15, 181nn12–14; divisive rhetoric of, 52–53, 54; and film theory, 30–31; hurricane images of, 131; and hyper-real, 56–57, 61, 71–72, 79, 80; and militarized images, 51–52, 52; participatory construction of, 55–56; and Santería, 77, 78, 80, 187n11; slogans of, 68–70, 186n8. See also Cuban revolutionary missions; Cuban state suppression of creative production
Cuban revolutionary missions: Algeria and Congo, 179n3; and Cuban Revolution as decolonizing event, xxv–xxvi; current forms of, 47, 48;

Cuban revolutionary missions *(continued)*
  El encanto del regreso on, 170; and enthusiasm, xxiv, xxvii–xxviii; and iterability of revolution, xxviii, 115, 179*n*5; nostalgia for, 29–30; and shared colonial history, xvii; and temporalities, 115–17; as threat to colonial regimes, xxvii, 181–82*n*15. *See also* Cuba's Angola mission
Cuban state suppression of creative production, 61–63, 109; and colonized time, 118–19; *El encanto del regreso*, 170, 171; in *El hombre que amaba a los perros*, 112, 114, 124–25, 171; and naïvete, 125–26; *quinquenio gris* term, 189*n*1; and silence, 171; and Soviet influence, xxxiv, 110, 124–25, 136
Cuba's Angola mission: and Alves coup, 7; cinematic depictions of, 60–61; de-isolating effect of, 62; documentaries on, 32–33, 57; and Ochoa scandal, xxxii–xxxiii, 30, 46, 171, 182*n*22; in Padura's work, 111; and race, xxxiv; recent literary works on, 173–77; and Santería, 79; and shared colonial history, xvii–xviii; silence about, xxxii–xxxiii, 7, 30, 36; and war film genre, 59; withdrawal, 171. *See also Caracol Beach*; *Kangamba*; *O Herói*
Cunha, Euclides da, 102
Curbelo, José, 70

Dávila, Jerry, 95
de la Nuez, Iván, xxix–xxx, xxxiii, 73
dechronicalization, 13–14, 20
Deckard, Sharae, 161
Desde la Habana: ¡1969! (From Havana: 1969!) (Guillén Landrián), 61
La deuxième mort de Ramón Mercader (The Second Death of Ramón Mercader), (Semprún), 126
dictator novels, 192*n*10
Diegues, Carlos, *Quilombo*, 189*n*16
disappointment: as collective feeling, xvi; as contingent, xxviii; critical approaches to, xx–xxiii; and disenchantment, xxvi, xxxiii–xxxiv, 3, 182*n*23; as fascination, xxii; and historical consciousness, xxiii; as loss of place in public sphere, xv–xix; and opening, 177; and structures of feeling, xx–xxi, xxii; as utopian loss, xxxv–xxxvi
disenchantment, xxvi, xxxiii–xxxiv, xxxv, 3, 13, 111, 170, 182*n*23
Dissidence (Gamboa), 40–41
Dorfman, Ariel, 132–33
dos Palmares, Zumbi, xxxiv, 82. *See also O Ano em que Zumbi Tomou o Rio*; Palmares
dos Santos, Eduardo, xviii
doubling, xxxiv; in *Caracol Beach*, 64–65, 73, 76; and Global South solidarity, xxxvi; in *O Herói*, 39, 42–43, 172. *See also* parallel structure
Doyle, Arthur Conan, 145, 148; *A Study in Scarlett*, 158–59
Dyer, Richard, 144

Eco, Umberto, 143, 186*n*2
El encanto del regreso (The Enchantment of Return) (Alcalde), 169–71, 173, 174
enthusiasm, xxiv–xxx; in *Bom dia camaradas*, 174–75; and colonized time, xxix–xxx; and Cuban Revolution as decolonizing event, xxvi–xxvii; and Cuban revolutionary missions, xxiv, xxvii–xxviii; and Global South solidarity, xxvi–xxvii, xxxiv; and multiplicity, 171–72; and postmodernism, xxiv, 181*n*11; and religion, 6; and repetition, xxx
Una epistemología del sur (Sousa Santos), 86, 188*n*8

Escrito sobre un cuerpo (Written on a Body) (Sarduy), 67–68
Espinosa, Juan García, 30
exile: in *Caracol Beach*, 72–74, 79, 172; in *El hombre que amaba a los perros*, 113–14, 120, 127; in *O Ano em que Zumbi Tomou o Rio*, 82, 88. *See also* marginalization

Fanon, Frantz, xxv, 41, 184*n*11, 185*n*17
feeling: and affect, xxi; collective, xvi; structures of, xx–xxi, xxii, 3
Fellini, Federico, *La Strada*, 73
Fernandes, Mário António, xxxi
Ferrari, Guillermina de, xxxvi, 47
Ferreira, Carolin Overhoff, 47
flashback, 41
Flatley, Johnathan, xxi
Fleitas, Miguel, *La guerra en Angola*, 32–33, 57, 169
Fleming, Ian, 143
Fornet, Ambrosio, xxxiii, xxxiv, 109, 110, 124–26, 182*n*23
Fornet, Jorge, xxvi, xxxiii, 46, 137–38, 182*n*23
fracturing, 13, 24
Freitas, M. M. de, 187*n*1
French Revolution, xxiv, 128, 131, 133, 190*n*10
Frente Nacional de Libertação de Angola (FNLA) (National Liberation Front of Angola), xxxi, 182*n*18
Frente Negra Brasileira (Black Brazilian Front), 94
Freyre, Gilberto, 90, 94, 101, 188*n*11
Fuentes, Norberto, 182*n*21
"Fuera del juego" (Padilla), 73, 186–87*n*10

Gamboa dos Passos, José Augusto Octávio (Zézé Gamboa): *Dissidence*, 40–41; *O Grande Kilapy*, 47. *See also O Herói*
Ganga, Maria João, *Na Cidade Vazia*, xiii–xv, 35–36, 179*n*2

García Borrero, Juan Antonio, 57, 169, 170
García Márquez, Gabriel, 57, 58, 74
Genette, Gérard, 143, 144
A Geração da Utopia (The Generation of Utopia) (Pepetela), xxxv–xxxvi, 139
Getino, Octavio, 31
Gil, Susana Pérez, 185*n*1
Gleijeses, Piero, xxxii
global marketplace: in Cardoso's post-independence novels, 5; and cinema production, 46–47; criticism of, 140, 158; and emergent sites of production, xii–xiii, 180*n*9; and ethical possibilities, 165; and Global South solidarity, 140; marginalization within, xxi–xxii; and post-independence colonial reproduction, 158, 192*n*8; and postmodernism, 159. *See also* capitalism
Global South solidarity, xvi, 177; and anticolonialism, xvii, xxx, 93; and capitalism, 37; and colonialism, xvii–xx, xxvii; and colonized time, xxx; critical approaches to, xxxiv; Cuban-Angolan mutual publication agreement (1978), xix, 179*n*4; and Cuban Revolution as decolonizing event, xxvii, 181*n*13; and documentary style, 34; and enthusiasm, xxvi–xxvii, xxxiv; and epistemology, 86–87, 105–6; and global marketplace, 140; and historical revisiting/revision, 92–93, 104; and iterability of revolution, xx, xxvii–xxviii, 115, 179*n*5; in *Kangamba*, 29, 30, 31, 34, 37, 47–48; and Mandela's Cuba visit, xix–xx; and multiplicity, xxxvi, 86–87; in *O Ano em que Zumbi Tomou o Rio*, 82–83, 84–85, 87, 92, 101, 104, 105–6; and post–Cold War transition, 30, 37; and post-independence colonial reproduction, 173; and racial equality,

Global South solidarity *(continued)* 95, 104; and Tricontinental Congress (1966), xviii–xix, xxviii, 115. *See also* Cuban revolutionary missions; Cuba's Angola mission
Goldberg, David Theo, 100–101
Gómez, José Miguel Sánchez (Yoss), xxxii, 182*n*22
González, Eduardo, 133
González Echevarría, Roberto, 129, 131, 190*n*10, 192*n*10
The Great Patriotic War (Karmen), 186*n*5
Grossman, Edith, 186*n*5
Guantanamera (Alea), 55
Guerra, Lillian, 56–57, 61–62, 63, 69, 71–72, 79
La guerra en Angola (The War in Angola) (Fleitas), 32–33, 57, 169
Guevara, Alfredo, 57
Guevara, Ernesto "Che": Congo mission, 179*n*3; and Cuban Revolution as decolonizing event, xxv, 181*n*12; and Global South solidarity, 179*n*5; on iterability of revolution, xx, xxviii, 115, 179*n*5; "Mensaje a todos los pueblos del mundo," 115–16; "El socialismo y el hombre en Cuba," xxv
Guillén Landrián, Nicolás, 61–62, 186*n*6; *Desde la Habana: ¡1969!*, 61
Guimarães, António Sérgio Alfredo, 94

Haitian Revolution, xxxiv, 128, 131, 191*n*14
Hamilton, Russell, 9
Hardt, Michael, 183*n*4
Harrow, Kenneth, 44
Hart Santamaría, Celia, 124
Hatzky, Christine, 35, 46, 47, 182*n*21
Hegel, Georg W. F., 113, 129, 130, 189*n*15
Hemingway, Ernest, 110–11
Henighan, Stephen, xix, xxvii, 7, 115, 140, 182*n*19, 192*n*8
Heredia, José María, 110

Hernández Salván, Marta, xxxiii, xxxv, 18–19, 36, 105, 113
Herrmann, Gina, 127
El hijo del héroe (The Son of the Hero) (Suárez), 173, 174, 175–77, 182*n*22, 192*n*1
historical revisiting/revision, xvi–xvii; and citation, 103–4; and closed histories, xxviii–xxix; and dialectical view, 129–30; and genre, 189–90*n*5; and Global South solidarity, 92–93, 104; in *Na Cidade Vazia*, xiv, xv; in *O Ano em que Zumbi Tomou o Rio*, 10, 92–97, 102, 103–4; and pastiche, 144; and silence, 189–90*n*5
El hombre que amaba a los perros (The Man Who Loved Dogs) (Padura), 109–38; broken temporality in, 110, 189*n*2; and Carpentier, 128–31, 132–33, 134, 190*n*11; dogs in, 127, 190*n*8; enthusiasm in, xxviii; feelings in, xxi; genre in, 119, 123–24, 127; historical context of, 112, 123, 173, 189*n*4, 190*n*6; historical revisiting/revision in, 129–30, 189*n*5; hurricane in, 130–34, 136–38, 191*n*13; marginalization in, 113, 154–55; petrified life in, 134–35, 138; plot of, 110; state suppression of creative production in, 112, 114, 124–25, 171; waiting/deferral in, 110, 113–14, 117–18, 119–20, 121–23, 136–37, 138; writing in, 123–27
Hong Kong, xii
Hook, Derek, 134–35, 138
Hurricane Iván, 130–32, 136–37, 191*n*13
Hutcheon, Linda, 143–44
hyper-real, 56–57, 61, 66, 69, 71–72, 79, 80, 186*n*2

ICAIC (Instituto Cubano de Artes e Industrias Cinematográficas/Cuban Institute of Cinematic Arts and Industries), 30, 56, 57, 61

imperfect cinema, 30–31
Informe contra mí mismo (Dossier Against Myself) (Alberto), 59, 68–69, 70–71
intercultural translation, 84, 85–88, 97–98, 101–2
International Book Fair (Havana, 2013), 169
internationalism. *See* Cuban revolutionary missions; Global South solidarity
irony, xxviii; in Cardoso's post-independence novels, 23, 24; in *O Herói*, 28, 38, 42, 46

Jaime Bunda novels (Pepetela), 139–67; colonial reproduction in, 142, 155–56, 158, 167, 173, 192n8; corruption in, 140–41, 149, 159, 161, 191n2, 192n10; counterfeiting in, 155; displacement in, xxii; ethical possibilities in, 164, 165–66; global marketplace in, 158, 165, 192n8; imitation in, 141–42; meta-textual awareness in, 159–61, 192n9; and *Mistério da Estrada de Sintra*, 150–56; pastiche in, 143–44, 152, 159–60; plot in, 139–40; and postmodernism, xxiii, 159; pseudo-author in, 161–64, 165; social order in, 147–49; stylistic imitation in, 144–47, 152, 155–56; urban landscape in, 156–57, 192n6
Jamba, Sousa, *Patriots*, 184n14
James, C. L. R., 191n14
James Bond novels, 143
Jameson, Fredric, xxi, xxiii, 143–44
Jesús, Carolina Maria de, *Quarto de despejo*, 189n18
Jeyifo, Biodun, 26, 185n17
Johnson, Randal, 102

Kangamba (París), 29–37; allegory in, 27–28, 31–32, 36; Global South solidarity in, 29, 30, 31, 34, 37, 47–48; historical context of, 28–29; and imperfect cinema, 30–31; International Book Fair recognition, 169; nostalgia in, 45–46; parallel structure in, 35–36, 37; production of, 46–47; revolutionary style in, 28, 32–34, 36, 172; and social criticism, 36–37; South African/UNITA opposition in, 29, 31, 34–35, 185n5
Kant, Immanuel, xxiv, 181n11
Karmen, Roman, *The Great Patriotic War*, 186n5
Knopfli, Rui, 103, 189nn19–21
Kurasawa, Akira, *Seven Samurai*, 59, 60, 61

Lara Filho, Ernesto, 102
Laranjeira, José Luís Pires, 105
Laura (Preminger), 59
linguistic authority, 5, 7–12, 184nn7–9
Lins, Paulo, *Cidade de Deus*, 189n14
Llarena, Alicia, 74
Loss, Jacqueline, xxxiv, 109, 124, 125, 189n3
L'Ouverture, Toussaint, xxxiv
Lueji (Pepetela), 139
Lusophone solidarity. *See* Global South solidarity
lusotropicalism, 90, 101, 188n11
Luuanda (Vieira), 9
Lyotard, Jean-François, xxiv, 181n11

Macedo, Jorge, 5, 6
Macêdo, Tania, 160–61
Maciel, Francisco, 95
Mãe, Materno Mar (Mother, Maternal Sea) (Cardoso): allegory in, 17–18, 20, 24–25, 174; collective narration in, 5; collective/plurivocal narration in, 22–24, 25–26; dechronicalization in, 20; divine authority in, 20–21; enunciation in, 6–7, 24; feeling in, xxi; historical context of, 3, 4, 5; historical elision in, 25; linguistic

Mãe, Materno Mar (Mother, Maternal Sea) (Cardoso) *(continued)*
authority in, 5, 7–10, 184n7; marginalization in, 10; multiplicity in, 3, 18–20, 22–24; nonlinear narrative in, 20; plot movement in, 4–5; silence in, 25; social criticism in, 5–6, 26
magical realism, 58, 74, 184n12
Maguire, Emily, 127
Mahler, Anne Garland, xix, 115
Maio, Mês de Maria (May, the Month of Mary) (Cardoso), 10–17; *assimilado* status in, 4, 10, 12, 183n2; collective/plurivocal narration in, 11–12, 13, 14–17, 25–26; dechronicalization in, 13–14; disenchantment in, 13; education in, 112–13; enunciation in, 6–7; historical context of, xxxi, 3, 4; historical elision in, 13, 14, 24, 25; linguistic authority in, 5, 7–11, 184n7; plot movement in, 4; post-independence colonial reproduction in, 12, 14, 184nn9, 11; silence in, 13, 14; social criticism in, 5–6, 26; utopian loss in, xxxv–xxxvi
Maldoror, Sarah, 186n7; *Sambizanga*, 43
"The Man Who Liked Dogs" (Chandler), 127, 190n8
The Man Who Was Thursday (Chesterton), 143
Mandela, Nelson, xx, xxviii
Margarido, Alfredo, xxvii
marginalization: in global marketplace, xxi–xxii; in *El hombre que amaba a los perros*, 113, 154–55; in *Mãe, Materno Mar*, 10; in *O Ano em que Zumbi Tomou o Rio*, 84, 187n4. *See also* exile
Martí, José, 70–71, 186n9
marvelous real, 184n12
Massip, José, *Angola, victoria de la esperanza*, 32, 57, 169
Mata, Inocência, xxxiii, xxxv, 4, 13, 184n11

Mateus, Álvaro, 182n20
Mateus, Dalila Cabrita, 182n20
Matthews, Sean, xxi
Matzke, Christine, 159
Mayombe (Pepetela), 139
McNee, Malcolm, 101
melancholy, xxxiii, 26, 113, 130
Melo, Francisco José Sampaio, 96
Méndez Rodenas, Adriana, 71, 72
Mendonça, José Luís, xxxv
"Mensaje a todos los pueblos del mundo (Message to the Peoples of the World)" (Guevara), 115–16
Mercader, Luis, 126–27
mestizaje/mestiçagem (racial mixing), xxvii, 85, 90, 94, 101, 187–88nn7, 11, 189n15
Michelena, José Antonio, 119
Milanés, Pablo, 70, 78
Mills, Charles Wright, 181n12
Mistério da Estrada de Sintra (The Mystery of the Sintra Road) (Queirós and Ortigão), 144, 150–56, 191nn3–4, 192n5
Monteiro, Ofélia Paiva, 153–54
Moorman, Marissa, 45, 185n6
More, Thomas, 20
Movimento Negro Unificado (MNU) (United Black Movement) (Brazil), 93–94
Movimento Popular para a Libertação de Angola (MPLA), xxx–xxxi, 179n1; and 1992 elections, xxxi–xxxii, 38; and religion, 19, 184n14, 185n16. *See also* Cuba's Angola mission; MPLA post-coup purges
MPLA post-coup purges, xxxi, 3; death toll, 182n20; and historical revisiting/revision, 88–89; and post-independence colonial reproduction, 89, 188n10; silence about, xxxii, 6, 9, 13, 89–90, 172, 183n6
Mueller, Eddy Von, 143, 148
Mühleisen, Susanne, 159

multiplicity, xxviii, xxxiv; in *Caracol Beach*, 71; in Cardoso's post-independence novels, 3, 10, 18–20, 22–24; and collective/plurivocal narration, 22–24; and enthusiasm, 171–72; and Global South solidarity, xxxvi, 86–87; in *O Ano em que Zumbi Tomou o Rio*, 102–3; and religion, 18–20
multitude, 183*n*4
"The Murders in the Rue Morgue" (Poe), 192*n*5
Les Mystères de Paris (Sue), 152, 191*n*3

Na Cidade Vazia (Hollow City) (Ganga), xiii–xv, 35–36, 179*n*2
Nação Crioula (Creole) (Agualusa), 85
"La narrativa cubana entre la utopía y el desencanto" (Cuban Narrative Between Utopia and Disenchantment) (Fornet), xxxiii
narratorial intrusions, 159, 160–61, 192*n*9
Nascimento, Abdias do, 94, 99
Navarro, Desiderio, xxxiv–xxxv
La neblina de ayer (Havana Fever) (Padura), 190–91*n*12
Negri, Antonio, 183*n*4
Neto, Agostinho, xxxi, 7
New Man: in *Caracol Beach*, 54, 75, 80; and concepts of revolution, 105; and disenchantment, xxxiii, 170; Guevara on, 181*n*12; in *Na Cidade Vazia*, xiv; in *O Herói*, 40
New York Accords (1988), xxxi
Ngai, Sianne, xxi
nonlinear temporalities, 20–21, 85–86, 92, 101–2
nostalgia, xxix, xxxv, 29–30, 45–46, 73
La novela de mi vida (The Novel of My Life) (Padura), 110
Nzinga Mbande/Ana de Sousa (queen of Angola), xxxiv, 105

O Ano em que Zumbi Tomou o Rio (The Year That Zumbi Took Rio) (Agualusa), xxii, 81–106; citation in, 102, 103–4, 172–73; concepts of revolution in, 83–84; contamination in, 85; enthusiasm in, xxviii; and favela stereotypes, 102, 189*n*18; Global South solidarity in, 82–83, 84–85, 87, 92, 101, 104, 105–6; historical context of, xxxi, 81–82, 88–90, 91, 93–94, 98, 187*n*3, 188–89*nn*10, 14; historical revisiting/revision in, 10, 92–97, 102, 103–4; intercultural translation in, 84, 85–86, 87–88, 97–98, 101–2; marginalization in, 84, 187*n*4; multiplicity in, 102–3; nonlinear plot movement in, 85–86, 92, 101–2; and Palmares, 81–82, 87, 93; patriarchal abandonment in, 90–91; post-independence colonial reproduction in, 89, 91–92; postmodernism in, 105, 173; protagonists of, 83, 187*n*4; racial epistemologies in, 98–101; and racial equality, 94–96, 99, 100; setting of, 91, 188*n*12; social criticism in, 91
O Grande Kilapy (Gamboa), 47
O Herói (The Hero) (Gamboa), 38–44, 48; allegory in, 27–28, 38, 40; children in, 41–43; colonial reproduction in, 43; doubling in, 39, 42–43, 172; form in, 28; and Gamboa's prior work, 40–41; historical context of, 28–29, 43; International Book Fair recognition, 169; irony in, 28, 38, 42, 46; plot of, 38–39; production of, 47; repetition in, 44; revolutionary style in, 38, 39; social criticism in, 40, 46; trash in, 44
Ochoa, Arnaldo, xxxii–xxxiii, 30, 46, 171, 182*nn*21–22
The Odyssey, 120–21, 124, 127
Oliveira, Emanuelle, 94
Oliveira Martins, Isabel, 151

Ondjaki (Ndalu de Almeida), xxxii; *Bom dia camaradas*, 173–75
orally-inflected syntax, 7–9
Ortigão, Ramalho, *Mistério da Estrada de Sintra*, 144, 150–56, 191*nn*3–4, 192*n*5
Ortiz, Fernando, 131
Our Lady of Fátima cult, 183*n*3. *See also* religion

Padilla, Heberto, xxv; "Fuera del juego," 73, 186–87*n*10
Padura, Leonardo Fuentes: *Adiós, Hemingway*, 110–11; background of, 110–11; and Carpentier, 112, 128–29, 132, 134, 190*n*11; and genre, 112, 119, 190*n*5; Mario Conde series, 46, 110, 111, 119, 133, 137–38, 190–91*n*12; *La neblina de ayer*, 190–91*n*12; *La novela de mi vida*, 110; *Paisaje de otoño*, 133, 137–38; "La Puerta de Alcalá," 111; "Según pasan los años," 111. *See also El hombre que amaba a los perros*
Paisaje de otoño (Havana Black) (Padura), 133, 137–38
Palmares: mythology of, 81, 96, 187*n*1, 189*n*16; and *O Ano em que Zumbi Tomou o Rio*, 81–82, 87, 93
Palmer, Margarita Mateo, xxiii, 180*n*10
Parábola do Cágado Velho (The Parable of the Old Tortoise) (Pepetela), 139
parallel structure: in *Kangamba*, 35–36, 37; in *Na Cidade Vazia*, xiv, 35–36; in *O Ano em que Zumbi Tomou o Rio*, 92, 101–2. *See also* doubling
Paranaguá, Paulo Antonio, 36–37
París, Rogelio: *Caravana*, 29, 37, 46, 169, 185*nn*4–5; third film by, 29, 185*n*1. *See also Kangamba*
pastiche, 143–44, 152, 159–60
Patriots (Jamba), 184*n*14
Pavón Tamayo, Luis, 125
Pélissier, René, 181*n*14

people, power of: as enunciation, 6–7, 24; and multiplicity, 22–24; Rancière on, 183*nn*4–5; and silence, 26. *See also* collective/plurivocal narration; linguistic authority
Pepetela: on Alves coup, 183*n*6; *As Aventuras de Ngunga*, xiv, 35–36; *A Geração da Utopia*, xxxv–xxxvi, 139; *Lueji*, 139; *Mayombe*, 139; *Parábola do Cágado Velho*, 139; *Yaka*, 139. *See also* Jaime Bunda novels
Pereira, Pedro, 189*n*15
Peres, Phyllis, 10, 184*n*8
Peters, Christabelle, xxxiv, 62, 77
petrified life, 134–35, 138
Petrov, Vladimir, *The Battle of Stalingrad*, 186*n*5
Phaf-Rheinberger, Ineke, 93
plurivocal narration. *See* collective/plurivocal narration
Poe, Edgar Allan, 145, 152; "The Murders in the Rue Morgue," 192*n*5
Pogolotti, Gabriela, 131
Ponte, Antonio José, 123–24, 131, 132, 190*n*7, 191*n*13
"Posposição (Postponement)" (Knopfli), 103
post–Cold War transition, 176–77; Cuban Special Period in Times of Peace, xxxiii, 111, 114; and disenchantment, xxxiii, xxxv; and genre, 140; and Global South solidarity, 30, 37
post-independence colonial reproduction, 184*n*11; and capitalism, 43, 142; and global marketplace, 158, 192*n*8; and Global South solidarity, 173; and historical revisiting/revision, 167; and MPLA post-coup purges, 89, 188*n*10; and race, 12, 184*n*9; and stylistic imitation, 155–56; and urban cartography, 91–92
post-independence transitions: Gamboa on, 41; importance of cinema to, 45,

57; and linguistic authority, 10–12, 184n9. *See also* Cuban Revolution; *Mãe, Materno Mar; Maio, Mês de Maria*

postcolonialism: and crime genre, 159; and global marketplace, xxi–xxii; as impasse, 26, 185n17; and limits of postmodernism, xxiii, 180n10; and pastiche, 144; and subalternity, xxiii; and urban landscape, 156–57, 192n6

postmodernism: and enthusiasm, xxiv, 181n11; and global marketplace, 159; and hyper-real, 56, 186n2; limits of, xxiii, 180n10; in *O Ano em que Zumbi Tomou o Rio*, 105, 173; and uncertainty, 179n6

Preminger, Otto, *Laura*, 59

public sphere, xv–xix, xxi–xxii, xxxv

"La Puerta de Alcalá" (Padura), 111

Quarto de despejo (Child of the Dark) (Jesús), 189n18

Quase dois irmãos (Almost Brothers), 189n14

Queirós, Eça de, *Mistério da Estrada de Sintra*, 144, 150–56, 191nn3–4, 192n5

Quem Me Dera Ser Onda (I Wish I Were a Wave) (Rui), xxxv

Quilombo (Diegues), 189n16

Quilomboje, 94

Quinney, Laura, xv–xvi

quinquenio gris, xxxiv, 62, 109; in *El hombre que amaba a los perros*, 112, 114, 124, 137; and Soviet influence, 110, 124; term, 189n1. *See also* Cuban state suppression of creative production

race: and Cuba's Angola mission, xxxiv; in *O Ano em que Zumbi Tomou o Rio*, 94–96, 98–101; and post-independence colonial reproduction, 12, 184n9; racial mixing, xxvii, 85, 90, 94, 101, 187–88nn7, 11, 189n15. *See also* slavery

Ramón Mercader: mi hermano: cincuenta años después (Mercader and Sánchez), 126–27

Rancière, Jacques, 6–7, 10, 183nn4–5

Rapi (Constante Alejandro de Diego García Marruz), *El corazón sobre la tierra*, 55

El reino de este mundo (The Kingdom of This World) (Carpentier), 128, 131, 184n12

religion: and anticolonialism, 21–22, 184–85n15; and capitalism, 18, 19–20, 22, 24; in Cardoso's post-independence novels, 5, 6; and collective/plurivocal narration, 5, 14–16; and colonialism, 8; divine authority, 20–21; and enthusiasm, 6; and fracturing, 13; and linguistic authority, 8; MPLA opposition to, 19, 184n14, 185n16; and multiplicity, 18–20; Our Lady of Fátima cult origins, 183n3; and social criticism, 6, 22; syncretic, 4, 6, 14–15, 17, 18

repetition: in *Caracol Beach*, 70–71; in Cardoso's post-independence novels, 8; and citation, xxx; and Global South solidarity, xxxvi; in *O Ano em que Zumbi Tomou o Rio*, 84, 86; in *O Herói*, 44. *See also* historical revisiting/revision

Retamar, Roberto Fernández, xxiv, 133, 182n17

revolution, concepts of, 83–84; and anticolonialism, 83, 105; Carpentier on, 128–30, 133, 190n10; dialectical view, 36, 129–30; iterability, xx, xxvii–xxviii, 115, 179n5; and temporalities, 113

Ribeiro, Raquel, xxxii

Ricoeur, Paul, 189n2

Rodríguez, Albita, 70

Rodríguez, Silvio, 70, 78

Rojas, Rafael, xxiv–xxvi, 28, 66, 111, 181*n*12
Rosales, Guillermo, *La casa de los náufragos*, 73–74
Rothwell, Phillip, 90, 175
Rui, Manuel, *Quem Me Dera Ser Onda*, xxxv
Ryan, Connor, 44

Sabine, Mark, 40, 47
Sambizanga (Maldoror), 43
Sánchez, Germán, 126–27
Santería, 76–80, 187*n*11
Sarduy, Severo, *Escrito sobre un cuerpo*, 67–68
Sarró, Ramón, 185*n*16
Sartre, Jean-Paul, xxv, 131, 181*n*12
Savimbi, Jonas, xxxi–xxxii, 38
Schurmans, Fabrice, 149, 191*n*2
Schweizer, Harold, 120–21, 124
Secco, Carmen Lucia Tindó, 6, 17–18, 19, 21, 25
The Secret Agent (Conrad), 143
secrets. *See* silence
"Según pasan los años (As the Years Pass)" (Padura), 111
Semprún, Jorge, *La deuxième mort de Ramón Mercader*, 126
settings, 71–73, 91, 188*n*12
Seven Samurai (Kurasawa), 59, 60, 61
Shakespeare, William, *The Tempest*, 133
Sherlock Holmes stories, 145, 148
Los siete contra Tebas (Seven Against Thebes) (Arrufat), 66
El siglo de las luces (Explosion in a Cathedral) (Carpentier), 128, 129–30, 131, 132, 190*n*10
silence: about Cuba's Angola mission, xxxii–xxxiii, 7, 30, 36; about MPLA post-coup purges, xxxii, 6, 9, 13, 89–90, 172, 183*n*6; and anticolonialism, 10, 25; and Cuban state suppression of creative production, 171; and historical revisiting/revision, 189–90*n*5; and linguistic authority, 10; and power of people, 26; as textual strategy, 10, 13, 25
Simenon, George, 148
slavery: and Cuba's Angola mission, xxxiv; and Global South solidarity, xviii, xxvii, 93; and *O Ano em que Zumbi Tomou o Rio*, 84; slave trade population, 93, 188*n*13. *See also* race
Soares, Francisco, 9
Soares De Oliveira, Ricardo, 161
soccer, 12, 184*n*10
"El socialismo y el hombre en Cuba" (Guevara), xxv
Soitos, Stephen, 158–59
Solanas, Fernando, 31
solidarity. *See* Global South solidarity
Someillan, Yamile Regalado, 56
Sommer, Doris, 10, 25
Sousa Santos, Boaventura de, 82, 84, 86–88, 91–92, 99, 101, 105, 188*nn*8–9, 191*n*14
South African invasion of Angola, xxxi, 29, 34–35
Soviet Union: and Alves coup, 7, 182*n*19; as colonizing power, 111, 173, 189*n*3; Cuban relations with, 109; influence on Cuba, xxxiv, 110, 117, 118, 124–25, 132, 136, 173; invasion of Prague, xxv, 117; and Spanish Civil War, 129
Spanish Civil War, 129
Sting, 70
La Strada (Fellini), 73
structures of feeling, xx–xxi, xxii, 3
A Study in Scarlett (Doyle), 158–59
Suárez, Karla, xxxii; *El hijo del héroe*, 173, 174, 175–77, 182*n*22, 192*n*1
subalternity, xxiii
Sue, Eugène, *Les Mystères de Paris*, 152, 191*n*3
Sumbe, 29, 169
syncretism, 4, 6, 14–15, 17, 18

Tavares, Ana Paula, xxxii
The Tempest (Shakespeare), 133
temporalities: asynchronicity, xv, xxix, 110, 173; colonized time, xxix–xxx, 118–19; and concepts of revolution, 113; and Cuban Revolution as decolonizing event, 114–15; and Cuban revolutionary missions, 115–17; dechronicalization, 13–14, 20; and historical revisiting/revision, xxviii–xxix, 92, 102; and hyper-real, 57; nonlinear, 20–21, 85–86, 92, 101–2; petrified life, 134–35, 138; and writing, 124. *See also* waiting/deferral
Teoria Geral do Esquecimento (General Theory of Forgetting) (Agualusa), 7, 89–90
Third Cinema, 31
third-world solidarity. *See* Global South solidarity
Thornton, John K., 93
Traverso, Enzo, xxviii–xxix, 113, 119
Tricontinental Congress (1966), xviii–xix, xxviii, 115
Trotsky, Leon, 109, 110, 113, 123, 124, 190n6. See also *El hombre que amaba a los perros*

uncertainty, 175, 179n6
União Nacional para a Independência Total de Angola (National Union for the Total Liberation of Angola) (UNITA), xxxi, 182n18; *Kangamba* on, 29, 31, 34–35, 185n5; and 1992 elections, xxxi–xxxii
Unión de Jóvenes Comunistas de Cuba (the Young Communist League of Cuba), 51–52, *52*, 53

Valente, Luis, 102
Vasconcelhos, Botelho de, xxxv
Vieira, Luandino, 9–10, 25, 184n8; *A Vida Verdadeira de Domingos Xavier*, 43; *Luuanda*, 9

waiting/deferral, 110, 113–14, 117–18, 119–20, 121–23, 135–37, 138, 191n14
Weppler-Grogan, Doreen, 62
Wheeler, Douglass, 181n14, 188n13
Whitfield, Esther, xxi–xxiii, xxxv, 37, 180n9
Williams, Raymond, xx–xxi, xxii
Winant, Howard, 98, 99, 104
Wittgenstein, Ludwig, 147
Wong Kar-wai, 180n8

Xitu, Uanhenga, 9

Yaka (Pepetela), 139
Yoss (José Miguel Sánchez Gómez), xxxii, 182n22

Zumbi, xxxiv, 82. See also *O Ano em que Zumbi Tomou o Rio*; Palmares

www.ingramcontent.com/pod-product-compliance
Lightning Source LLC
Chambersburg PA
CBHW030536230426
43665CB00010B/918